MW00528916

BISON
BOOKS

James Fillis

BREAKING AND RIDING

WITH MILITARY COMMENTARIES

James Fillis

TRANSLATED BY

M. H. Hayes, F. R. C. V. S.

INTRODUCTION BY

Barbara Burkhardt

WITH SEVENTY ILLUSTRATIONS

University of Nebraska Press
Lincoln and London

Introduction © 2005 by the Board of Regents of the University
of Nebraska
Manufactured in the United States of America

First Nebraska paperback printing: 2005

Library of Congress Cataloging-in-Publication Data
Fillis, James, 1834–1913.
Breaking and riding: with military commentaries / James Fillis;
translated by M. H. Hayes; introduction by Barbara Burkhardt.
p.   cm.
Includes index.
ISBN 0-8032-6915-3 (pbk.: alk. paper)
1. Dressage.   I. Title.
SF309.5.F55   2005
798.2'3—dc22   2004022680

Barbara Burkhardt

INTRODUCTION.

Although James Fillis (1834–1913) is often remembered for his accomplishments as a circus rider and military instructor, he was in fact a great innovator in horse training and riding. Many of Fillis's techniques are still applicable today, and he could be called the father of modern competition dressage, this by way of his influence on military equitation. François Baucher (1796–1873) is the man accredited with "inventing" the high school form of riding, adding a greater variety of movements in closer succession and showcasing the new style in the circus. It was James Fillis, however, who perfected the high school techniques and brought academic equitation into the twentieth century. And James Fillis's methods have never been as controversial as Baucher's.

By the time James Fillis began working with horses in the mid-1800s, the heavy cavalry horse had fallen out of favor. This was in response to changes in military tactics to a lighter, more mobile and agile "hot-blooded" horse from England—the thoroughbred. The English thoroughbred's true superiority in speed and its characteristic refinement contributed to its popularity for racing, hunting, and sport riding (an adaptation of the instinctive, athletic way of English riding).

It was also in the mid–nineteenth century that horsemanship split into two extremes: horse racers, hunters, and the cavalry embraced piercing forward movement as their style, whereas a small group of circus riders introduced, for entertainment, a new genre they called high school riding. Bringing thoroughbred or thoroughbred-crossed horses to perform brilliantly inside a ring thirteen and one-half meters in diameter was the challenge the circus offered, and it was a challenge Baucher, Fillis, and others masterfully met. It is to the circus that we must look for the origination and perpetuation of high school riding, or what much of the equestrian world today recognizes as "dressage riding." For this innovation, we can thank James Fillis.

Fillis's career and achievements cover a span of seventy years. Fillis was born in 1834 in London; his family moved to France when he was quite young, and it is believed his father was a solicitor. We first hear of the young Fillis riding at the age of eight at the stables of a dealer in Le Havre. There he was put up on many rough and untrained horses and told only to "make them go." He said himself that those were his first lessons in impulsion, which later was to become such an important part of his system.

When he was still young, Fillis met the great master Baucher and later trained under Baucher's pupil François Caron. As a result, some of Fillis's work is based on Baucher's teachings. But being the innovator and dedicated artist he was, Fillis introduced new techniques of his own. In *Breaking and Riding* (or *Principes de dressage et d'équitation* in French) he tells us the good and the bad advice he received amid all the confusion of the conflicting ideas of his time; he also explores his own experiments and innovations in the book.

Fillis had no military training and did not graduate from a school of equitation. What he knew about training horses came from his own observations, study, and reasoning. He made his living training horses for five francs (about one dollar) per horse per day, a pretty good wage for the era. Later he showed his own finished horses in circuses and gave private lessons and exhibitions. At that time the circus was the only place for highly skilled riders to exhibit themselves. Granted, the circus showcased many unnatural movements, such as the canter on three legs, the canter backward, the Spanish walk, and the Spanish trot; but it also showcased canter lead changes at every stride (invented by Baucher), piaffe and passage, and lateral (two-track) movements. These movements are practiced to this day in the upper levels of dressage competition.

In his day Fillis was acknowledged throughout Europe as the greatest high school rider of all time. In fact, he had the honor of giving private riding exhibitions before the emperor and empress of Germany, the tsar of Russia, the queen of Belgium, the king and crown prince of Denmark, the emperor of Austria, and other gentry of the day, all of whom accorded him special praise for their appreciation of his unrivaled ability.

In addition to working for the circus, Fillis managed and supervised the stables of the queen of Naples. He also taught riding to ladies and gentlemen of the aristocracy as well as to military officers, who, likewise, were from families of class. In 1870, at the time of the Franco-Prussian War, Fillis was engaged to train horses for the French Thirteenth Army. Despite this role with the French army, he was never officially employed at Saumur, the main French cavalry school; nonetheless, Fillis is remembered there, his name inscribed on the roll of Écuyers Célèbres.

After the war of 1870 Fillis returned to his circus work, where he could then command a very high fee. It was at the Ciniselli Circus, performing in St. Petersburg, Russia, that the Grand Duke Nicholas saw Fillis riding. So impressed was the grand duke that he invited Fillis to take a course for officers of the Imperial Guard. Fillis's success in the course resulted in him being taken on in 1898 as chief instructor, with the rank of colonel, at the Russian cavalry school. During his stay, Fillis developed the manual for the Russian cavalry, which was copied by other military schools in Europe and America.

It is interesting to note that Fillis was already sixty-four years old when he received this important appointment. Historic documentation suggests that three hundred horses a year, together with a large number of riders, received his instruction. Fillis stayed in Russia until 1910; he had been due to retire two years earlier but was persuaded to stay on.

One must remember that the cavalry schools where Fillis and other talented masters taught were for officers only. The cavalry used the basic principles of the manège (school riding) to increase the maneuverability and obedience of their mounts. What use, then, were the high school movements? To show off the officers' skills at horsemanship, of course. The manège recipe was regarded as "art for art's sake." Riding masters assured their students that "managed" horses were perfectly reliable at war—the long marches made them soon forget their high airs!

Fillis's influence on the world of equitation during his twelve years with the Russian cavalry was enormous, although the impact may not have been felt beyond Russia's borders until after World War I. After the war people like Col. Paul Rodzianko, Vladimir Littauer, and other Russian officers went to England and the United States and spread Fillis's techniques.

Before leaving France for Russia, Fillis had been persuaded to write a book. The book, *Breaking and Riding*, is a classic, and one reason for Fillis's longstanding reputation in equitation. (*Breaking* is the British word for *training*.) In this text Fillis presents a method of schooling for a horse to learn in one year to walk, trot, and canter indoors, outdoors, to go hunting, or to go into the military. With that foundation, the horse could then be taught high school movements, such as the Spanish walk and trot, pirouettes (turns around the haunches at the canter), piaffe (trot in place), passage (a highly collected trot), as well as various circus "tricks" if the rider so desired. Although he was famous as a circus rider and trainer, Fillis worked with all kinds of horses; sections of his book are devoted to trotting race horses and flat racing, the requirements of a hack (a late-nineteenth-century term for an elegant riding horse for gentlemen or ladies of high class), as well as training a horse to be used as a hunter (fox hunting), a military officer's mount, or an exhibition horse capable of doing various high school and/or circus movements on cue.

Fillis's system, simply put, is based entirely on balance, lightness, and impulsion. He controlled the distribution of the horse's weight through the placing of the horse's head and neck. Fillis (and Baucher before him) changed the position of the horse by taking it off its haunches and placing it into horizontal balance. Horizontal balance, or bearing an equal load in front and behind, made the horse far easier to manipulate and enabled it to perform a greater variety of movements in closer succession.

Fillis writes at length about the importance of putting the horse "on the bit" by getting "flexions in the jaw" before a rider is ever put on the horse's back. This is so the horse will know how to respond to the bits when he is mounted. Fillis also teaches response to the whip (to be replaced later by the rider's leg) while on the ground.

One point to remember is that prior to Fillis's era, the masters of classical equitation usually trained horses in collection only, and they used Spanish-type horses that excelled in that work. But Fillis, in accordance with the fashion of the day, preferred thoroughbreds or thoroughbred-crossed horses, which could collect *and* extend their gaits. (The "warm-blooded" horse, bred specifically for sport and dressage competition, is a cross between the thoroughbred and the fashionable, high-stepping carriage horse and would not appear until after World War II.)

Fillis writes about suppleness, balance, and impulsion, all tenants of modern dressage horses. Fillis could ride a horse in great extension, either at trot or at gallop, then bring it back, raise its neck, and show the most elevated, elegant high school movements. Those who remember him at the end of his career in France, after he had finished his work in Russia, say his horses seemed to float through the air. Fillis was such a believer in impulsion that, unlike Baucher and others, when he practiced those flexions to relax the horse's jaw, he always kept the horse moving. He was adamantly opposed to the "old-fashioned" method of flexions at the halt.

Many of the horses Fillis owned had come off the racecourse and had learned to go truly forward before he started to school them in dressage. He was thus able to start by putting them in a double bridle— a practice he used with all of his horses—and raising the neck with various flexions. Skeptics who question using a double bridle on a green horse must remember that Fillis was an accomplished rider and trainer; if this method is carried out incorrectly, the horse can easily end up with a ewe-neck, and the practice can result in no action at all. As with any training system, an inexperienced or crude trainer can ruin the horse.

Dressage competition today owes a great deal to turn-of-the-century military schools and to their instructors, such as Fillis. Dressage as a competition was introduced into the modern Olympics in 1912, the year before Fillis died in Paris. The Olympic equestrian competition was restricted to military officers until the 1950s. Many of these officers may have been Fillis's students, either directly or indirectly.

In the beginning the dressage competition was not particularly demanding on the horse or rider. The test was simply an evaluation of the well-trained officer's mount. It called for lengthening and shortening at trot and canter, half turns on the haunches, and four flying lead changes on straight lines in a ten-minute freestyle. This was followed by five small jumps. By the 1920 Olympic Games the emphasis was less on the utility horse and more on a highly trained officer's mount. As a result, the competition requirements changed considerably. A test comprising individual movements was devised and included the half pass at trot and canter, serpentines, and changes of leg every four, three, two, and single strides. The piaffe and passage were added in 1929, thus incorporating most of the elements in today's Grand Prix test—and all elements taught and practiced by Baucher and Fillis. Fillis would be proud.

James Fillis's legacy does not end there, however. James Leon Fillis, his son, came to the United States in 1912 and entered vaudeville with a horse act. Much later, the younger James trained J. Shirley Watt's mount, Connecticut Yankee, for the 1956 Olympics in Stockholm, where the pair finished thirteenth. Watt was one of only two Americans at that Olympics; her teammate was Maj. Robert Borg.

In conclusion, the master James Fillis influenced modern riding and modern dressage competition in a way that is strongly felt today—in part because of his mastery and understanding of the horse and in part because he was able to record his instructions in writing. *Breaking and Riding* may have been written in a very different era, but there are many pearls of wisdom to be gleaned from its pages. Although some of Fillis's methods are today regarded as controversial (for instance, starting a horse in a double bridle and employing flexions of the jaw from the ground), the book is still well worth studying for its historically significant information and, in many cases, timeless instruction.

PREFACE.

IN this book, I do not presume to discuss scientific subjects. I am simply a horseman who has been among horses for sixty years, who knows them, loves them, and is capable of reasoning about them.

The fundamental principle of the studies which I submit to the public is that it is necessary for a horse to be correctly balanced and light in forward movements and propulsion, in order that the rider may obtain the most powerful effects with the least exertion.

My method of equitation consists in distribution of weight by the height of the neck bent at the poll and not at the withers; propulsion by means of the hocks being brought under the body; and lightness by the loosening of the lower jaw. When we know this, we know everything, and we know nothing. We know everything, because these principles are of universal application; and we know nothing, because they have to be applied practically.

Practice cannot be taught in a book; but I will try to set forth principles. Probably, I would not have had the boldness to do this, had not one of my pupils entreated me to write this book; because he had been greatly struck with the aptness of the explanation which I gave him respecting the details of the breaking lessons.

In judging this work, I trust that my readers will give it the attention it deserves, as the result of sixty years' serious study and hard practical work.

I crave the indulgence of the public, and the impartiality of my reviewers.

JAMES FILLIS.

TRANSLATOR'S PREFACE.

MR. FILLIS, at whose request I have had the pleasure of translating his *Principes de Dressage et d'Équitation*, is acknowledged throughout Europe as the greatest high school rider of all time. In fact, he has had the honour of giving private riding exhibitions before The Emperor and Empress of Germany, The Tsar, President Carnot, The Queen of Belgium, The King and Crown Prince of Denmark, and the Emperor of Austria, all of whom have accorded him special marks of their appreciation of his unrivalled ability.

Having fortunately had many opportunities of seeing Mr. Fillis ride both in Germany and at the St. Petersburg Cavalry Riding School, where he is *Écuyer en chef*, I can fully endorse the correctness of the good opinion held about him by his most enthusiastic admirers.

A school rider obtains control and guidance by the combined action of hands and legs ; but an ordinary horseman depends almost entirely on the reins for collecting and directing his mount, and consequently his power over the animal is insufficient for military and polo requirements. With extremely few exceptions, school riders abuse their power, and sacrifice freedom of movement to exaggerated control, with the result, in many cases, of getting their animals behind their bits and straining their hocks. Such men ride in a mechanical manner, which is inelegant in a school or circus, and is entirely unsuited for work in the open. Mr. Fillis, on the contrary, acting on his motto "*en avant*" (forward), has succeeded in showing how a horse can be made clever in his movements, without in any way diminishing his usefulness on the road or over a country. I therefore trust that all English-speaking horsemen, and especially cavalrymen and polo players, will profit by the valuable instruction which he now puts before them.

M. H. HAYES.

CONTENTS.

CHAPTER I.

HORSE AND MAN.

CHAPTER II.

ORDINARY RIDING.

CHAPTER III.

HORSES WITH VICES.

LIST OF ILLUSTRATIONS.

BREAKING AND RIDING.

CHAPTER I.

HORSE AND MAN.

The Horse—Feeding—Intelligence of the Horse—Influence of a Man's expres-
sion of face on a Horse—Influence of the Human Voice on a Horse—
Making much of a Horse—Punishment—Bitting—Martingale—Saddle—
Stirrups—Cutting Whip—Spurs—Man's Seat—Lady's Seat.

THE HORSE.

ALTHOUGH I break in only thorough-breds for my own use ;
I in no way assume that three-quarter or half-breds cannot be
good riding horses.   I do not care for very big animals, and
prefer those about 15.2, or, say from 15.1 to 15.3.   When
examining a horse, I at first take a general view of him at
a distance of a few yards.   If the first impression is pleasing,
I go over his various points in detail, with a fairly liberal spirit,
as regards trifling faults ; but if it is not favourable, I become all
the more critical.   In any case, it is hopeless to expect perfection.   In this first general examination, we should be particularly
careful to see how he moves at the walk, trot and canter, both
when led and ridden.

Some horses appear badly shaped when standing still ; but
become good-looking, light and active as soon as they begin
to move.   Others, which seem almost perfect in repose, are
heavy and awkward in their paces.   I prefer the former to the
latter, because they can utilise what they have got.

I

I like a handsome head, long and light neck, prominent withers, short and strong back and loins, long croup, long and oblique shoulders, close coupling between the point of the hip and the last rib, hocks well let down, short canon bones, long fore arms, and the pasterns fairly long. These desirable points are rarely found in one animal. A horse should be close to the ground, which he will be when the distance from the brisket to the ground will be equal to that from the withers to the brisket. A horse which is high off the ground is generally clumsy in his movements, and liable to stumble.

I would have nothing to do with a horse whose fetlock and pastern joints are stiff, because he would be deficient in elasticity, would drag his feet, and would consequently be liable to trip.

I take particular care to see that the heels are not contracted. In order to prevent my horses acquiring this defect, I do not have them shod when they work on soft ground, in which case the heels remain well apart, on account of the frog being subjected to pressure. I always have my horses shod with tips, the ends of which are imbedded into the wall at the heels; and I thus prevent them having their heels contracted and their feet becoming diseased.

Horses are like men; having obtained physical perfection in them, we further require good temper and courage.

The highest mental qualification of a horse is to be a freegoer; because such an animal, contrary to what is often thought, is neither irritable nor sulky. I will again refer to this point. At present I confine myself to stating that such a horse is valuable, even if his make and shape are only moderate. If an animal has not the essential requirement of being always ready to go forward, he is useless, although he may be a perfect picture to look at.

I like to begin breaking a horse when he is two off and not more than three years old, and to buy if possible in or near

September, at which time the animal would be about two and a-half years old. At that age he would have done little or no work, and would consequently be sound. Besides, it is easy to get such horses, because there are a large number of young thorough-breds which are capable of becoming marvellously good horses for riding-school purposes and other work, although they might be of no use on a race-course. Also, for many other reasons, we can get a large choice of thorough-breds at that age.

I never buy mares, because they often become peevish, especially when touched with the spurs. I always have my horses "added to the list," because thorough-bred entires are greatly inclined to rush at every animal they meet, which is a habit that is not pleasant for their riders, and they are always ready to get on their hind legs. Besides, many of the horses which I break are required for ladies, who should never be allowed to ride a rearer. These objections do not generally apply to Arab and Trakene (German) entires, which live with mares and pay little or no attention to them. In course of time the thorough-bred entire gets heavy in front and becomes poor behind. A riding horse should, on the contrary, have his hind quarters well developed and his forehand light. Thorough-bred stallions which are used for stud purposes preserve their proper proportions, although they get very fat. Everyone knows that a gelding is much more quiet than an entire.

After the hot weather, I send my young horses to be castrated at the Veterinary College of Alfort, where they remain a fortnight, and afterwards I turn them out to grass for three months and a-half at a place where they are properly looked after. I do not put even a saddle on their backs during these four months, after which I begin their education in the quietest manner possible.

When I have taught them to go collectedly when walking,

1*

trotting, cantering, turning, reining back, and moving from one side to the other for a few steps, I begin to take them outside, and they will then need only a few days to make them pleasant to ride in the open. In this way, I first of all make them into hacks. During the following two or three months I repeat, in the open air, the work which my horses have learned in the school, so as to make them light and supple in their natural paces. Thus, from September to the end of December, nothing but care and repose ; from January to March, breaking in the school ; from April to June, confirmation, outside, of the work learned during the preceding months. In July I send my horses for their holiday to grass, leave them loose in the fields, and give them oats.

In August I resume work in the open, and as the animals have rested and got strong, I begin at the same time high school riding. My horses being handy, light and well balanced, their progress is rapid, and I generally finish their school training towards the end of December, with a limit of two or three months one way or the other, according to the difficulties which I have to overcome and the extent of the instruction. I then give them another holiday of a fortnight and immediately after that I take them out hunting if possible. I do not consider their education complete until I have tested them in all these ways.

In this manner I obtain an excellent hack for spring and summer, a hardy hunter for autumn, and a pleasant school horse for winter.

<h3 style="text-align:center">FEEDING.</h3>

I feed my horses liberally, especially as regards oats, of which I give them 10 quarterns a day. This makes them lively, but not more so than I wish. I give them only a small quantity of oats in the morning, so as not to overload their stomachs ; but I allow them all they can eat in the evening,

which is their time of rest.   Not being disturbed, they eat
slowly and thoroughly chew their food, which on that account
becomes properly digested.

I give one-and-a-half quarterns in the morning, three-and-a-
half at noon, and five in the evening.   The morning oats is
given at least two hours before work, so that the stomach of
the animal may be empty at that time.   For the same object
I rack him up, so that he may not eat his bedding.   Half an
hour after work I give each horse 2 or 3 lbs. of hay ; at noon
three-quarters of a bucket of water ; and after that, oats.   At
four o'clock in the afternoon, each horse gets a bundle of straw
as bedding ; at five o'clock, 2 or 3 lbs. of hay ; and finally, at
seven o'clock in the evening, the same quantity of water as at
noon, and the evening ration of oats, instead of which I give,
twice a week, a bran mash.

INTELLIGENCE OF THE HORSE.

The great difficulty in breaking is to make the horse understand what we want him to do, which is no easy matter,
because a horse, contrary to what many think, has only a small
supply of intelligence.   His only well-developed mental quality
is his memory, which is particularly acute, and should therefore be specially utilised.

A horse is incapable of affection for man : he possesses only
habits, which he often acquires far too easily, and frequently
sticks to them with too much persistence, a fact we should
always bear in mind.   On this subject I have made hundreds
of experiments.   For instance, one of my friends had a horse
which went to him when he called him, neighed when he
entered the stable, etc.   He averred that this animal was particularly attached to him, and that the horse would pine away
if he left him.   Having learned all about the habits of the
horse from the owner, I begged him to lend me the animal,
which I took to my stable, where I treated him exactly as he

had been treated in his own stable.   On the following day I
worked him during periods of time similar to those his owner
had adopted ; I gave him carrots according to established
custom ; I imitated the voice of his master ; and brought him
his food at the accustomed times.   On the following day I
re-assumed my natural tone of voice, and in forty-eight hours
the animal made similar manifestations of affection to me as
he had done to his master, whose loss he did not appear to
feel in the slightest degree.

After the morning lesson I give a large quantity of carrots
to my horses, who neigh the moment I speak to them on
entering the stable.   If a stranger accompanies me on these
occasions, he will always tell me that the animals recognise me
and love me, which is a mistake ; because if another person
takes my place in distributing the carrots at the usual hour, the
horses will not notice my absence.   This can easily be proved
by the fact that if I go into the stable a few minutes after they
have finished eating, they will not take the slightest notice of
my arrival.   I could give a hundred other instances of the indifference of horses towards those who tend them or ride them.
This is not a matter of regret ; for if horses were differently
constituted, they would be willing to obey only one master.

INFLUENCE OF A MAN'S EXPRESSION OF FACE
ON A HORSE.

Despite many arguments to the contrary, I am thoroughly
convinced that the human expression of face has no influence
on a horse, who pays no attention to one's look, whether it is
hard, angry, soft or caressing.   I have proved this fact by
many experiments on young and old animals ; and I can
certify that if a person who is looking at a horse works only
the muscles of his face, without moving his body or limbs, the
animal will not take the slightest notice of the changes of
expression.

I have scores of times tried the effect of giving a horse an angry look and of smiling on him without any result whatsoever. If you make the most horrible grimaces at your horses or stick your tongue out at them, you will find that they will take absolutely no notice of such a proceeding, but they will be quick to perceive any movement of the body, and especially of the hand.

INFLUENCE OF THE HUMAN VOICE ON A HORSE.

The human voice has a great influence on a horse, but of course it is only the tone which he remembers. The sweetest words, repeated in a short, high tone, will frighten him, and the most horrible threats, uttered in a soft voice, will soothe him. The voice is the most useful help for breaking a horse " at liberty," in which case he is turned loose in a riding school, circus, or other suitable enclosure. Thus, to teach a horse at liberty to move forward at a walk, trot or canter, one says : " walk," in a comparatively weak voice ; " trot," in a higher voice ; and " canter ! " in a tone of command. You may say " canter " in a soft voice, and the horse will remain at the walk ; but if you say " walk ! " in a high tone, the animal will immediately strike off into the canter.

The voice is also of great use when breaking a horse which one is riding. For instance, if my mount kicks, rears, or plays up in any other way, I correct him with whip or spurs, and speak to him, at the same time, in a tone of reproof, and he thus soon becomes attentive to my voice. If he makes a mistake, or tries on a " defence," it will generally be enough for me to raise my voice, which, by reminding him of the previous punishment, will make him quiet. By acting in this manner, I save him from fresh punishment.

The voice can be used not only for correction, but also to encourage and quieten a horse, in which case a pat on the neck of the horse will help to aid its good effect.

Its action is all the more useful because it can be employed in all cases with a varied choice of tone. A rider cannot, on the contrary, always bring his hands and legs into play.

Let us suppose that a hot-headed, impetuous horse which one is riding, gets startled and becomes maddened in a place where there are several carriages, and that one cannot get him out and steady him by means of the reins and legs. The voice, however, will calm him down, if he has been trained to obey it.

The effect of the voice has often been a great help to me, and has brought me out of many a difficulty.

I like impetuous horses, and I rarely use any others. I make them sufficiently quiet to carry ladies ; but I never employ them for this purpose until I am certain that my voice will soothe them when they are excited. I have avoided accidents by always acting in this manner.

MAKING MUCH OF A HORSE.

The good effect of "making much" of a horse should not be neglected, as we shall see further on. The education of the horse is based on the principles of reward and punishment. Making much of a horse gives him confidence, by placing the rider in direct contact with him otherwise than by impulsion.

All horses, even the most impatient, accept a pat on the neck, which is therefore the place the rider should caress. The pats on the neck should be given forcibly enough to attract the attention of the horse, but without hurting the animal. We should avoid touching him too lightly, which might only have the effect of tickling him.

A pat on the neck should be given at an appropriate time, that is to say, *immediately* after an act of obedience on the part of the horse, in the same manner as punishment should promptly follow disobedience. The moment he yields, give him his proper reward by patting him on the neck and slackening the reins, which will greatly facilitate the process of breaking. To obtain its full effect, a pat on the neck should be accompanied by the voice. A combination of these two soothing means will produce the best possible effect and, as a rule, will accomplish its object.

PUNISHMENT.

The education of a horse, as I have already said, depends entirely on the manner in which the rider applies the principles of reward and punishment ; the appropriate application of the latter being even more essential to success than that of the former. Above all things, the rider of a difficult horse should never lose his temper. When a horse deserves punishment, he should get it with an amount of severity which might be regarded as the outcome of anger, but which should be proportionate to the offence. In fact, we should treat horses as we do children. We all know that nothing is worse than to punish a child when we are in a rage. A horse can in no case understand the feeling which prompts a man to punish him, and he will remember only the pain he has suffered and the occasion on which it was inflicted. His intelligence enables him to connect his action with the punishment it provoked ; but it does not allow him to go further than that. On this account, if punishment is not administered at the precise moment the fault is committed, it will lose all its good effect, and will be an element of confusion in the memory of the animal. For instance, if a horse which kicks receives punishment when his hind legs are off the ground, he will remember that he got hurt for kicking. If, on the contrary, the punishment is received after his hind legs have come down, he will be unable to connect in his mind the ideas of these two acts ; in fact, the probability is that he will try, by a fresh kick, to get rid of the person who is hitting him.

I have said that every deliberate act of disobedience committed by a horse should be punished ; but I do not hesitate to add that it is better not to punish him than to do it too late. Both are bad, but it is necessary to choose the lesser of the two evils.

It is also important to find out what is the motive which has caused a horse either to wilfully disobey or to act on the defensive ; in other words, to find out whether he is vicious or in pain. Thus, if a horse kicks because his loins or hocks are painful, we would not be justified in punishing him, and should do everything to relieve his suffering. But if the kicking is a vice, we ought to severely correct him the moment it is practised, and, to prevent it, we should forcibly raise his head and neck in order to put the weight on his hind quarters.

BITTING.

I have nothing particular to say about the snaffle, except that it ought to be rather thick, so as to reduce its severity, and that it should be placed at about an equal distance from the bit and the corners of the mouth.

The form of a curb bit and the position it is placed in the mouth are points of great importance. It is impossible to decide at first glance what kind of curb will suit a young horse best, and what position it should occupy in his mouth. Baucher says that he would use the same kind of bit for all kinds of horses, which statement is the consequence of his pet theory that all horses have the same kind of mouth. I will discuss this theory further on, and I will here content myself with saying that even the most inexperienced horseman will state that horses go better in one bit than in another, and that certain animals will go kindly in a snaffle, but will resent

the use of a rather severe curb. This is a generally accepted
fact which has been amply proved. We can find the best
curb for a horse only by trial. But there are always certain
general principles to help us in making our experiments,
which we may sum up as follows :

The curb which is used at the beginning of the breaking
should have a thick mouth-piece, low port, and short cheek-
pieces, so that it may be easy to the mouth. Its width
should be proportionate to that of the mouth of the horse. If
it is too narrow, the lips will be compressed by the cheek-
pieces. If it is too wide, the horse, either in play or to relieve
the bars of his mouth from pressure, will bring it too much
over on one side of his mouth, so that a part of the port will
rest on one of the bars, and consequently the mouth-piece
will exert an uneven pressure, which will almost always cause
the horse to carry his head sideways.

In order that the curb may fit properly, it should be wide
enough for the cheeks to keep clear of the lips on each side.
The mouth-piece should have an even feeling on both sides of
the mouth, and should be mid-way between the tushes and
the corners of the lips, and consequently it will be lower in
the mouth than the snaffle in the case of a double bridle.
Later on I shall point out some exceptions to this rule. The
lower ends of the cheek-pieces, yielding to the pull of the
reins, cause the upper ends to revolve forward, and thus to
produce pressure on the bars of the mouth. The curb-chain,
which prevents the upper ends of the cheeks from revolving
forward, increases the pressure on the bars proportionately
to its shortness. Hence, the length of the curb-chain should
be proportionate to the lightness of the horse's mouth, which
we are unable to estimate in the case of a perfectly "green"
horse. With such an animal, we should at first leave the
curb-chain very loose, as there will always be time to take it
up. It would not, on the contrary, be right to say that there

is always time to slacken a tight curb-chain, which causes
pain that will continue to be felt by the horse after the curb-
chain has been let out.   If, however, we begin with a loose
curb-chain, and gradually shorten it to the desired extent, we
shall avoid hurting the bars of the mouth and irritating the
horse to resistance, and we gain time.   But if, at the beginning of the work, we hurt or even irritate the bars by undue
pressure, we shall fail to obtain any of the required indications.   By artificially increasing the sensitiveness of the bars,
we fail to estimate it correctly, and work on a wrong method
from the beginning.   The bruising or even the mere irritation
of the bars does not disappear as soon as the work is finished
and the bridle taken off, but continues for a more or less long
period.   Consequently, when the next lesson is given, the
bars are congested and painful.   The rider will then be apt
to form an opinion of the effects he produces on the mouth of
the horse without taking into consideration that it is in an
abnormal condition, and he will increase the evil which has
been done, and he will become more and more unable to
correctly estimate what is the natural condition of the mouth.
In a word, he will do the very things he ought not to do.
From the foregoing observations we can see that, at the
beginning of the breaking, the curb-chain should be loose.
In fact, it is better to take it off.

The knowledge of the mouth of a "green" horse is an
important and delicate matter.   In order to gently feel the
mouth without spoiling it, we must begin with great lightness
of hand, and gradually increase the pressure up to the point
of making the horse feel it, which sensitiveness varies in
degree according to the animal.   If a horse yields to the light
pressure of a curb which has no curb-chain, of what use is the
curb-chain, and what is the good of seeking for a more powerful means of restraint?

I have thoroughly broken horses, not only for the *manège*,

but also for outdoor work, without using a curb-chain, which may remain hooked up on one of the curb-hooks, so that it may be instantly used in case of need. As a rule, it should not be employed unless the rider finds that he needs its help. When he uses it, he should never put more tension on it than is actually required ; the proper maximum being when the curb-chain is tightened up, so that it makes an angle of 45° with the lower jaw.

As the tension of the curb-chain should be proportionate of the sensitiveness of the bars, so should the pressure caused by the pull of the reins be proportionate to the resistance. If this resistance is slight, the effort to overcome it should be light, and the point of its application should be high up on the jaw. If the resistance is great, the effort should be energetic, and it should be applied low down. Therefore, without greatly altering the middle position which the mouth-piece should occupy between the tushes and the corners of the lips, we may raise or lower the mouth-piece so that the horse may yield his jaw by, respectively, a light feeling of the reins, or by a strong pull on them. In other words, the softer the mouth is, the higher should be the mouth-piece ; and the harder, the lower should it be placed. In no case, however, should it press on, or even touch, the corners of the lips or the tushes.

We learn from the foregoing remarks that the proper tension of the curb-chain and the right position of the mouth-piece in the mouth of a young horse can be found only from experience, which should be gained from very slight effects that can be gradually increased in severity as the case may demand.

MARTINGALE.

The martingale prevents a horse from star-gazing and throwing up his head, and helps the rider to guide him. If a

horse is well broken he will not require its use. I would
recommend its employment only when the teacher has not
time or knowledge to properly break in a horse. It would be
well to put it on a horse which we are going to ride for the
first time, whether for hacking or for hunting, if we had
reason to think that he threw his head about or carried it
too high.

There are three kinds of martingales, namely, the *standing*
or *fixed martingale buckled on to the nose-band*, the *running
martingale*, and the *standing martingale buckled on to the
rings of the snaffle.* The first is the only one I would
recommend, because it produces its effect on the animal's
nose and not on his mouth, and, being unconnected with the
rider's hands, its use is consequently free from danger. It
ought to be long enough to allow the horse to carry his head
high, and short enough to prevent him bringing his nose in a
horizontal position, in which case the curb, by revolving from
below upwards, would produce no effect on the mouth. If
the martingale is too short, it will interfere with the movements of the horse, and can then become dangerous,
especially if he does not go freely forward ; because when it
is fixed in this manner, he will draw his chin in towards his
breast so as to escape from its action.

The running martingale has two rings, through which pass
the reins of the snaffle, and occasionally those of the curb,
which is a very dangerous arrangement. It is therefore
connected with the hands of the rider and the mouth of the
horse. It may be of great service to experienced riders, but
on account of the strong effect which can be produced with it,
it is particularly dangerous for other people.

The martingale which buckles on to the rings of the
snaffle, being unyielding, is always dangerous, particularly if
the horse runs back ; because, in this case, it will continue to
pull on his mouth. If he rears, which he will have a ten-

dency to do, in order to escape from the pressure of the mouth-piece, this martingale will be liable to make him fall backwards.

SADDLE.

I would not advise the use of a new saddle, which rarely gives satisfaction to the rider. New leather is hard and stiff, and consequently the seat of the saddle will not be comfortable. It is best to try several second-hand saddles, one of which is certain to give satisfaction.

The seat of a saddle ought to be fairly straight. If it is too high at the pommel the rider will be thrown back, and if it is too high at the cantle he will be thrown forward. I am also of opinion that a saddle should have very little stuffing, so that the rider may get close to his horse.

The length of the flaps should be proportionate to that of the thighs of the rider. If they are too short, the rider might hurt the calves of his legs. If too long, he will not be able to feel the sides of the horse with his legs. The rider can please himself as regards plain flaps or knee rolls, which are a matter of habit and firmness of seat. I believe I was the first to use a plain flap saddle for high school riding.

I always begin with a pupil by putting him on a French saddle in preference to an English one, as he is able to get better into it, and is consequently more at his ease. After the beginner acquires a firm seat in a French saddle, I put him in an English saddle covered with doeskin, and when he is able to trot, canter and turn without rolling about, I give him a plain English saddle to ride on.

STIRRUPS.

I never allow a pupil to use stirrups until he has acquired a good seat at all paces, and in this respect I follow the example of all the old riding masters, French and foreign. We must admit that formerly riders had quite a different seat to those of the present time. Stiffness has replaced the pliability, ease and grace of the olden time, because pupils have fallen into bad habits from the commencement of their instruction, either from want of comprehension or on account of being badly taught.

Not only the premature, but also the excessive use of the stirrups has other faults. I am of opinion that the great majority of dangerous falls are caused by their abuse. For example, Mr. X—— is run away with by his horse in the Forest of Saint-Germain ; he sits well down into the saddle, succeeds in stopping the animal, and starts into a trot on his stirrups ; unfortunately, a stirrup leather breaks at this moment, and Mr. X—— falls on his head and is killed. Every horseman knows that the breaking of a stirrup leather can cause a rider to fall on his head, only because the man had put all his weight on the stirrups, and was consequently more or less out of the saddle. If he was not bearing his weight on the stirrups he might, no doubt, roll off, but the severity of the fall would be more or less broken by the fact that the knees would be gripping the flaps of the saddle. I would go further and say that if a rider did not depend on his stirrups, he would hardly ever fall off on account of a stirrup leather breaking.

Let us take another example. Mr. Z——, at Toulouse, rides out of his stable at a walk ; his horse falls, and Mr. Z—— is thrown forward on to his head and is killed. We need no knowledge of riding to understand that if he had been sitting in his saddle he could not have been thrown forward with such violence. I hasten to add that I recall these two well-remembered accidents, not in a spirit of criticism, but in order to explain the sad consequences which may arise from the abuse of the stirrups, and in the hope that my modest advice may render such accidents rare in the future.

Standing on the stirrups is like standing on a spring-board, in which case, if any violent movement is produced by the horse, the rider is liable to be shot forward as if from a catapult, and always on to his head. Even when the horse plunges forward, the rider will be rarely unseated if he is sitting well into the saddle, with the weight resting on his seat. Then the worst thing that can happen to him is to be shifted on to the horse's neck, in which case he will fall softly; but if he is bearing his weight on the stirrups, with his legs straight, nothing will be easier for the horse than to send him between his ears. When the rider adopts this faulty position, his body is carried forward, and the horse is able to plunge as he likes, on account of the weight being taken off his loins.

The rider who stands on his stirrups is in the position of a gymnast standing on the hands of a comrade, whose business is to give him the necessary propulsion for making a dangerous leap. In order for him to be projected very far, it is necessary for him to keep his body and legs straight, but if he bends his knees he cannot go far. The stirrups play a *rôle* similar to that of the hands of the gymnast who is ready to give the propulsion. Hence, if the rider bends his knees he will remain in the saddle.

We should bear in mind that if the pupil, before his legs have got well down, is allowed to use the stirrups, he will not be able to keep his feet in them. He will then make all sorts of contortions in order to retain them, in which case, not only the muscles of the legs, but also those of the body and face, will become contracted, and the neck and the shoulders will assume a characteristic form of stiffness.

Notwithstanding all the care which the teacher may take later on to correct these faults, the pupil very rarely succeeds

2

in getting rid of them ; because it is extremely difficult, if not
impossible, to leave off a bad habit.

CUTTING WHIP.

I use the cutting whip only in work on foot, in order to
teach the horse to go forward, and to give way to the spur, but
I discard it the moment I mount.   True horsemen require legs
and hands ; incompetent riders need a whip.

SPURS.

The box spur is the only spur of which I approve, because it
remains fixed in its place, and it can therefore be applied with
precision.   All the other kinds are liable to become displaced,
either up or down, so that one is never certain of touching the
horse on the spot one wishes.

We ought to use dummy spurs (spurs with round heads), if
they are sufficient for our purpose, and we can replace them by
spurs with very blunt rowels, the sharpness of which should
be increased only when necessary as, for example, when the
horse does not answer to their touch.

Without trying them, it is difficult to find out the proper
length for the neck of the spurs, which should be short, if the
legs of the rider are short ; because, in this case, his heels will
always remain close to the animal's sides.   If the rider has
long legs, he will be obliged to raise his heels when he wants
to use the spurs, which should have proportionately long
necks, so that he may have to shorten his legs as little as
possible.

MAN'S SEAT.

As a rule, every one can acquire a good and strong seat,
but every one cannot become a fine and graceful horseman.

A pupil who has been well taught from the beginning, has
done his best to learn, has trotted without stirrups for several

months, has ridden horses that were lively and difficult, without being dangerous, will of necessity acquire a firm seat. He will hold his head in a free and unconstrained position, so that he can move it with ease in every direction. He will keep it high in all ordinary paces and when jumping, and will lower it a little, with the chin towards the breast, when going fast. His eyes should preserve their mobility, and should not become fixed in any one direction, so that they may take notice of all the inequalities of ground, fences and other difficulties which the horse may meet. He should keep his neck supple, and his shoulders down and without contracting them, as is often done. His arms should hang naturally down to the elbows, which should be kept close to the sides, and should on no account be turned outwards; for the hands cannot be kept light if the elbows are in this position. Lightness of hand is absolutely necessary for using the reins with precision and without jerking them. With the elbows firmly fixed to the sides, it is easy to prevent the hands from moving about.

A rider who has a good seat will keep his elbows at the height of his waist, the insides of the wrists facing each other and the fingers turned inwards. He should avoid rounding the wrists, which would tend to bring the elbows away from the sides, and would prevent him having a straight line of communication with the horse's mouth. The action of the bit on the mouth of the horse should be produced only by the tightening and slackening of the fingers on the reins. A rider who works his hands a good deal, does not know how to use them; but a man with good hands produces the necessary effect by a simple movement of the wrist and fingers.

The rider ought to keep his body upright, but without any stiffness, which prevents the independent action of the "aids" (hands and legs). Stiffness in one part produces muscular contraction of the whole body, which is a condition entirely

2*

opposed to good horsemanship.   He should in no case hollow
out the back, because that will produce stiffness which is the
thing we should avoid.   The loins (not the shoulders), on the
contrary, should be slightly rounded, so as to preserve their
elasticity.   The chest should be kept in a natural position,
without being pressed out in any way, and the muscles of
the pelvis relaxed, which is the only means of obtaining ease.

The weight of the upper part of the body should be carried
by the buttocks, which are its only proper support.   The legs
should be stretched well down, the thighs flat, the knees close
to the flaps of the saddle, and the toes turned slightly outwards, so that the horse may feel the leg before he is touched
with the spur.   When the toes are turned too much inwards,
the calves of the legs will be forced outwards, and then the
rider will be able to use the spurs only by prods.

The fact of the knees forming a kind of fixed pivot will
give great mobility to the lower portion of the legs, which
should fall naturally from the knees, and should not be kept
close to the animal's sides.   In order for the rider to be at his
ease, he should sit well down in the saddle, without hanging
on by his hands or gripping by his knees, which should grip
only when occasion demands.   By always gripping with the
knees, the rider is made to assume a cramped position on
horseback.   On the contrary, the seat should be maintained
by balance and not by grip.   When we use the leg, we should
use it from the knee to the heel.   Fatigue of the muscles
above the knee is caused by stiffness and is a sign that the
seat is bad.

The rider will also appear cramped if his knees are too
high, if too low he will rest not on his buttocks, but on the
inner part of his thighs, which fact will increase the firmness of his seat, because the entire length of the legs will be
applied to the horse.   This seat can be used with advantage
by cavalry when charging, only at the moment of meeting

the enemy, because it helps them to avoid being displaced by the shock. With this seat, it is difficult to keep close to the horse when he changes from the canter to the trot. In conclusion, I may point out that a rider who has a good seat sits on a saddle in the same manner as he would do on a chair.

When the rider uses stirrups, his toes ought to be higher than his heels. Without stirrups, the feet ought to fall naturally, and consequently the toes will be lower than the heels. We may see that with the feet out of the stirrups, it is impossible to keep the toes up without contracting (stiffening) the muscles of the legs. In Germany, pupils are taught to keep the toes higher than the heels, when riding without stirrups, which practice gives German horsemen their characteristic stiffness. I am aware that Germans are naturally stiff. Even a Frenchman made to ride in that manner would become stiff.

The length of the stirrups should be proportionate to that of the legs. The traditional plan of measuring the length of the stirrups by that of the arm, affords a useful approximation which one has always to rectify when mounted. To do this, it is necessary to take the feet out of the stirrups and to leave the legs hanging down. Then the stirrup leathers will be the correct length when the " tread " of the iron comes just below the ankle joint. It is generally recommended to keep the foot in contact with the internal side of the stirrup iron. I place my foot at an equal distance from both sides of the iron. We can give great suppleness to the ankle joints by working them in various directions, and can then let go or pick up the irons very easily. In the open I ride with the leathers one hole shorter than in the school, and then obtain a better support in quick paces, especially when rising at the trot. In the *manège* one requires to have the legs lower down than in the open, so as to get the legs round the horse, and it is also necessary to be entirely on the buttocks, in

order to catch each movement of the horse. We all know
that this feeling can be acquired only by long training.

Many physical qualities are necessary for obtaining a
strong and graceful seat. For instance, it is evident that
a stout, short man is less likely to ride well than one who is
sufficiently tall and slight. I say " sufficiently tall," because
it is a common error to think that one must be tall in order
to ride well. On the contrary, the taller the horseman, the
more difficulties will he have in riding. First of all, the
longer the body, the more easily can it be displaced, on
account of the height of the centre of gravity, and the harder
will it be for the equilibrium to be restored. Also, long legs
cannot adapt themselves to the sides of the horse so well as
those of medium length, because the feet are below the sides
of the horse, and if the rider wishes to use the spurs he is
obliged to bend his knees, in order to shorten his legs, which
action is ugly, and weakens the seat.

I recognise the fact that every man can acquire a strong
seat if he works hard. The remarks I lately made about
German stiffness also apply to the English. Nations of
Teutonic origin have justly earned the reputation of being
the best horsemen, which they have become by their great
perseverance and love of work. The Latin races, being of
middle height, are better fitted, by their suppleness and
agility, to work in harmony with a horse, and if they were
industrious they would certainly be the finest horsemen in
the world. But, unfortunately, they are content with being
nearly the best. It goes without saying that I am speaking
generally, and that there are good and bad horsemen in
every country.

The ease, firmness of seat and confidence of the rider
generally depend on the first lesson which he has received ;
and, as I have said, a good seat is acquired only by trotting
without stirrups for a long time.

The only horses beiginners should ride are those which have easy paces and very good tempers. One cannot take too much pains to give confidence to a novice. It is only the confidence which he gets in his first lessons that will enable him later on to ride with entire absence of stiffness. A man whose movements on horse-back are stiff, may remain on the outside of his mount, but does not ride him. Stiffness of arms, legs and body makes fine horsemanship impossible. How can contracted or stiff limbs keep in touch with the horse while they are occupied in holding the body on the saddle? When they become supple, and when the body maintains its position in the saddle by balance, they will acquire a delicate feeling with the horse, which they had not at first. Flexibility of the limbs and a good seat are indispensable conditions for attaining "equestrian tact."

Being merely stuck on a saddle is not riding. Generally the pupil gradually gets out of this faulty position only by acquiring confidence in his seat. I need hardly say that a man may be very brave and yet have no confidence in the saddle.

Slight horses are best for the first lessons, especially in the case of boys and men who have short legs. A too great separation of the legs might have grave results, and it fatigues the groins without benefiting the rider in any way. I have seen malformations of the hips caused by this practice. Later on, the rider becomes accustomed to this form of gymnastics, and he will be able to ride a horse of any shape without discomfort.

I think that beginners should not ride with a double bridle, and that it is better for them to use an ordinary snaffle, with a rein in each hand. If they are at first given a double bridle, the body will probably follow the movements of the hands, because, at the beginning, they almost always carry the hands and also the arms either to one side or the other.

This faulty practice is avoided when the snaffle reins are held one in each hand. We should bear in mind that it is easier to put a beginner into a good position than to rectify a bad seat later on.

To sum up, I may say that the chief good point about a rider is firmness of seat, which is obtained by a correct position and practice. The rider should have, not merely blind pluck, but self-confidence and coolness, without which he will not be able to utilise the useful things he has learned.

It is not necessary to know all about horses in order to ride well. I prefer an unscientific man who can stick on any rideable horse, to one who is strong in theory but weak in practice. The purely theoretical man almost always succeeds in making restive horses which he pretends to break in. He may have enough firmness of seat to give the horse an indication to move, but not sufficient to enable him to enforce his orders when the animal " plays up."

Nothing is worse than to provoke a horse to resistance if the rider has not the pluck to make him give in.

LADY'S SEAT.

Except as regards the legs, a lady should sit on a saddle exactly like a man. For some time there has been talk of ladies riding astride, which practice would deprive her of all feminine grace, and would afford no useful result. The great want in a man's seat is firmness, which would be still more difficult for a woman to acquire if she rode in a cross-saddle, because her thighs are rounder and weaker than those of a man. Discussion of this subject is therefore useless. Ladies who ride astride get such bad falls that they soon give up this practice.

At all paces the shoulders should be parallel to the ears of the horse, which is possible only when the hips occupy a similar position. Therefore the position of the lady depends entirely on that of the hips. The two legs being on the left, the right leg is hooked round the upper crutch, and is more advanced and higher than the left leg, which presses against the leaping-head, a little above the knee, and the foot rests in the stirrup.

It has been proposed that ladies should sit on the right side of the saddle. English and American journals have dwelt on the bad effects of girls on only one side of the horse, and they have tried to make out that this practice causes curvature of the spine. As I judge only by practical observations, I cannot say how it would affect children of five or six years old; but as I have often taught beginners of twelve or thirteen years old, I can certify most positively that girls of that age have nothing to fear on that score.

I am well aware that in England and America young girls are given their first lesson in riding by coachmen and grooms, who are apt to teach wrongly and to pass over, and even accentuate faults. The same remark applies to many riding masters who have studied both theory and practice, and who succeed, only after a long course of teaching, in correcting small mistakes, which are apt to become greater.

I maintain that if a lady is taught by a good master, her figure, instead of being spoiled by riding exclusively on the left side of the saddle, will increase in grace and suppleness. We may therefore continue to make ladies ride only on the left side. Placing her on the right side would be accompanied by the serious inconvenience of making her hold the whip in her left hand, which she cannot use as easily as her right. Her whip hand acts the part of a horseman's leg.

The position of a lady on the left side of a saddle, causes almost all the weight of her body to be carried to the right side; consequently, the left hip being freer from weight, is apt to be stuck out behind the right hip, which is a fault that ought to be avoided. The weight of the body ought to be equally distributed on both sides. Like a man in his saddle, she ought to sit in her saddle exactly as she sits in a chair, namely, with the hips and shoulders parallel to the ears of the horse. This is a question not only of correct attitude, but also of strength of seat, which is the main thing.

A lady is rarely thrown to the left, because she is supported on that side by the crutches, and, if need be, by the stirrup. All the danger of a fall is therefore on the right, and it increases in proportion as the left shoulder is drawn back.

It is easy to understand that if a horse makes an abrupt movement, or makes a shy from the right to the left, the upper part of the body will be forcibly thrown to the right, a displacement which can be easily prevented by the lady holding herself in a correct position, that is to say, if her shoulders are placed as I have just indicated. If, on the contrary, the left shoulder is not so far advanced as the right one, her equilibrium will be unstable and she will be in danger of falling off, which kind of fall should be provided against, because it is dangerous; for the lady will fall on her head, supposing that she gets clear of the crutches and stirrup. If, in falling, her foot catches in the stirrup, or if her skirt becomes hooked on the crutches, she will become dragged without having any means of freeing herself.

That which gives firmness of seat to the horsewoman also endows her with elegance. Consequently, she need not sacrifice either of these advantages for the other. It is necessary: *Firstly*, that the knees are brought as closely together as possible, the right leg being firmly hooked round the upper crutch, with its pressure acting from front to rear. The left leg, on the contrary, by reason of the fulcrum afforded by the stirrup, exerts its pressure from rear to front. *Secondly*, the left shoulder should be carried well forward, and the body slightly bent forward, so as to make it more supple.

If the left shoulder is drawn back when the horse is at a

walk, and consequently when all the weight is on the saddle,
the position of the lady is bad and particularly ungraceful.
When rising at the trot, her seat is still worse ; because the
left shoulder is jerked forward when she rises, and goes back
when she comes down on the saddle.   This is the well-known
ungraceful cork-screw movement.

When the lady sits evenly on both sides of the saddle and
has a good position at the walk, her hips and shoulders will
easily remain well placed at the trot.

She should keep her body well under her when rising at
the trot.   The upper part of the body makes no effort, but
allows itself to be raised by the movement of the horse.   The
foot rests in the stirrup iron without stiffness, and the ankle
and knees act only as hinges.   The slightest muscular contraction, or the least effort made by the ankle, knees or loins
will give the rider a stiff and ungraceful appearance, and will
cause fatigue.   If the lady will carry out these rules, she will
ride in two-time, namely, one on the saddle and one in the
air.   Otherwise she will come down too quickly, and will
mark two-times on the saddle, which will give her a useless
and fatiguing shock.   I will refer to this fact at greater
length when discussing the position of a horseman at the trot
(p. 146).

A horsewoman should have great pliability of body, which
she will acquire by practice in riding and other preliminary
exercises, of which dancing is the best.   It also depends on
certain small details of dress, about which I may give the
following advice.

A lady on horseback is apt to cut herself.   The slightest
crease in her clothes may cause an abrasion.   For a long ride,
and still more for hunting, she should wear a short chemisette,
made of very fine material, and fitting close to the body.
The collar and cuffs ought to be strongly connected to this
chemisette, and not fixed to it merely by pins, which are liable

to fall out or hurt the wearer.   I strongly advise that she
should wear socks instead of stockings ; because a garter is
always inconvenient and may cause serious wounds.   The
socks should be furnished with a close-fitting collar of some
soft and elastic material, such as knitting or jersey, lined with
silk, or, still better, very fine doeskin.   The trousers should
be strapped with india-rubber and should fit rather closely, so
that they may not wrinkle.   The boots should have elastic
sides and not buttons, which might cause wounds.   I prefer
ordinary boots to long boots, which are too hard, and are
consequently apt to cut the wearer under the knee, and to
prevent her feeling the horse with her leg.   The corset should
be very short and low.   A long busk is not only inconvenient,
but is also dangerous.   I would not have touched on these
details but for the fact that the dress of the horsewoman is
closely connected with her strength of seat and ease in the
saddle.   I have seen so many ladies returning from a ride in
pain, and condemned to spend many days in a long chair, that
I am certain the points to which I have drawn attention are
important.

The head-dress of the lady should be firmly arranged, so that
it may not occupy her attention, in which case she will think
too little of her horse.   Then, if she loses her hat, she will
probably lose her head.

The choice of a saddle is of great importance, both for the
rider and for the horse.   Its seat should be quite level, so that
the knees of the rider may not be higher than her seat, and
it should have but little stuffing, so that it may fit close to the
horse, and may not become shifted.   The smallest displacement of the saddle may seriously injure the animal's withers.
If the cantle of the saddle is too short, it will certainly hurt
the rider, and if too long, it will hurt the horse's loins.

A lady's horse should have high withers, so as to prevent
the saddle turning round.   Great care should be taken that

the mane at the withers does not become pressed upon by the pommel of the saddle, the irritation from which often causes the animal to "play up."

A few words about putting a lady into a saddle may be useful, not only for horsewomen, but also for men who have the somewhat parlous honour of touching a lady's foot. I regret to say that when being "put up" a lady generally does the very opposite of what she ought to do. She places the left foot in the hands of her male attendant, and jumps from the right foot on to the left foot, while carrying the body forward, with the result that all the weight falls suddenly on the hands of the man, who is inevitably pushed backwards and away from the shoulder of the animal. On the contrary, when her left foot is on his hands, she ought to use the right leg only to make a slight spring which will enable her, by straightening her left knee, to hold the body upright and a little inclined to the rear. This is a very simple movement, and is exactly similar to that which one makes when getting up a rather high step of a staircase. The lady should not try to jump up, but should limit her spring to straightening the left knee, while keeping the upper part of the body well bent forward ; and she should use her arms, her left hand resting on the shoulder of her attendant and her right hand on the upper crutch. In acting thus, she will mount quite straight by the impulse given by the hands, and will come naturally on the saddle, and will carry the seat a little to the rear. She should not try to place herself on the horse, which is the business of her attendant, but should merely occupy herself with sitting down. If a lady attempts to jump into the saddle, she will generally strike it and fall on the man.

I cannot help adding that the old practice of giving the left foot is bad, and am unable to explain its origin or the reason of its continuance. In fact, to be put on the saddle with the left foot on the hands of the attendant, the lady, when she is

raised up, ought to carry her seat from front to rear, and from
left to right, while the man at the same time makes a
movement from rear to front and from right to left.
Here we have a double displacement.   If, on the contrary,
the lady gives her right foot, which is nearer to the
horse than the left, she need make only a very slight spring
with her left foot and to straighten the right knee, to come
naturally on the middle line of the saddle, and to sit down
without the slightest displacement.   I do not claim the merit
of having discovered this simple method, which has long been
practised by many of the best horsewomen.   I have had the
honour of putting into the saddle sovereign ladies who always
mounted in this manner.   Ladies, without having previously
made up your mind, please try for a week this method of
being put up on the saddle, and I am certain you will
adopt it.

As soon as the lady is in the saddle she ought to place her
right leg over the upper crutch without waiting to settle her
skirt, so that she may avoid falling off in the event of the
horse starting to one side.   I may add that the hands of the
man ought not to quit the foot of the lady until her right leg
is in its right place.   To dismount, the lady takes her foot
out of the stirrup and gives her left wrist to the attendant.
She thereupon removes her right leg from the upper crutch,
gives him the right wrist, and lets herself slip down to the
ground, while supporting herself a little with her arms.   She
ought to alight on her toes, and should bend her knees, so as
to avoid any concussion, which, without this precaution, she
is apt to receive after a long ride, on account of her legs
being stiff and numbed.   I repeat that the lady ought to give
her wrists, and instead of jumping ought to slide down.   It
often happens that the lady throws herself from the saddle
and the cavalier takes hold of her by the waist.   Not being
able to hold her up with his outstretched arms, he lets her

slide through his hands, which is ungraceful and not particularly decent.

The question is often asked whether the lady's cavalier should ride on her right side or on her left? I do not think that a fixed rule on this subject would work well. Under ordinary conditions the man should be on the right, because the lady, in order to turn her head towards him, is obliged to carry the right shoulder back, which is the correct position, as I have already said. Further, the gentleman, being on the right, can, in case of necessity, help the lady, to whom he cannot come close enough, on account of the position of her legs, if he is on the left. If it happens that there is danger on the left to the lady, by reason of the presence of horses or carriages, he ought to place himself on that side in order to protect her legs.

CHAPTER II.

ORDINARY RIDING.

Lunging a Horse—Close work, advancing—Collecting a Horse and direct Flexion
—Objects to be obtained by direct Flexion—Making a Horse quiet to mount
—How to hold the Reins—Teaching a Horse by the Whip to obey legs and
spurs—Horse mounted, first Defences, means for overcoming them—The
Walk—To halt and stand still—Changes of Direction—Lateral flexions—
Objects of Lateral flexions—Rotation of the Croup and Shoulders—School
Walk—The rein back—The *ramener*, collection, *rassembler*, and equestrian
tact—Side steps and two tracks—The trot—The canter—Voltes and demi
voltes at the canter—Changes of leg—The Hack.

LUNGING A HORSE.

I WORK all horses in the same manner. The animal
which is to be broken being brought into the school saddled
and bridled, I pass the reins of the curb and snaffle through
the throat-latch, so that the horse may not catch them with
his feet. I then buckle a lunging rein to the left ring of the
snaffle and let the horse walk at ease.

For every lesson the horse should have flannel bandages on
his forelegs, from the fetlock to the knee, so as to support
the flexor tendons and to guard the horse from getting
splints which are often caused by a green horse hitting
himself.

Immediately after the lesson I take the bandages off the
forelegs and put them on the hind ones, and leave them on
for three or four hours, which period is sufficiently long to

prevent the legs filling and windgalls forming. If flannel bandages are constantly left on, the tissues of the legs are apt to become softened and the tendons to become stretched by the action of the heat.

If he tries to get away from me I let him go, my object being to make him keep close to the wall. If he does not try to get away and turns towards me, I show him the driving whip, the sight of which will make him get away as far as the lunging rein will allow him. I hold the whip in my right hand, the rein in my left, and I let the horse free to go at any pace he likes. The object of walking the horse in this way round the school is to make him examine the ground and all the surrounding objects which are new to him.

If he is lively he will probably plunge, and then canter or trot, but he will soon steady down. If he is sluggish he will be disinclined to go forward, and it may be necessary to make him go on by showing him the whip. If that does not produce the desired effect, we may touch him lightly on the hind quarters, so as to make him trot or canter for about five minutes. We should most carefully avoid making any abrupt or rough movement which might frighten him.

I have said that I would give the animal five minutes' work at a fast pace, but, of course, would not do so unless he was in good condition. If he was not fairly fit, the duration of the work would be shorter during the first few lessons, and would be gradually increased up to the five minutes' limit.

When the horse has circled for five minutes to the left— that is to say, with the left shoulder towards the inside of the school—I throw the whip down and try to steady the horse by my voice. I then shorten the lunging rein until he is close to me. I speak softly to him and pat him on the neck, which is a form of caress that all horses like. I also stroke his head, if he will let me do so, and then unbuckle the lunging rein and fix it to the off ring of the snaffle.

After a short rest I begin the same exercises to the right for five minutes. When the work is over I again throw down the whip, and call the horse to me, while at the same time gently drawing him towards me by the lunging rein, and then pat and stroke him as before.

In my opinion the foregoing exercise is the indispensable first step in breaking, and, as I attach great importance to it, I will give my reasons at some length as follows.

A young horse is almost always restless and timid; shadows, walls, and all sorts of trifling objects frighten him. He rushes away from anything that startles him, and goes to the part of the school which is unoccupied, while I remain by myself in the centre. If I show him the whip, while advancing towards his side, he instinctively flies away and goes to the wall, against which he can be easily kept by pointing the whip towards his shoulder.

Being placed between the threat which I make and an object which he fears, and from which he has fled, he returns to this fixed object, which appears to him to be less terrifying than the driving whip. When, thanks to this procedure, he has several times crossed the place of which he was afraid, he will eventually have no fear of it. We may note that it was not necessary to use punishment, which should be our last resort.

Further, if the animal is too lively, I would give him a good long turn at the trot, or even at the canter, if he prefers that pace, in order to get rid of his excess of energy. If he is dull, I teach him, by means of a few cuts of the whip, to go forward. We must draw a distinction between a horse that is soft and one that is sluggish. If the former is properly fed and exercised he can become lively; but the latter, although he may be full of muscular vigour, does not like to put forth his strength except when he pleases, a fact which makes him dangerous to an inexperienced rider. We are

never certain except with a free-going horse. Although an
impetuous animal may get out of control and run away, I
prefer him to a sluggish horse. Pluck is the best quality in a
horse.

I have always obtained a good result with my equine pupil,
who quickly loses fear of the things which surround him,
because he has no one on his back to hamper his movements
and upset him. I easily obtain my result without a struggle,
and without having to put up with the plunges and shies of a
horse which has been mounted too soon, and which is liable
to roll over on the ground with me, on account of the
awkward use of his feet.

It is of great advantage to teach a horse to know, bear and
fear the lunging whip; because if, later on, he refuses to go
forward when ridden by an indifferent horseman, the use of
the whip will make him obey. The sight of it will often be
sufficient to make him go forward. If he refuses to do so,
we should touch him lightly and carefully behind, because
any roughness or abruptness is apt to make him resist.

Lunging has the further advantage of enabling us to make
a horse trot out, by driving his hind quarters forward with
the whip. In fact, we can thus make a horse acquire the
habit of collecting himself. By being lunged in freedom, he
will gain suppleness, confidence, cleverness and sure-footed-
ness, which are the best qualities in a horse. A harnessed
horse puts his weight on the collar and a mounted animal
puts it on the hand of his rider; but a horse which is
lunged is obliged to balance himself independently of all
support.

A horse which is lunged at a fast pace for five minutes to
the right, and for another five minutes to the left, gets in good
wind, on account of the work his lungs have to do. If he
was ridden, he would not get this exercise during his first
few lessons; because they would be given at a walk.

During the first two or three lessons, I let the horse go at any pace he likes, provided that it is fast and that he keeps to the wall.   I make him trot in the subsequent lessons.

It is so easy to make a horse trot, that one ought to do so with any horse in the third or fourth lesson without an assistant.   The old custom, recommended in almost every book on the subject, of having two men to lunge a horse is faulty, because it is impossible to have perfect harmony in the movements of these men.   It often happens that the man with the whip touches up the horse when he ought not to do so, and that the man who is holding the lunging rein, stops the animal at the moment when his comrade is making him go on.   Of course, such a discord could not happen if the breaker was by himself.

Supposing that the horse is at the wall, and going to the left ; the breaker, who is at the centre of the school, ought always remain facing the horse and at a line with his shoulder, thus keeping him enclosed in the angle made by the lunging rein and whip, the former held in the left hand, the latter in the right hand.   The breaker should always *accompany* the horse, but should not *follow* him, and should place himself so as always to keep the horse between the lunging rein in front and the whip behind.

In order to *accompany* a horse without *following* him, while constantly remaining in a line with his shoulder, we need only follow the diagonal, while alternately extending and drawing back the arm.   This precaution is essential, because if we describe a circle, when following the horse round the school, we shall get giddy and become unable to carry out the work properly.   By moving diagonally we can accompany the horse as long as we like.

To make the horse trot, I touch him lightly behind with the whip.   It is better to touch the shoulder, but we should not try to do so, especially with a young horse, unless we have great experience in using the whip. If, instead of lightly dropping on the shoulder, the lash touches or brushes by the head, the horse will start back, and we shall then obtain a movement which is the exact opposite of what we wanted. Also, if the horse is a bit lively, we may stimulate him with a click of the tongue, which is a form of stimulus we should not use too much, because it might upset other horses when we are in company.

If the use of the driving whip makes the horse plunge or go off into the canter, as it often does, I soothe him by lightly shaking the lunging rein and speaking to him at the same time. The lunging rein should never be kept tight, but should remain in touch with the mouth only by its own weight, and by the vibrations which the breaker gives it.

I have already said that the voice is a powerful help in breaking. If, when we shake the lunging rein to make the animal adopt a slower pace, we call out loudly " trot ! " no matter how stupid he may be, he will soon connect in his mind the effect produced on his mouth and the sound which falls on his ears. At first he will obey only the combined impression, but he will soon learn to obey the voice by itself.

When I have obtained a free trot which is kept up for the time required, I bring the horse to the walk by lightly shaking the rein, in the same manner as I made him change from the canter into the trot. Here also I use the voice rather loudly, though mildly, in saying " whoa ! "

The next step is to make the horse come up to the breaker. To do this, I gently shorten the rein and draw the horse towards me, while walking backwards with very short steps, so that he gradually gets closer to me. When he has arrived within reach of my stretched-out arm, I pat him on the neck and soothe him with the voice. I take great care to avoid making the slightest forward movement with the

body, my wish being to give him confidence. If I were
to make a step forward, he would immediately spring back,
which result would be the opposite to that which I wished
to obtain. If nothing has frightened him while he is coming
to me, and if my pats on his neck and my voice have shown
him that he need not fear my presence, he will soon gain
confidence, and will of himself try to come to me, and all the
more readily when he finds that tranquility is to be obtained
only at the centre of the school. He ought to have sufficient
confidence to come up to the breaker without fear, but he
should do so only at a given signal. Our object is to make
him understand this signal without the use of the lunging
rein, which will be discontinued later on.

I use the driving whip to make the horse come up to me
in obedience to my order, and I give him light and repeated
flicks on the buttock, ribs, or shoulder, while always seeking to
block the side from which he tries to escape. In order to
make the animal go forward, I sometimes touch him on the
breast, in which case his first movement is to run back ; but
I continue to hold him tightly with the lunging rein, and
while preventing him from running back, I call out "whoa!"

If he runs back, he does so because he is afraid of the
whip. An unbroken horse does not fly from a sting, flick, or
prod ; on the contrary, he goes up to it and lies against it.

We shall see further on that the effect obtained on a
mounted horse by the pressure of the leg or by a touch of the
spur is due solely to education. A horse in a state of nature
will do the very opposite to what he will do when broken.
For instance, stung on the right flank by a fly, he will bring
himself round to the right, until he meets some object against
which he can rub himself or even lie upon.

The sight of the driving whip makes him run away from it,
but its touch makes him go forward. As soon as the tension
of the lunging rein has shown him that he cannot get away

from the sight of the whip by running back, his instinct will cause him to go forward. If at that moment the whip is lowered and a pat on the neck given, he will gain confidence, will understand what we want him to do, and will obey our wishes. Although we cannot obtain the result at the first attempt, we shall do so in a few lessons, especially if the breaker does not frighten the horse by some abrupt movement when the animal is advancing.

We can dispense with the lunging rein as soon as the horse will come freely up to us, when we show him the driving whip. This first lunging work is only preparatory. It has been used in all times, but has been applied and utilised in different ways. It was employed in excess before the days of Baucher, who disliked it. I think it is useful, supposing, of course, that it is not employed to fatigue the horse.

In order to make a horse come up to me without the help of the lunging rein, I use the same methods as when lunging. At the beginning of the work I employ the rein a good deal and the whip only a little. According as the horse progresses I diminish the use of the rein and increase that of the whip, while always blocking up with the whip the side at which the horse tries to escape from me, so as to make him come up to me. Finally, he gets into the habit of coming up to me on seeing the whip, and without my using the rein in any way. I then teach him to follow me all over the school, while always stopping him with the whip from getting away, and making him promptly go on by light flicks on the hind quarters.

Finally I discontinue the use of the lunging rein. If, as always happens, the horse refuses to obey the whip and tries to escape from me, there is a battle, which consists in my flicking the horse on the hind quarters until he comes up to me, which result may at first appear improbable. However, when the horse is pursued by the man round the school for a sufficiently great number of times, his only idea will be to stop. As the whip follows him all round the track of the school and allows him rest only at the centre, he finishes by coming to it, in the same manner as he learned when being lunged. In order to facilitate this movement on his part, the breaker ought to seize the moment when the horse appears inclined to slacken his speed, to make him come away from the wall, by showing him the whip in front, and at the same time calling out "whoa!" which, from his lunging work, he will have learned to regard as an order to come up to his breaker.

If the horse refuses to come up and remains at the wall, we should again follow him up, so as to bring him to the centre, and should continue to do so until he obeys.

I may add that the breaker, by keeping himself out of reach of kicks and blows with the fore feet, will make his authority felt at a distance, and the horse will learn to obey without being provoked into resistance.

I am not a believer in the caveson, except for really vicious horses. If it is used, it should be light and well stuffed.

Having obtained the foregoing important result, I will pass on to "close" work.

CLOSE WORK ; ADVANCING.

Having given up lunging, I take hold of the snaffle reins, after having passed them over the animal's head. I replace the driving whip by a cutting whip, which I use along with the snaffle in the same way as I employed the lunging rein and driving whip.

Having the horse with his right side parallel to the wall of the school, I place myself close to his left shoulder and take hold of the whip and the end of the snaffle reins with the left hand. It goes without saying, that the reverse aids are used when going round the other way. I conceal the whip from the sight of the horse by placing it along the outside of my left leg. With the right hand I catch the snaffle reins close to the animal's mouth and just below his chin (Fig. 1), and then take a few paces forward. If the horse also advances, I pat him on the neck ; but if he refuses to do so, I touch him up behind, close to the girths with the whip. Occasionally, a green horse at first refuses to advance and requires a touch of the whip, which is generally sufficient. Some horses refuse

Fig. 1.—Leading a horse forward.

to go forward, especially if we make them bend their necks, in which case I replace the cutting whip by the lunging whip, with which I hit the animal on the hind quarters and always succeed in making him go on.

I wish to direct my readers' special attention to this decisive moment, on which contest depends our future success with the horse. It is important to understand that at this moment the animal pays no heed to the demands of his breaker and is ignorant of the breaker's means of coercion. He has not yet learned to fear punishment, and knows little about the reassuring nature of pats on the neck.

Appropriate punishment and reward are the two great principles of successful breaking.

If my horse refuses to advance, it is evident that, from the position I am in, it will be difficult for him to run back, but not impossible, and it is necessary to look out for any movement which a green horse may make.

To make him go forward, I extend my right arm, while always holding the snaffle reins with the right hand at the chin-groove, over which the curb-chain passes ; and I push, instead of drawing forward, whilst holding the end of the snaffle reins with my left hand behind my back.   I lightly touch the horse with the tip of the cutting whip a little behind the girths.

If the horse is quiet and not too nervous and excitable, he will go forward without rushing.   He will often, however, answer to the cuts of the whip by plunging, rearing, shying violently to one side, or running back, which are the four "defences" which a horse can offer in this case.   Let us now examine the best means of thwarting them.

If the horse plunges, we have only to raise his head, so as to put the weight on his hind quarters, taking care to keep close to his shoulder, so as to avoid being struck by his fore feet.   A horse cannot plunge with his head high.

Rearing is more dangerous, because the horse may hit the breaker a blow on the top of the head with one of his fore feet, to avoid the bad consequences of which accident it is well to wear a chimney pot hat, which has often saved me from a blow on the head.   When the horse rears, the right hand should quickly let go the snaffle reins, only the end of which should remain in the left hand, and then, if the breaker turns to the right about, he cannot be hit, as his distance from the horse will be equal to the length of the snaffle reins and that of his left arm.   Having allowed him to regain his feet, go up very quietly to him, while carefully concealing the whip.

If he again rears, bear strongly on the snaffle, but without jerks. When he has tried to rear three or four times without being able to succeed, he will soon give up the attempt, and perhaps may throw himself on his side, which he can do only to the left, as the wall is on his right. A touch of the whip on the left side, and shaking him up with the left snaffle rein will be sufficient to make him get up.

When the horse runs back, we should place ourselves in front of him, and should pull strongly on the snaffle reins, while slightly bending the knees and carrying the weight of the body back, so that the horse can drag us back only with difficulty, and consequently will soon become tired. I have had so much practice in letting myself be dragged, while keeping on my feet, that I can almost always stop any horse at his second or third step. When he finds that we passively and not actively resist his efforts, he will generally stop and give a deep sigh. Fix him in this position, and try to find out, which we can easily do with a little practice, if he is going to yield or to continue his resistance.

The lesson should never be interrupted, and it should on no account be terminated by reason of the resistance of the horse.

When the horse has given in, I again gently try, as in the previous manner, to make him go forward and do not stop until I have succeeded. Almost always the animal promptly gives in.

In the first part of this breaking, Baucher used to try to make the horse come forward by lightly touching him on the breast with a cutting whip, while he held the snaffle reins at half-length and stood facing the horse. As I have explained in the chapter on lunging, I do not object to this method, although it is open to the serious objection of rendering the man liable to be hit by the horse's fore feet and of making the animal ticklish. Besides, touching the horse on the breast is of no further use in breaking ; but touching him on the sides, as I have described, is the best preparation for the use of the spurs.

According to the system of Baucher, one pulls the horse by his forehand, and if the animal is thus made to move, he will drag his hind quarters after him ; but by my method the horse gets his hind quarters under him, and by their means he pushes the forehand forward, which is the essential principle of good riding.

COLLECTING A HORSE AND DIRECT FLEXION.

As soon as my horse goes well with me round the school to the left, I make him change and begin similar work to the other hand.   Then, when I am satisfied with him, I commence collecting him.   While going to the left and keeping myself at his left shoulder, I take the bit reins in my right hand, at five or six inches from his mouth.   Keeping the buckle of the snaffle reins in the hollow of my left hand, I seize with its fingers the snaffle reins at about eight or nine inches from the mouth, and I carry the left hand in advance of the animal's head, in order to draw him forward.   It is absolutely in-dispensable to hold the snaffle reins in this way, if we wish to prevent the horse from stopping, when we feel the curb reins. Merely holding the snaffle reins horizontally will not do, because we want to do more than to simply pull the animal forward.   It is also necessary that the pull of the snaffle is in an upward direction ; because it ought to raise his head and neck at the moment when the pressure of the bit prompts him to flex his lower jaw (Fig. 2, jaw contracted ; and Fig. 3, jaw and bit free,) which action on his part should be counter-balanced by the pressure of the snaffle, in order that it may not make him lower his head and neck.

I feel the snaffle reins in order to raise the head and neck, and I then put equal tension on the curb reins, in order to make him bend his neck and loosen his lower jaw.   If the

horse does not go freely forward, I take a stronger feeling of
the snaffle reins, and if he stiffens his neck and lower jaw, I

Fig. 2.—Jaw contracted.

make more use of the curb reins.   I particularly recommend
that the tension of the reins should not be of a uniform and
continuous nature, but should consist of light pressures
sufficiently prolonged, so as not to form a jerk, and sufficiently

short, so that the horse may not be inclined to bear his weight
on the bridle.

If he yields, even in the slightest manner, I give to him
and pat his neck. I then try to get him to yield still more,
without asking too much from him. I again give to him and
pat him ; and so on.

We should take particular care to get the horse to give to
us, not only with his neck, but also with his jaw, which he will
do by opening his mouth. The bending of the jaw is the last
stage of flexion. Several horses, in yielding the lower jaw,
whether in direct or lateral flexions, bring the jaw from one
side to the other side. Although the jaw in this case does not
resist the hand, it yields by going to the right or left, instead
of yielding in the direction of the axis of the head. This incomplete method of yielding can be corrected only by stimulating the animal to go forward.

We can easily understand that if the lower jaw is carried to
the right or left, the horse will not be correctly in hand,
although his head and neck will be in a good position. His
appearance of being in hand is not real, because the contraction of the muscles of his lower jaw makes it impossible for his
mouth to be light. In these conditions the horse will never go
freely up to his bridle, despite the stimulus of the legs. If I
require an increase of impulsion, it is because the horse, by
escaping from the straight line, brings his head too near his
breast, in which case he will have a tendency to get behind his
bit. It is therefore necessary to send him up to it.

Finally, if the jaw does not yield, the bending of the neck
will only cause the weight to be brought back, and consequently to make the horse rein back or get behind the
bit.

The entire principle of direct flexion consists in the alternate
opposing actions of the curb and snaffle. Whilst the snaffle
draws the forehand forward, a light pressure of the curb

steadies and bends the head, and causes the jaw to yield without stopping the forehand.

To obtain this result, combined with lightness, we must con-

Fig. 3.—Jaw and bit free.

tinually practise the great principle of *taking* and *giving ;* the
former to stop resistance, the latter to reward obedience.
Having obtained it, we should again take, so as to make the
horse yield still more ; and so on.

A horse should not only champ his bit, but should also relax his lower jaw to it (Fig. 3), which concession proves that the bending of the head and neck is perfect. With this object, when the lower jaw readily yields to the tension of the curb, we should prolong this tension until the horse completely loosens his hold on the curb, and we ought to keep touching him lightly on the side, so as to prevent him stopping (Fig. 4).

It is, of course, understood that this work ought to be done with great lightness of hand. We can gauge the sensibility of the mouth by an alternative feeling of the curb and snaffle, and can thus at once find out if the horse has a hard or soft mouth. In this manner we readily get *good*, that is to say, *light hands*, with which we can manage almost any horse by the continued play of "take and give." It is a great advantage to have good hands, which will be sufficient for all ordinary work. But we can take and give for all our life without being able to render an account of what we are doing, in which case neither the hand nor the horse makes any progress. Finally, the action of the hand would be limited to giving when the horse pulls, and pulling when he gives. This faculty may be called the possession of a bell in the hand, and is in fact the movement of a bell in all its beauty.

The *well-trained hand* acts in the contrary manner, because its *rôle* is to break in the horse, that is to say, to advance his education. It remains fixed in position by strongly closing the fingers when the horse pulls, but the moment the horse yields his lower jaw, the fingers should be relaxed with the rapidity of an electric flash.

A *good hand* gives when the horse takes, and takes when he gives. A *well-trained* hand gives when the horse gives, and takes when he takes, and that instantaneously.

In all cases we ought to guard against confounding hardness

of mouth with the resistance which is due to a faulty position of the head. A horse which carries his head low is always heavy in hand, because he puts all his weight forward, but it does not therefore follow that he has a hard mouth. If we simply change the position of his head, and place it high, it will not bear on the hand, and we will be able to find out what kind of a mouth he has.

Fig. 4.—Going forward when mobilising the lower jaw, so as to prevent the horse getting behind his bit.

It is a mistake to think, as many do, that a horse which slavers or foams at the mouth has a good mouth. To produce this soapy foam, a horse must contract his tongue, and will not then be able to have his mouth free, at rest, and ready for the fingering of his rider. A horse produces this foam by constantly turning his tongue, or by rubbing it against his hard palate, by passing it over the bit, or by making it into a ball at the back of his mouth. In all these cases, the only

4

remedy is to put a small movable plate of the shape of a
figure of eight, with its centre on the top of the port of
the bit, upon which it can revolve.   This apparatus will
also prevent horses letting their tongues hang out of their
mouths.

Sometimes a horse foams at the mouth by playing with
one of the cheeks of the bit, which we can prevent by putting
the mouthpiece a little higher up in his mouth and tightening
the chin-strap, so that he cannot reach the cheeks of the bit
either with his tongue or lips.

A *good mouth* will always continue fresh during work without being either dry or wet.

If the flexion has been made in the manner I have indicated,
and by the methods I have described, the horse will have his
neck high and bent at the poll ; the axis of the head will be a
little beyond the perpendicular, the mouth open, and the curb
free (Fig. 3).   In order that the flexion may be irreproachable,
it is necessary that the muzzle should be on a line with the
upper part of the shoulder (Fig. 5).   The bending of the neck
should bring the direction of the head near to, but not behind
the perpendicular, which faulty position can be produced only
when the neck is bent at a point too near the withers.   By this
position I have my horse very lightly *on the bit.*   Whereas
Baucher, who liked to have his mount *behind the bit*, drew the
animal's head back beyond the perpendicular, and thus put the
horse into this position.

I will now describe the mechanism of direct flexion, as I
understand it, and as I have practised it, with this single
difference, that, for the sake of clearness, I take for granted
that the horse is halted ; although I will explain later on,
that at first I make the direct flexion while going forward.

The majority of riding masters practice this flexion in
an entirely different manner.   To give an account of what
ought to be the direct flexion, which is the fundamental

principle of riding, we must first know what is the desired result to be obtained from making it.

OBJECTS TO BE OBTAINED BY DIRECT FLEXION.

1. *To balance the horse by the height of his neck.* It is very rare that horses are naturally well balanced. On account of

Fig. 5.—Muzzle on a line with upper part of shoulder.

their conformation, all horses have a tendency to be heavy in front, and the majority of them have this defect ; the cause being the distance which the head is removed from the base of support. The further the head is away from the centre of gravity the lower it is, and the more weight is on the shoulders. The result of raising the neck, so as to bring the head near to the centre of gravity, is to more or less equalise the distribution of weight. As good horsemanship depends

4*

on the distribution of weight, as we shall see further on ; the first step in breaking ought to be the equal distribution of weight, so that good equilibrium maintained during progression may later on give lightness to every movement.

Raising the neck and putting equal weight on the forehand and hind quarters will allow them full freedom and energy, and will put the horse in such a position that he will only require to be stimulated. With the neck high, the hocks are easily brought under the centre of the body, and the action of the fore legs becomes lofty. In a word, raising the neck gives good equilibrium and grace by lightness.

In racing, one's sole object is to gain in length without paying any attention to high action. Consequently, in training, one guards against raising the neck. Here we prove the principle that a horse extends himself as much as possible by " daisy cutting."

But there are horses which are heavy behind, and one might think that if it is good to raise the neck of a horse which is heavy in front, it would be necessary to lower the neck of the animal which is heavy behind ; but this is not so. As I have just explained, the conformation of the horse and the relations between his levers are such that the equilibrium of his mass can be obtained only by raising the neck.

The horse which is heavy behind is inclined to get behind his bit, and has his hocks either too far removed or too near his centre. In the former case the horse is too much stretched out, and in the latter the croup is unduly lowered, and the points of the buttocks are much further back than the hocks.*   Here, instead of a naturally bad distribution of the weight of the mass, as with a horse heavy in front, we have

---

* This position is dangerous, because the horse is ready to rear. The danger of being behind the bit is restiveness, which causes rearing, with the probability of the animal falling backwards.

a bad voluntary distribution of the forces in an animal which holds himself back and which does not wish to advance ; and his hocks do not do their work of pushing the mass forward. If we overload the forehand by lowering the neck, we add still more to the weight, and consequently we increase the difficulty of the work required from the hocks.* We must therefore raise the neck in order to lighten the forehand ; but we should raise it from below upwards, and not from front to rear, while taking care not to exaggerate the movement and to keep the hand very light. A high position of the neck is the first condition of good equilibrium, and having obtained it, we should seek to give freedom to the hind quarters, while bringing them into action, and making the horse go freely forward, which we do by the flexions of the well-placed head, by the loosening of the jaw, and especially by the legs. A horse which is heavy in his hind quarters is behind his bit, and if he does not wish to go forward, he is *behind the legs.* With such an animal we must employ great lightness of hand and great energy of the legs, so as to change his distribution of weight by making him go up to his bit.† We cannot obtain this result by a low position of the neck, which is the chief obstacle to lightness.

2. *To fix the neck in the axis of the body by connecting to the shoulders the head rendered light by flexion.* The unbent head is heavy at the end of the neck, which has become too movable. Hence the proverb, " Heavy head, slack neck." This is a case similar to that of holding a fishing-rod by its thin end. The flexed head, on the contrary, moves with lightness on the high neck, which is kept without stiffness on the axis of the body by the sole action of the good

---

* Without taking into consideration that a depressed position of the neck will give only more spring to the act of rearing.

† In such cases the driving whip, which obliges the horse to go forward, is a good preparation for the use of the legs.

equilibrium of the levers. Head, neck, and shoulders fixed in the axis of the well-balanced body, and making a supple and homogeneous whole. This is the action of flexion.

3. *To obtain lightness by the relaxation or flexion of the jaw.* Having the body balanced and connected in all its parts, the flexion of the jaw enables us to regulate collectively with extreme lightness all the movements from rear to front, and from front to rear, by receiving on the hand the impulsion of the mass which the legs throw on the bit, and which the hand, in its turn, partly sent back to the rider's legs. The hand only retains and sends back to the centre the amount of impulsion which is necessary to maintain equilibrium. The greater portion of the impulsion is naturally employed to propel the body forward. The flexibility from front to rear of the arm of the bent and jointed lever formed by the neck, head, and jaw, progressively increases from rear to front ; that is to say, from the shoulders to the neck, from the neck to the head, and from the head to the jaw. In other words, we hold the fishing-rod by its butt end.

Thus, all the force developed by the horse is concentrated in the hand, the slightest action of which on the bars bends, first, the jaw, proportionately to the impulsion ; secondly, the head* by the jaw ; and thirdly, by the head, the neck ; the neck reacting with its greatest effect on the shoulders. The expression employed to define the reciprocal position of the horse and rider is most exact. We have really our horse *in hand.*

With respect to these remarks it is necessary to point out that the position of the head is singularly favourable to the action of the reins. In fact, the curb, which acts almost like

---

* The head ought to oscillate from a position a little beyond the perpendicular to the perpendicular, but never in rear of it. The position which I have indicated enables us to get by the shortest way to the end of the lever, and to obtain the greatest effect by the smallest effort.

Fig. 6.—Correct preparation for direct flexion.

Fig. 7.—Preparation for Baucher's direct flexion.

a second snaffle, if the head is low, presses freely on the bars, and develops all its power when the head is raised, provided always that the head is kept a little beyond the perpendicular. The moment the axis of the head comes behind the perpendicular, the action of the curb is false, because it works from below upwards. Then the horse begins to draw his chin into his breast.

Such, I consider, is direct flexion and its object.

We can see that this flexion, as I practice it, is not done by chance or simple routine. On the contrary, I have carefully given my reasons, and I have touched on all details to justify my practice.

Unfortunately Baucher, who was the first to improve the art of flexions, by making it the base of his method, did not give a complete account of its mechanism. This did not matter much to him, because his marvellous equestrian tact remedied every deficiency. Where his theory was false, his hands and legs by themselves rectified, more or less conscientiously, the error of his doctrine.

Baucher, however, could not put his tact into his books, in which he left his good and bad doctrines. I consider that by criticising him and by showing where he has failed, I shall render increased homage to the great horseman. I maintain that the flexion which Baucher has described, and which is practised every day,* has done much to discredit in the minds of horsemen this most useful exercise, which I consider to be the first condition of good equitation.

Baucher's faulty flexion, which is in very common use to-day, is made at the withers instead of at the poll. It lowers the neck, and causes the horse to place the weight on his shoulders, that is to say, it aggravates the natural fault in equine conformation, and it makes him liable to fall by

---

* Alas ! the faults of masters are acquired more easily than their good qualities.

Fig. 8.—Incorrect and frequently employed flexion.

Fig. 9.—Lowering the head—a faulty practice.

carrying his head low, and to draw his chin into his breast
by bringing his head behind the perpendicular. We must
note that this fault was originated by Baucher, who, during
the greater part of his career, made the flexions at the
withers by lowering the neck. Compare Fig. 6, which
shows the flexion I have described, with Fig. 7, which
illustrates Baucher's flexion, and which I have taken from his
book. It is well to note that Baucher's horse in Fig. 7
has his legs stuck out in front, and consequently it is impossible for him to go forward. Nothing could be worse!
Compare the correct flexion, shown in Fig. 5, with that
in Fig. 8, which is the more frequently practised of
the two.

Towards the end of his life Baucher recognised this
mistake (see his last edition, 1874); but he restricted himself
to raising the head of the horse, without making the flexion
when it was high. Whatever he did and whatever errors he
made, he was an incomparable horseman. The people of
to-day who make faulty flexions succeed only in ruining
their horses. There is no reason for stopping when one has
started on this road. Certain authors have thought it right to
systematically lower the neck, than which there is no better
means of ruining a horse! As a great curiosity, I have
shown in Figs. 9 and 10 two illustrations which appeared
in recently published books, and which show the lesson of
lowering the neck. That could be called the art of teaching
a horse how to break his knees!

This explains how it is that many people say that they
have made their horses perform flexions without any good
result, a fact which should not surprise us. As we have just
seen, the flexion is such a delicate thing that an incapable
horseman who practises it, will often spoil a horse instead
of improving him. If, on the contrary, the reader understands the principles and practice described in this chapter,

59

Fig. 10.—Lowering the head—a faulty practice.

Fig. 11.—Direct flexion when going forward.

he will always be certain to obtain by flexion the benefits
which he has a right to expect.

To thoroughly explain the mechanism of flexion, I have
been obliged to suppose that the horse was halted. But
I must explain, contrary to what is everywhere practised,
that I begin the direct flexion while going forward. With
this object, I place myself at the shoulder of the horse,
which I stimulate by a click of the tongue, while drawing
him forward by a stronger feeling of the reins of the snaffle
(Fig. 11). Apart from this, the flexion is done exactly as
I have indicated.

When I have obtained a certain number of flexions of
the jaw, I let the horse walk freely beside me for a few
moments, and I carefully avoid prolonging the flexions,
although I frequently begin them again. When the
horse has got into the habit of readily doing the direct
flexion at the first indication of the reins by relaxing his
jaw, the breaker should modify his method in order to
make the animal assume as nearly as possible the conditions
he will be under when mounted. This will be a new form
of work.

The breaker, always in the same position, and being on
the near side of the horse, holds the reins of the curb and
snaffle in his right hand at about six inches from the jaw.
The left hand holds the end of the snaffle reins and the
cutting whip, the point of which he keeps on a level with
the animal's side. Under these conditions, at the moment
when the right hand demands the direct flexion, the whip
performs the office of making the horse go forward, as before
described (Fig. 4).

We are then placed under the same conditions as when
mounted. No longer, as was recently done, the forehand
draws forward the hind quarters, which now get under the
body, and propel the forehand on the head held by the

reins,* *i.e.*, by the hand of the rider.   In this manner the
horse learns to go forward without leaning on the bit, and
is then perfectly light, in the same way as we ought to
make him later on when he is mounted.   The work which
I have just described not only prepares the mouth of the
horse in an admirable manner, but also makes the hand of
the rider skilful.   There is no doubt that it is easier to make
the jaw supple when standing still than during movement ;
but there is the risk of making him keep behind the bit,
which inconvenience, or rather danger, is avoided when going
forward (Fig. 4).   I insist on this point ; because, if the work
of loosening the jaw during movement is certainly longer and
more difficult, it guards us against the great danger of putting
the horse behind the bit, which is always the inevitable result
of the first flexions.   Therefore, take your time and do well.

Although, as a rule, I maintain that it is of the greatest
importance for the whole of this work to be done when going
forward, I am obliged to admit that it would be impossible or
at least extremely fatiguing to do it with certain horses which
throw themselves suddenly on the hand, or which have their
heads too low.   Personally, I have never found these faults
carried to such an extent that I have been unable to obtain
direct flexion and relaxation of the jaw while going forward.

If the work is stationary, we should take the utmost care to
prevent, at all hazards, the horse from getting behind his bit.
If he reins back ever so little, we should immediately send
him forward by touching him on the side with the whip, while
holding the end of the snaffle reins in the left hand (Fig. 4).
If the horse stretches out his hind legs behind, or his fore legs

* We will notice in Fig. 4 the manner in which the right hand of the
breaker holds at the same time the reins of the snaffle and those of the curb.
The former are held between the thumb and closed index finger, and keep the
neck high by their upward pull.   The latter are held more or less horizontally,
and serve to loosen the jaw, the left curb rein being passed between the middle
finger and the ring-finger ; and the right, underneath the little finger.

in front, he is also behind his bit, and should be immediately sent forward.

A horse may be behind his bit without backing, and this may happen even without the animal moving his feet. He will have this tendency if a perpendicular dropped from the point of his buttocks comes behind his hocks, in which case the weight will be on his hind quarters. We should then act energetically on the snaffle, in order to bring the body forward and maintain the balance of the body during flexion, or to avoid a return of the tendency to get behind the bit.

After this preparation, direct flexion becomes easy when mounted, especially as the action of the legs in propelling the horse on the hand is more energetic and effective than that of the whip.

Here the chief point is to begin, not by the action of the hand, but by that of the legs, which ought to be used progressively. In mounted work, as in flexion on foot, it is, of course, necessary that the hand makes the concession at the moment when the horse yields, in order to retake its action immediately afterwards. The entire practice of flexions is comprised in timely *taking* and *giving*. It is, of course, understood that the legs should always remain close to the animal's sides, as much for obtaining a definite concession of the jaw as for avoiding the tendency to get behind the bit. It is also taken for granted that the flexion should never be made at a halt, when the horse is mounted, which is a most objectionable practice. As we can obtain relaxation of the jaw only by light touches of the spur, the horse contracts the habit of resting on the spur when standing still. As we have then no means of making him go forward, or of preventing him from reining back, he becomes restive.* This result is all

* Baucher made the mistake of practising the flexion when mounted at a halt. He naturally proceeded by light touches of the spur. Only his great tact saved him from making his horses restive.

the more certain when the horse no longer dares to go up to his bridle when moving forward, on account of the preponderance which the hand has on the legs, whenever the animal wants to advance.

Fig. 12.—Baucher's flexion when mounted.

Finally, the work of making the horse go forward constitutes the great difference between my system of equitation and that of Baucher.

My first lesson has been to make the animal go forward.

In his *Dictionnaire raisonnée d'équitation* (1833), page 112,

ORDINARY RIDING.

Baucher writes : "During the first lessons the entire half-hour should be occupied in stationary work, except the last five minutes, during which the rein-back will be practised." Twenty-five minutes of stationary work and five minutes of reining back is a deplorable waste of time. For a lesson of

Fig. 13.—Correct flexion when mounted.

half an hour's duration I would devote thirty minutes to forward work, without any stationary work or reining back.

We shall subsequently see that this difference in method is found in all the work.

Naturally, Baucher's flexion is as incorrect in mounted work as in work on foot. Fig, 12, which is borrowed without any change from his book, enables us to judge his work by comparing it with Fig. 13, which represents correct flexion.

Fig. 14, which is taken from a recent work, shows in an exaggerated form all the faults of Baucher's bad flexion. In it the head is low, far from the centre of gravity and behind the perpendicular; the horse has all his weight on his

Fig. 14.—Exaggerated example of Baucher's incorrect flexion.

shoulders, and is ready to bring his chin into his breast; the muscles of the jaw are contracted, and the action of the curb is in a downward direction, and is consequently false. This caricature of breaking is simply perfect! The exact opposite of all these conditions is what we should seek to obtain from direct flexion.

5

MAKING A HORSE QUIET TO MOUNT.

To make a horse quiet to mount, we must adopt a method by which we can easily stop him from annoying the rider, or preventing him from getting into the saddle.   Let us examine the means we should employ, and let us place ourselves in such a position that we will be able to circumvent any defence which his instinct or bad habits may prompt him to make.

The vicious or restive horse rears, lashes out, strikes with his near forefoot, or cow-kicks with his near hind.   With such an animal we should make use of the lunging rein and driving whip, and make a feint of putting a foot in the stirrup while standing close to the near shoulder.   If he rears, we can hit him thoroughly with the lash of the whip across his buttocks. As he is held by the lunging rein, we can remain sufficiently far away from him to avoid being struck.   Every time he rears we should begin again until he yields.   If he reins back, we should employ similar methods.   If he kicks, raise his head and loudly scold him.   If he strikes out in front, cut him with the driving whip on the offending leg.

Besides horses which resist in this manner, there are others which are simply timid, nervous, restless, ticklish, or irritable, and which do not remain as quiet as they ought to do, although they do not really "show fight."   What will they do?   They will perform only four movements—namely, go forward, run back, shy off to the right or to the left, against which we should act as follows :

I take the near rein of the snaffle in my left hand, and with the same hand I catch hold of the mane at about the middle of the neck in such a manner that there is a slight tension on the rein which I hold.   I pass my right hand, in which I have my cutting whip, over the neck, seize with it the off snaffle rein, which I draw up only slightly, and finally take hold of the pommel of the saddle with the right hand (Fig. 15).

I then face the left shoulder of the horse.   If he runs back,
a cut on the croup with the whip will bring him forward.
This can be repeated twenty or thirty times till he yields.
If he goes forward, I bring him back by feeling the reins.   If
he shies to the left, I draw his head to that side, and consequently bring his hind quarters to the right.   Similarly, if he

Fig. 15.—Proper way to mount.

shies to the right, I draw his head to the right, so as to make
him carry his hind quarters to the left.

He makes his defences, when the rider touches the stirrup
with his foot, when he puts his foot into the stirrup, or when he
raises himself by his straightened left knee, and before he has
passed his right leg over the saddle.   We should not go to
the second or third of these movements until we have made
the horse perfectly steady in the preceding movement.   We
should not place ourselves in the saddle until the animal
remains steady during all the time we are standing on the

5*

near stirrup iron, at which moment it often happens that
the horse attempts one of the defences already described.   If
the movement is only slight, we can correct it by the action
of the reins without changing our position.   If it is violent,
we can place our foot on the ground and correct him with the
whip.

Finally, we should bear in mind that as soon as we are in
the saddle, we should have the snaffle reins in their respective
hands, and we should hold them only just short enough to
enable us, by a light feeling on them, to steady the horse, in
the event of his "playing up."

I ought to admit that my method of getting into the saddle
is contrary to the principles which are generally taught.   In
fact, it is always laid down that to mount, the rider ought to
take both reins of the snaffle and a lock of the mane near the
withers in his left hand ; place the right hand on the centre of
the saddle, raise himself on the stirrup, and, when his left knee
is straight, carry his right hand quickly from the cantle to the
pommel, while passing his right leg over the horse.   He then
sits down.   By this system the rider is unable to counteract
any movement made by the horse.   Further, at the moment
when the right hand passes from the cantle to the pommel, the
equilibrium of the rider is as unstable as possible, and can be
upset by the slightest cause.   Precisely on account of this want
of equilibrium, the rider falls, instead of sits, down on the
saddle, and by falling in this manner he can unfortunately
hurt himself, especially on the pommel, if the horse makes a
single step to the rear.

With the method which I advocate, the rider is able to avoid
any accident, to stop any "playing up," or even any movement
on the part of the horse ; because he holds a snaffle rein in
each hand.

When I lunge a horse, I take care to girth him with a
moderate degree of tightness before putting him into a trot.

And as he gets a bit slack from trotting, the girths do not in-convenience him when I mount. I always carry out this procedure when mounting a difficult horse for the first time.

Grooms are in the habit of girthing up their horses very tightly, and it would be contrary to a knowledge of the weak-nesses of human nature to think that they would give up this practice on the very day when I try to succeed at what they have failed to do. On that day they girth up more tightly than ever. They know that the tighter a horse is girthed up the more he will plunge, and therefore they feel certain that they will presently have the innocent pleasure of seeing me chucked over the ears of the horse. Nevertheless I encourage them to girth up more tightly, and after they have squeezed him as tightly as they can I take him by the bridle, walk him about for a few minutes, and the moment before putting my foot in the stirrup I let out the girths one or two holes. I am then in the saddle, and the animal gives a great sigh of relief, which for the moment prevents him from thinking of playing up.

I never allow my horses to be held when mounting them. All horses become quiet if not held, and they will gain confi-dence if we mount and dismount several times consecutively, while patting them on the neck. We ought to mount as quietly and lightly as possible. Above all things, we ought to avoid bustling the horse when starting ; because, if he expects we are going to do this, he will never stand quietly to be mounted.

I never require anything from the horse which I mount for the first time. I am content if he walks straight on. I keep the reins separated, I feel only those of the snaffle, and I never touch the horse with the spurs for the first few lessons. I ride him a few times round the school to the right and to the left, while leaving him as free as possible, supposing, of

course, that he does not play up, which he will very rarely do
if I require almost nothing from him.

If he carries his head too low, I try to raise it by almost
imperceptible touches on the snaffle reins, which I draw
upwards, and not from front to rear.   If he holds his head too
high, I feel the curb reins very lightly, and in such a way. as
not to stop his forward movement.   If he stops on account of
the action of the curb, I let the reins loose and apply my legs
behind the girths.   In this case the legs have an effect similar
to that of the cutting whip during work on foot.   I keep on at
the horse until I have obtained forward movement, which is
the great end that has to be obtained at any price.

Having obtained this forward movement, I prolong it, as I
have said, for a few turns round the school, while trying to get
the head into a good position ; but I work very lightly, and
always in such a manner as not to stop the horse.   If I obtain
only a little play in the mouth, I get off, and make a few
flexions on foot until he obeys.   I then give him some carrots
and send him to the stable.

Carrots ought always be cut lengthwise and never across,
in which case they might stick in the animal's throat.   I have
seen a horse almost choked by swallowing carrots cut across.
I do not give sugar to a horse, because if he is bridled and plays
with his bit, it will produce a foam that will soil one's clothes,
which is the smallest objection.   A more serious one is that
sugar given in the stable predisposes a horse to crib-bite.
He begins by licking his manger, and, finding the taste
agreeable, he finishes by persistently biting it, which is a
habit that will often make him crib-bite or wind-suck.

In this mounted lesson, I have asked the horse only to go
forward, while making him lightly work his jaw.   Further, as a
general rule, we should not demand from him several things at a
time, because he will be apt to confuse them, and we may mistake
for disobedience a simple want of comprehension on his part.

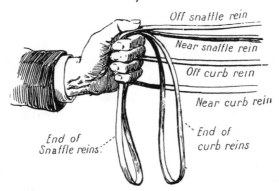

Off snaffle rein

Near snaffle rein

Off curb rein

Near curb rein

End of
Snaffle reins

End of
curb reins

Fig. 16.—Equal tension on all four reins.

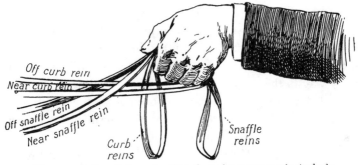

Off curb rein

Near curb rein

Off snaffle rein

Near snaffle rein

Curb
reins

Snaffle
reins

Fig. 17.—Action of the curb ; little finger brought towards the body.

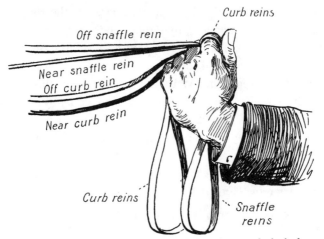

Curb reins

Off snaffle rein

Near snaffle rein

Off curb rein

Near curb rein

Curb reins

Snaffle
reins

Fig. 18.—Action of the snaffle ; thumb brought towards the body.

HOW TO HOLD THE REINS.

There are three orthodox ways for holding the reins, namely, the *English*, *German*, and *French*. I do not hesitate to say that the French way is the best.

As the snaffle is higher in the mouth than the curb, its principal action is to raise the head of the horse, and that of the curb to lower it. In other words, the snaffle is an elevator ; the curb, a depressor. Therefore, the reins should occupy the same respective positions in the hand, as the snaffle and curb do in the mouth, namely, the snaffle reins should be above the curb reins.

Contrary to this very simple principle, the English place both reins at the same height in the hand and hold one rein between each finger. The Germans act in a still more contrary way to the principle in question, by holding the snaffle reins below the curb reins, supposing that the hand is in a vertical position. It appears that the Germans have even less common sense than the English.

Reason tells us that the reins should be held in the French manner ;* the hand vertical, the left curb rein under the little finger of the left hand ; the right rein between the ring finger and the middle finger, while their ends pass between the thumb and index finger. The two reins of the snaffle are joined in the same hand, and taken between the thumb and index finger (Fig. 16). With the reins held in this manner and without displacing the hand, we are able, by the mere play of the wrist, to obtain the movements which are indispensable for acting on the mouth ; supposing, of course, that the animal is broken.

1st. The hand placed in position exerts an equal tension on all four reins (Fig. 16).

* Is it not strange that in the French army the German method of holding the reins is adopted, namely, the snaffle rein under the curb rein ?

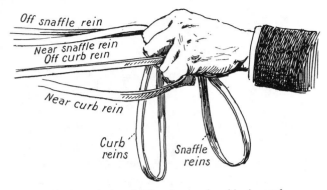

Off snaffle rein

Near snaffle rein
Off curb rein

Near curb rein

Curb reins

Snaffle reins

Fig. 19.—Action of off curb rein ; knuckles lowered.

Curb reins

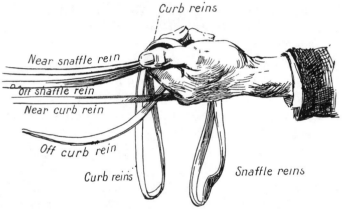

Near snaffle rein

Off snaffle rein

Near curb rein

Off curb rein

Curb reins

Snaffle reins

Fig. 20.—Action of near curb rein ; knuckles raised.

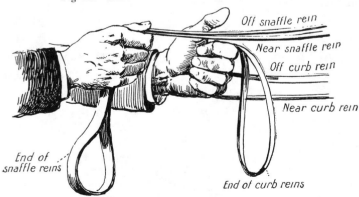

Off snaffle rein

Near snaffle rein

Off curb rein

Near curb rein

End of
snaffle reins

End of curb reins

Fig. 21.—Separating the curb and snaffle reins.

2nd.   Action of the curb ; the little finger brought towards
the body (Fig. 17).

3rd.   Action of the snaffle; the thumb brought towards
the body (Fig. 18).

4th.   Action of the off curb rein; the knuckles lowered
(Fig. 19).

5th.   Action of the near curb rein; the knuckles raised
(Fig. 20).

We can obtain all the necessary effects on the mouth of the
horse by the rotation of the wrist from rear to front (Fig. 17);
from front to rear (Fig. 18); from left to right, *i.e.*, prona-
tion (Fig. 19); and from right to left, *i.e.*, supination (Fig. 20).

When the reins are held in this manner, they are kept
apart as far as possible, supposing that they are in one hand.
The effect obtained is almost similar to that which would be
produced if the reins of the curb were held in the left hand
and the snaffle reins in the right hand, a little above them.
We can easily, if required, use both hands ; because the right
hand can take up the snaffle reins or put them back into the
left hand without disarranging or even touching the curb
reins (Fig. 21).

Finally, if we wish to have all four reins separated, namely,
the near ones of the curb and snaffle in the left hand, and the
off ones in the right hand (which is often necessary), we have
only to take the off reins in the position in which they are, by
placing the right hand between the reins of the curb and
those of the snaffle in such a manner that the off rein of the
curb will come under the little finger of the right hand, and
the off rein of the snaffle between the thumb and index finger
of the same hand, in exactly the same position as the reins
are in the left hand.*   We thus keep in the two hands the

---

*Fig. 22 shows the right hand being passed between the off rein of the curb
and the off rein of the snaffle, and Fig. 23 shows the right hand being closed
on these two reins.   Fig. 24 shows the reins separated.

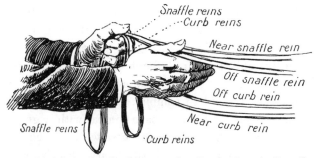

Snaffle reins
Curb reins
Near snaffle rein
Off snaffle rein
Off curb rein
Near curb rein
Snaffle reins
Curb reins

Fig. 22.—Passing the right hand between the off curb rein and off snaffle rein.

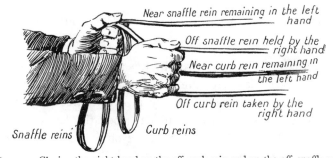

Near snaffle rein remaining in the left hand
Off snaffle rein held by the right hand
Near curb rein remaining in the left hand
Off curb rein taken by the right hand
Snaffle reins
Curb reins

Fig. 23.—Closing the right hand on the off curb rein and on the off snaffle rein.

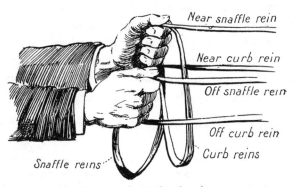

Near snaffle rein
Near curb rein
Off snaffle rein
Off curb rein
Curb reins
Snaffle reins

Fig. 24.—Separating the reins.

same distance between the reins of the curb and those of the snaffle as determined by the little finger and thumb.

By an inverse movement, we can replace the four reins in the left hand, in the position which they previously occupied. I need hardly add that, until the breaking of the horse is fairly well advanced, we do not draw up all four reins, which would consequently tend to combine and sometimes even to confuse their effects. When we have to deal with a green or insufficiently broken horse, in which case we may require to produce very quickly precise and particularly decisive effects, it is well to separate the reins.

TEACHING A HORSE BY THE WHIP TO OBEY LEGS
AND SPURS.

I invariably begin my lesson by repeating the former exercises, but every day I require something new from the horse.

As soon as the horse goes freely in every direction with a slight play of the jaw, I teach him to obey the leg and then the spur. This work should be done on foot and by means of the cutting whip.

While facing the horse, I take the snaffle in the left hand* close to the mouth so as to hold the head high. With the whip, which I hold in my right hand, I touch the horse very lightly just behind the girths, at the place where the spur will act, and at the same time I carry his head to the left.† The horse should thereupon carry his haunches to the right. He will show that he obeys by taking one or two steps in that

* The buckle of the bridoon rein ought to remain in the left hand during all the work on foot.

† This is what is termed *lateral effects*, because the effect on the forehand and that on the hind quarters are produced on the same side. In *diagonal equitation*, which is rational equitation and the consequence of good breaking, the effect on the forehand is always on the side opposite to that on the hind quarters. It is the only way to secure the movements in their entirety.

direction. I then stop him and pat him on the neck. If, on the contrary, he strikes out in front or kicks, on account of being touched by the whip, I rate him loudly and hold his head very high, which will oblige him to lower his croup.

It is of the greatest possible consequence that the patting on the neck should immediately follow the act of obedience on the part of the horse, in the same way as punishment should follow disobedience. This is the fundamental principle of breaking.

If the horse throws himself on the whip, that is to say, to the left, which ticklish horses are inclined to do, we must carry his head forcibly to the left, so as to bring his hind quarters to the right ; but should not punish the animal, because, as I have already pointed out, his action is instinctive. When we have put him several times through this work, which does not fatigue or trouble him, he readily yields, and does it on both sides. I recommend the breaker to be content with two or three steps. He should stop and pat the horse on the neck each time the animal obeys. I recommence this work very often.

When the horse readily yields to the whip on both sides, we should not turn his head to the side opposite to that towards which he turns his hind quarters. He should be kept straight, so that he may obey only the indication of the whip.

This work with the whip prepares the horse to bear and understand the action of the leg and spur. At the same time, it places the head in a good position, and it is an excellent and indispensable suppling exercise before coming to the lateral flexions which we will presently consider.

Baucher practised the lateral flexions before teaching the horse to yield his hind quarters to the whip. This method is wrong, because, when we begin the lateral flexions, the instinct of the horse makes him carry his hind quarters to the side opposite to that towards which we bend the neck. If we

have not taught obedience to the whip, how can we straighten
the hind quarters ?

HORSE MOUNTED—FIRST DEFENCES—MEANS FOR OVERCOMING THEM.

In the preceding chapter I have taken for granted that
when I am mounted, the horse will go forward, if I want him
to do so. As the animal will not always be obedient, it is
well to be forearmed against any probable or even possible
resistance which he may make. It is therefore necessary to
keep the legs close to his sides, in order to avoid being taken
off our guard by an abrupt movement, and, above all, to lean
the body well back, so as to put the weight on our seat. We
are then ready for anything that may happen.

If the horse tries to buck, we should press him forward with
the legs and hold his head high. It is not hard to sit a forward plunge when the head is kept high.* But the rider is
easily displaced if the horse bucks without going forward,
places his head between his fore legs, and arches his back. In
this case, as the rider is not able to make the horse go forward, he should turn him to the right or left by means of the
snaffle. Each time he tries to stop by lowering his head, he
should be turned afresh ; but it is not necessary to insist on
turning him more to one side than to the other side.

All horses have a soft and a hard side to their mouths. At
first, if the horse resists when we try to turn him to the right,
we should content ourselves by trying to turn him to the left.
The great thing is to prevent him from bucking without going
forward, his bucks being made in order to get rid of his
rider.

Later on, when the horse has made some progress in his

---

* Bucking without going forward is the most difficult of all movements to sit.
If the horse cannot be made to go on and if he continues to buck without
advancing, it will be impossible to sit him.

breaking, it would be evidently wrong to let him turn to the right, if we wanted him to go to the left; but at present we should consider only his acts of resistance. It is certainly a great point gained to be able to prove to him that he cannot get us out of the saddle. If he succeeds in doing this, we may be certain he will continue to try on the same form of defence.

The danger of at first requiring the horse to turn to whichever side we wish, consists in the fact that by doing this we run the risk of prompting the animal to add a second act of resistance to the first one. In fact, when we wish to turn the horse to the left, for instance, we are obliged to take a strong pull on the left rein, and may thus make him *pointe* (half rear) or rear* by throwing too much weight on his hind quarters.

The *pointe* or *lançade* is a forward spring in which the forehand is kept higher than the croup. Like all other forward movements, it is not dangerous, because its displacing effect is not great.† The movements of the loins and croup are, however, very disconcerting to the rider. When the horse *rears*, he stands up on his hind legs, which he keeps fixed on the ground. This is a very dangerous form of resistance and may cause the animal to fall backwards.

In my youth, when my horse reared, I used to put both arms

* We may succeed in preventing the rear or the "*pointe*" by the vigorous use of the spurs. But to do so, we should seize with precision the fleeting moment when the horse holds himself back and is about to throw his weight on his hind quarters. If the spurs are driven in at this moment, they will send him forward in a disordered manner, no doubt; but that does not matter, because they will have prevented him from fixing his hind legs on the ground. If the rider allows this critical moment to pass, the use of the spurs will be dangerous, because i will still further prompt the animal to rear.

† In the half-rear the rider ought to bring his body forward, keep his legs close to the animal's sides, hold his hands low, and leave the reins slack (Fig. 65). In this illustration, the off reins are lightly felt because I was trying to make the horse canter to the right on three legs. We can see that the near snaffle rein is quite loose.

round his neck and bring my head to the right ; consequently, the horse's head was against my left shoulder. I subsequently saw the inconvenience of this position, in which one is too far forward on his neck when he brings his fore legs down on the ground. And as we are then obliged to give him his head, he is at liberty to send us over his ears by a strong kick with both hind legs, or to give us a blow in the face or chest with his head, in the event of his throwing it up.

From a very long experience I have found the following to be the best means of avoiding accidents which may happen from rearing. Separate the reins—as one should always do, when a horse rears—and take hold of the mane in the left hand at about the middle of the neck. When the horse stands up on end, bring the body well forward by the left arm ; and when he comes down again, push the body back into its place by quickly straightening that arm. If the animal makes another attempt at rearing, again bring the body forward, again push it back ; and so on, until he ceases to rear. From the moment we stop trying to make the horse go forward, we are able by this means to put up with the horse's rearing for any length of time without difficulty. If he kicks, our straightened-out arm will act as a prop, and if he springs to the right about or left about, it will furnish a support which will keep us in the saddle, and will enable us to avoid hanging on to the reins, which is the usual cause of accidents. I feel certain that the foregoing position is the best for keeping the rider in the saddle, when a horse rears, or, rather, it is the least bad, because the position of the rider is never good in such a case.

I have had good luck with regard to rearing ; for although I have ridden a great number of rearers, none of them has upset me.

I do not believe that horses voluntarily throw themselves backwards. As far as I can see, they simply lose their balance. Usually the following happens: The horse by suddenly getting up, causes the body of the rider to go backwards, which is sufficient to upset the animal. When a horse is standing up on his hind legs, he may be compared to the centre rod of a pair of scales which is in equilibrium ; and then the slightest movement of the body of the rider, whether forward or backward, forcibly draws the horse in the former direction or in the latter.

I have said that I do not believe that horses voluntarily throw themselves backwards. I mean that a horse will not deliberately throw himself backwards as a means of resistance. His instinct of self-preservation will be sufficient to prevent him doing this. But I know that horses which are suffering from disease of certain nervous centres fall backwards, and sometimes dash their head against a wall. Here we have no concern with animals which are affected by a disease similar to madness in man, and which are unsuitable for any kind of work.

I have, however, broken, and seen broken by other breakers, horses which had *immobilité* or megrims. But they were only violent and irritable, and their eyes became injected with blood if upset in the slightest. In fact, they had only the appearance of megrims. To succeed with such animals, we require to have all the good qualities of a breaker and rider, especially pluck.

Some horses which are affected with only a certain degree of *immobilité* can be broken. Gaulois, which was a superb Hanoverian horse, was supposed to suffer from this disease. I made him into an excellent school horse, and rode him for several years. It is true that Gaulois, like many other horses which are reputed to have *immobilité*, showed symptoms of it only when he " played up."

I am greatly surprised that very few of all the authors who have written on equitation say nothing of the struggles which one always has with horses to a lesser or greater extent. To believe many of them, the breaker is on a bed of roses, and if he will use only their methods, he will be certain to make the horse obey. What is the reason of this silence on their part? Are they afraid to frighten their readers, or do they wish to make them believe that there are no struggles? I cannot say; but in any case it seems to me preferable to speak the whole truth, and to forewarn my readers of the accidents that may happen during breaking, so that they may not be surprised if the animal does not immediately submit to every demand.

I have seen a great number of good breakers at work, and they all had battles to fight; Baucher more than any of the others, because he required more.

The true talent of the breaker consists in making himself master of the horse, especially in the event of a fight, by suppling him, and by the employment of a rational method of breaking; because we must not forget that the horse always struggles against his rider, more or less openly, until his education is complete.

But we do not arrive at this result without more or less violent struggles. Those who have not had experience of these battles, upon the result of which depends the submission of the horse, begin by provoking the animal to resistance, but they do not dare to continue the attack. In this case the horse quickly understands that he is master. He will renew, as often as he likes, the form of defence which has served his purpose, and thanks to which he is certain to have the last word. This is the way to spoil the breaking.

My practice is altogether different. The moment the horse shows fight I shake him up vigorously, but rationally.* We should not tickle the horse with the spur, which would

---

* To stop a horse " playing up," lean back and lower the hands. Raising the hands, which will also raise the centre of gravity, will be certain to cause a fall.

only aggravate the animal's resistance. On the contrary, our attack on him should be somewhat brutal, so that he may immediately feel that his strength must yield to superior force. Here the real difficulty is to have the pluck to attack vigorously. Very few people make up their minds to do this, in which is the only means of security; because the horse, astonished at the brutality of the attack, will submit, although, if lightly tickled with the spur, he will increase his resistance, and will soon get the best of his rider.

It is evident that whereas the attack should be vigorous, it should be made in as rational a way as practicable, that is to say, in a manner which will overcome the horse's defence by "oppositions."* But, I repeat, the chief thing above all others is the vigour, the energy of the rider. As regards myself, once in the struggle, I pay little heed to lateral or diagonal equitation. I don't care if I increase the commotion; my great point is to be master, and to make the horse understand that his defence is in vain. To achieve this grand result, when a horse contents himself by merely indicating a resistance, I do not hesitate to provoke him to carry it out fully, so as to bring him to reason. Here is the true secret of breaking, namely, to obtain the absolute submission of the horse. A horse's breaking is not definitely completed if he has made no show of resistance, because there may be struggles for supremacy in the future. The object of breaking is the destruction of the free will of the horse. As long as a breaker hesitates to provoke struggles which he feels are close at hand, and which he knows are inevitable, his breaking is not complete.

We must also say, in a general way, that the *tact* of the

---

* To make an " opposition " is to do an action contrary to that which the horse wishes to do. We succeed in this simply by combining the " aids," so as to *oppose* the forehand to the hind quarters, or the hind quarters to the forehand, namely, to carry one of them to one side, in order to throw the other on the opposite side

6*

breaker ought to consist, throughout the whole course of breaking, in discovering the defences which the horse is preparing, and in anticipating and counteracting them before they are made. This is more especially necessary in the properly-called defences of the horse, which are not always produced in the form of violent or unruly movements. It constantly happens during breaking, that the horse, in order to refuse to do what is asked of him, obstinately does what he was previously taught. This is the history of every lesson. During all the breaking, the defences of the horse are produced alternately to the right and left. When, by the force of insistence, we have rendered one side supple, we may be greatly astonished to see the horse use, as a defence, what we have just taught him with much trouble, and to refuse to do that which he did without any hesitation the day before. In this case we must recommence the work and carry it on until obedience is equally obtained on both sides. If there is a difficulty in making such a horse canter with, for example, the near fore leading, as soon as we make him do so, we will find that in every case he canters with that fore-leg leading, and refuses to lead with the off fore. In order to make him canter with the off fore leading, we must begin over again all the work we did in teaching him to canter with the near fore leading, and alternate these two forms of canter, while making him do the canter in which there is greater difficulty, more frequently than the other kind of canter. We should continue in this way until obedience is perfect on both sides.

When a horse makes a defence always on the same side, we may be sure that he does so on account of pain or of faulty conformation.

Later on, when the breaking is more advanced, we shall see the horse use, for example, the Spanish trot as a defence against doing the *passage* or the *piaffer*. In every case he will try a less energetic work, in order to escape from a more fatiguing one. The ruses of a horse are infinite. The breaker has to checkmate them by tact, art and energy.

THE WALK.

It is most important that a horse should walk with long, regular and free steps, which can be obtained only by allowing the animal great liberty of head and neck. If the horse is lazy or dull, he should be made to go on, by closing the legs. If he is impetuous, impatient, or fidgety, he should be patted on the neck and encouraged by the voice. He should be at once stopped if he begins to trot. No mistake should be made between the trot and jog, which are entirely different paces. Jogging, which is often adopted by the horse, is very difficult to correct when it has become a habit. It spoils the long striding walk, and is very fatiguing to the rider. Keeping the horse in hand shortens the steps of the walk, which become higher and shorter, according as the neck is raised and the head is brought into a vertical position. The same thing occurs in the trot and canter. The well-collected horse is handsome, but he does not cover much ground.

TO HALT AND STAND STILL.

It is absolutely necessary to be able to stop the horse when one wishes. As a rule, the halt ought to be made progressively and not abruptly. It can be made at any pace, and often even in cases when a sudden halt is indispensable.

The means for stopping the horse is always the same—namely, raise the snaffle reins while drawing them back with an equal feeling on both reins, so as to bring the weight on the hind quarters ; at the same time, close both legs strongly to bring the hocks under the animal's body, and feel the curb reins. The horse is then *between the hands and legs.*

I cannot say that these three movements should be absolutely simultaneous. They certainly come one after another, but so closely together that the intervals are imperceptible. Anyhow, they ought to be executed in the order I have indicated. If, for instance. the movement of the legs precedes ever so little that of the snaffle, the effect will be to make the horse go forward, which will be the opposite to what is wanted.

This method of stopping the horse is the best and should be the only one used. The halt should be made without concussion. It is then painless for the rider, saves the horse's loins and hocks, and is easy, because the hocks and pasterns bend. To stop himself, the horse acts simultaneously with all the parts of his body, makes no local effort, and preserves all the elasticity of his loins, which bend and become slightly concave. If we stop the horse only by the hand, and without the help of the legs, the forehand will become arched in order to resist the impulsion received, and will push back the hind quarters by a counter stroke in removing it from the centre. In this case the loins become stiff and convex. The shock which results is painful for the rider, and often dangerous on account of its violence, and is very bad for the horse, on whom it inflicts pain in his mouth, shoulders, loins, and fetlocks.

A halt, no matter how sudden it may be, should be smooth; if it is not so, it is badly executed.

The halt ought to be done by the same means at every pace. It is, of course, understood that the faster the speed, the more difficult is the halt, and the more should the rider lean back.

The horse ought not only stop himself as quickly as his rider wishes, but should also remain standing still as long as he is required, wherever he may be. It is somewhat difficult to make an impatient, nervous, or excitable horse stand still at this time. We should calm him down, so as to gradually accustom him to his surroundings. We should begin in the school when we are alone, and should pat him on the neck and speak to him. Each time he wishes to advance or go side-ways, we should put him back in his place, and should not allow him to take a step in any direction. If we allow him to go to one side or the other, no matter how little, the first movement will probably be followed by a second one; and so on. I repeat, that the best way to calm him down and get him to stand steady, is to pat him on the neck and speak kindly to him.

If the horse is alone and in an enclosed place, he will readily give in, but to teach him to stand steady in a street, we should bring other horses into the school and make them move about. When he stands steady under these conditions, we should renew the exercise outside, in some quiet place, and should then, little by little, try him in places where there is more traffic. I have already said that habit is every-thing for a horse. Therefore it is only necessary to accustom him to stand in the middle of the noise and movement of the street, and to make him understand that he will get pats on the neck for so doing.

After all, great gentleness, patience and gradual training are the best means for making a horse stand still in any place as long as we like.

CHANGES OF DIRECTION.

At first, all changes of direction should be taught at the walk.

To turn to the right, we should lightly draw the off snaffle rein with the right hand to the right, and not towards our body, so as not to stop the horse.

We find that the animal slackens his pace when he turns; because the forward reach of his shoulder which begins the movement is decreased, so that the off fore leg of the horse, if the turn is made to the right, covers only about half the distance of an ordinary step. This period of arrest causes

the croup to swerve, because it cannot go forward, notwithstanding its acquired impulsion. But if, at the moment
when the animal yields his head and neck to the pull of the
right rein, we slacken the hand, while supporting the legs,
we thereby force the right leg to take a pace as long as usual,
and shall consequently avoid the period of arrest, by obliging
the croup to follow the shoulders.

The rider can thus straighten the croup when it swerves
in turning, and can do it easily, because he feels to
what side the swerve is made, and consequently knows which
leg to employ. As we do not know to which side the
deviation of the croup may be made, we would run a great
risk of making a mistake, if we were to say in advance what
leg we ought to employ.

The question of using the outward or inward leg in
turning has been greatly discussed. The old school recommended the inward leg, because they said that it helped the
turning movement. Baucher maintained, on the contrary,
that we ought to use the outward leg, so as to prevent the
hind quarters being swung round to the outside.

The practice of Baucher has been generally adopted.
The old teachers were wrong. They said that to turn to
the right, the rider had to bring the animal's shoulders to the
right by feeling the right rein, and to push the hind quarters
to the left by the right leg. This is lateral equitation in
all its beauty. But they did not take into consideration
the fact that the direction, not only of the shoulders, but of
the entire horse, had to be changed, and that consequently
the animal should remain straight.

The following is the simple solution of this problem. We
should apply an equal pressure of both legs. Then, if the
horse swings his hind-quarters round to one side, we can
keep them straight by the pressure of the outward leg.
The hind-quarters ought to follow the track of the

forehand without deviating from it in the slightest degree *The horse ought always to keep his hind-quarters in the same direction as the shoulders.* It is the rider's business to decide whether he should apply a more or less strong pressure with one leg or with the other leg, according as the horse swerves to one side or the other.

As a general rule, when we turn to the right, the hind-quarters are inclined to swing round too much to the left; and *vice versâ.* Therefore, unless in exceptional cases, we ought to apply the outward leg somewhat more strongly than the inward one when we turn.

In turning, the action of the leg, the office of which is to prevent any deviation of the croup, should never precede that of the hand, but should immediately follow it.

Another way is at first to turn the croup inwards, by doing which, the movement of the head, and immediately afterwards that of the neck and shoulders, is made difficult. Besides, the arched condition of the croup and shoulders will prompt the horse to resist the action of the rein.

We occasionally meet horses which naturally or by habit go sideways. In this case, they always bring their croup to the same side. If, for instance, they carry it to the right, that is to say, inwards, when we turn them to the right, we shall be obliged to apply the inward (right) leg more strongly than the outward one. But if, in turning such a horse to the left, he continues to carry his croup to the right, a stronger application will have to be given by the outward (right) leg. Therefore, with the same animal we may sometimes have to apply the inward, and at other times, the outward leg.

To get the horse to readily change direction, and to give him the required mobility, we should make him perform in the school, different exercises, such as *doublers, voltes, demi-voltes,* and changes of hand.

The *doubler* is a straight line which we take, either across or down the centre of the school, after having started from some spot in the wall.　Having arrived at the opposite wall, we turn, and continually go on to the same hand. (Fig. 25).

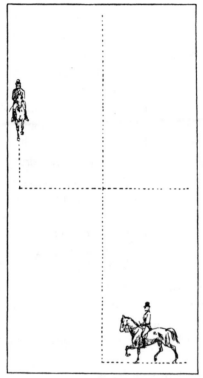

Fig. 25.—*Doubler.*

The *volte* is a circle which we describe on some point. But, at the beginning, it is best to do the volte by leaving the end of one of the long sides of the school.　As a horse has always a tendency to enlarge the circle, he will keep in bounds by the angle formed by the two walls which face him.　(Fig. 26).

The *demi-volte* is made in the middle of one of the small sides of the school. As it finishes on two tracks, we should not ask the horse to do it before teaching him to move on two tracks, which I will explain further on. (Fig. 27).

Whatever may be the pace at which the demi-volte is

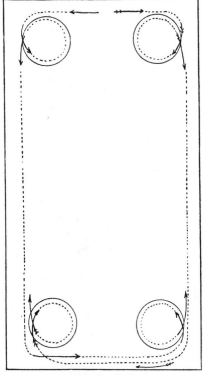

Fig. 26.—Volte.

made, the shoulders should be the first to leave, and to arrive at, the wall; that is to say, the horse should always remain on an oblique line. The demi-volte is usually done in a very incorrect manner. Nothing is rarer than a well-executed demi-volte.

It often happens that the rider uses his outward leg too

much in a change of direction, or that the horse, of his own accord, carries his croup to the inside, or simply goes down the centre. To remedy this, we should start, as for a demi-volte, from the usual place; but should continue to " double," while taking care to keep the horse very straight. If this

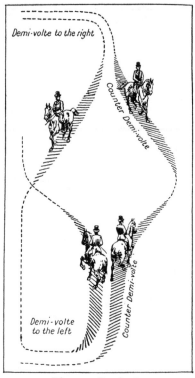

Demi·volte to the right

Counter Demi·volte

Demi·volte to the left

Counter Demi·volte

Fig. 27.—Demi-volte.

does not suffice, we should deceive the animal by a demi-volte; thus doing, as I term it, a *counter-demi-volte*. (Fig. 27.)

We start, for instance, to the right, as for a demi-volte; but having arrived at the middle of the school, we finish the demi-volte to the left on two tracks. The horse, who was wanting to carry his croup to the right, is obliged to carry it to the left by the vigorous action of the right leg, which at first was the inward leg, but which in this manœuvre becomes the outward one. There is no better exercise than this for keeping the horse always straight and attentive; because, by alternating the demi-voltes and the counter-demi-voltes, it is impossible for him to become " routined."

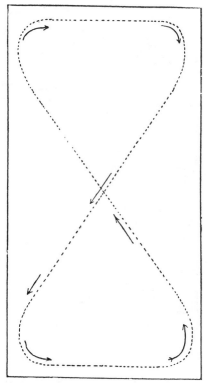

Fig. 28.—Diagonal change of hand.

There are three changes of hand. The most simple is the *diagonal change of hand*, in which we go along one of the diagonals of the school, on leaving the wall *at the beginning of one of the long sides*. (Fig. 28.)*

* If we start diagonally at the end of one of the long sides of the school, we will cross the school from one angle to the other, without having changed the hand.

To do the second or *reversed change of hand*, we start as in the preceding movement, from one of the angles of the school, always beginning at one of the long sides ; but having arrived at the centre, we return by a half circle to the wall of the long side which we left, and which we, of course, take on the left

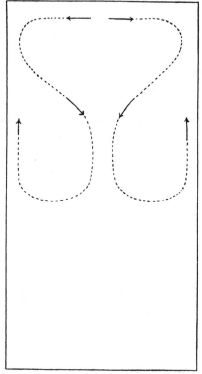

Fig. 29.—Reversed change of hand.

hand, if we had it on the right hand, and *vice versâ* (Fig. 29.)

The *counter-change of hand* is the most complicated one. In doing it, we start by entering the long side on two tracks, and, having arrived at the centre of the school, we return to the other end of the long side from which we started, while keeping on two tracks for the whole time.   At the canter, this movement requires two changes of leg, the first in the middle of the school, and the second at the wall.   If the rider is going on the right, as in Fig. 30, he will begin at the canter with the off fore leading.   Having arrived at the centre of the

Fig. 30.—Counter-change of hand.

school, he will make the horse change, and canter with the near fore leading, up to the wall, where he will make him change to the off fore.   We can see that in the *counter-change of hand* there is no change of hand.

In a like manner we describe circles and figures of 8 in the middle of the school.   This is the best kind of work for sup-

pling the horse, and is also the most certain means for making
the rider use his two legs in a timely way.

We do not learn to always keep our horse straight by continually "going large"; because in this case the croup can
swerve only to one side. Also, I often work my horses, while
keeping them at one yard, and in large schools, at two yards
from the wall.

We may further note that during the entire period of
breaking, the horse tries to keep as little straight as possible.
He will understand that if he carries his croup to one side he
will escape being collected, which consists in the hind quarters
propelling the body in the direction of its axis.

The best work for suppling the horse is the figure of 8 performed a yard from the wall, at the walk, trot and canter; but
it should be done with the greatest possible correctness, namely,
with a light inward flexion of the neck, an energetie application of the outward leg, and support from the inward leg.

By preparing a horse to readily change the diagonal at the
walk, we also prepare him to start into the canter, and to
change his leg. On arriving at the centre, we make the horse
take two or three steps to the side, and we start him in the
required position on a new diagonal. We should take great
care to keep him straight, especially at the canter, because at
this delicate work, the horse has always a tendency to throw
his croup inwards, so as to escape the outward spur, which has
helped to straighten him, and against which he tries to guard
himself. Hence the necessity, as I have recommended, of
opposing the inward leg. Finally, we can obtain impulsion
only by closing both legs.

LATERAL FLEXIONS.

Up to the present I have made the changes of direction
only in a rudimentary way. In the same manner, as my first
lesson was to drive the horse forward, I only require him at

first, for the changes of direction, to turn and follow the line
on which I place him.   In every case I go from simple things
to complicated ones.   When the horse unresistantly obeys
everything, from the first indication to all the changes of
direction, we have to solve the new problem of displacing the

Fig. 31.—Preparation for lateral flexion ; jaw contracted.

entire body of the horse, while keeping it in equilibrium and
lightness.   Lateral flexion is the preparation for the movement
thus executed.   To make the lateral flexion to the right,* for
instance, we should stand at the near shoulder of the horse,
and take the bridoon reins in the left hand and the bit reins

* We may note that I here recommence the work on foot.   I always practise
the foot work and the mounted work in the same lesson.

in the right, in exactly the same manner as for the direct flexion ; and, having placed the hand and neck in the same position as we would do for the direct flexion, we make that flexion. When the jaw is relaxed and the flexion complete, we push the head of the horse to the right, by light pressures of the left hand on the bridoon reins, which we hold high, and drawn from rear to front, in order to prevent both the lowering of the neck and any tendency which the horse may have to get behind his bit.*

At the same time, the right hand lightly feels the curb reins from behind, while carrying itself to the right in such a manner as to principally tighten the right rein,† until, the lateral flexion of the neck to the poll being complete ; the two reins of the curb acting equally in giving and maintaining the play of the jaw (Figs. 31 and 32), which ought to be the same as in direct flexion.

At the beginning, we ought to be content with even the appearance of obedience, and we should not want the horse to do more than to turn his head slightly, while opening his mouth. We must practise him very often at this work, and try to progress by requiring more exactness each time in these suppling exercises. We will certainly finish in obtaining complete flexion, by never employing force and contenting ourselves with a small degree of progress at each lesson.

In equitation we obtain much by requiring only a little at

* See Fig. 31, preparation for lateral flexion, jaw contracted; Fig. 32, lateral flexion, jaw relaxed.

† The left rein of the curb, however, remains slightly tense. If the right rein only acts, it will pull the muzzle, and the head will no longer be in a vertical position.

We may note that I give here the first lesson of obedience to the two similar impulsions in the changes of direction. Up to this I have used the right rein only to turn to the right. I now begin to teach the horse to obey the two simultaneous impulsions acting in the same direction, namely, the near snaffle rein which pushes, and the off curb rein which pulls, both acting from left to right.

a time. Patience then, and no roughness, which will always prevent us from obtaining our end.

The exact position for the lateral flexion is the same as for

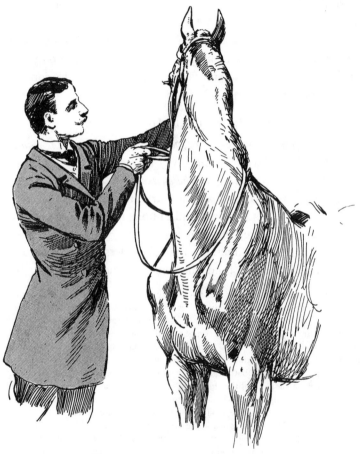

Fig. 32.—Lateral flexion ; jaw relaxed.

the direct flexion, except that the neck, while remaining flexed at the poll, from front to rear, is also bent to one side (always at the poll), in such a manner that the direction of the head is perpendicular to what it was in direct flexion,

7*

and faces the side upon which the flexion was made. The
neck, of course, remains high, as in direct flexion, the
muzzle being at the height of the upper part of the shoulder,
and the head in, or a little beyond, the perpendicular *
(Fig. 33).

Thus, as we have seen by the right flexion, this flexion is
generally done in quite a different manner. The only way
to find out what the lateral flexion ought to be, is to consider
the result we wish to obtain from it.

OBJECTS OF LATERAL FLEXIONS.

1. *To preserve, by the high position of the neck, the equilibrium of direct flexion in changes of direction.*

2. *To strengthen and bind the entire forehand in the changes
of direction*, by arranging all the parts in such a manner as to
make the whole as compact and supple in the turning movements, as in the direct movements.

In changes of direction, the shoulders naturally cover
the ground, while the hind quarters give the propulsion ; but

---

* In doing the lateral flexion we should take care not to alter the distribution
of weight. To counterbalance the effect of the flexion, the horse has a natural
tendency to make an opposition with the shoulder of the side away from which
the head is turned, and to put the weight of the forehand on the left leg if the
head is bent to the right. This is inevitable as long as the jaw resists, but the
moment it yields, its flexion, involving that of the neck, brings about an equal
distribution of weight on both legs. If we allow the horse to contract the habit
of opposing the shoulder of the side opposite to the flexion, the equilibrium, and
consequently the lightness, will be destroyed. In changes of direction, as in
movements on two tracks, the shoulder of the side opposite to that of the flexion
will always be late. The great difficulty in these exercises is to make this
shoulder move. Hence we should always try to relieve it by making only a
slight bend, whilst the snaffle rein of the side opposite to the change transfers the
weight to the inward shoulder (which has less ground to cover), by throwing the
weight at each stride to the side towards which the animal is proceeding. This
method enables us to obtain great propulsion in work on two tracks. A too
complete flexion will stop this propulsion by overloading the outward shoulder.
At first one is always astonished to learn that the flexion to the right overloads
the near shoulder, which is the natural result of the attempt made by the horse to
counterbalance the effort demanded of him.

the rider has no direct action on the shoulders. He acts only on the neck through the mouth, and on the shoulders through the neck. Lateral flexion, by strengthening and binding all the parts together, places them in a state of reciprocal dependence, which enables the rider to act on the entire forehand. Without flexion, the fishing-rod, as I have already said, will be held by the thin end ; that is to say,

Fig. 33.—Correct lateral flexion.

there will be a heavy head (because it is far from the centre of gravity) at the end of a slack neck. The action of the reins, instead of directing the mass, is therefore limited to bringing the head towards the forehand, which remains fixed on the ground, in proportion as the horse is on his shoulders.

3. *To preserve lightness in the changes of direction by the flexion of the jaw.*

In all movements, impulsion makes the horse a single whole.

It is the hind quarters which, by getting under the centre, bind themselves to the forehand.* If all this propulsion was accumulated on the bars of the flexed and movable lower jaw†— which should be connected to the entire forehand in such a way that the flexibility‡ of the arm of the lever would be always increasing from the shoulders to the jaw—the hands, both in the changes of direction and in direct movements, would send back with extreme lightness§ to the legs, a part of the propulsion which they have received from them. We can thus make the entire body of the horse into an energetic and harmonious whole by the good equilibrium of the levers, and by the well-regulated use of the forces in changes of direction. We will thus obtain lightness, and will continue *to have the horse in hand* in all the changes of direction.

In the foregoing remarks I have described what I consider to be the nature and object of lateral flexion, and have tried, as in the description of direct flexion, to give reasons for my practice. Unfortunately the greater number of those who teach horses flexions, do the work in a hap-hazard way, without accurately understanding the nature of the result which they ought to try to obtain.

I must say that Baucher did not give a better account of the mechanism of lateral flexion, than he did of direct flexion. Or, rather, he committed the same fault in lateral

* Many authors speak of connecting the forehand to the hind quarters, which is an absurdity, because the hind quarters throw themselves on the forehand during propulsion. The " aids " keep the body in good position by restraining or regulating the force which comes from the hocks.

† When the jaw does not yield, nothing yields, and the horse changes his position all in one piece during the changes of direction. He turns like a boat.

‡ The only lateral movement in *lateral* flexion is done by the poll ; the jaw bends exactly as in direct flexion.

§ In lateral flexion, as in direct flexion, we should work the levers in such a manner as to obtain the maximum effect by a minimum effort.

flexion as in direct flexion, because the latter is a preparation for the former.   This faulty flexion, which is adopted by those who have followed him, is made at the withers instead of at the poll.   Here, again, as in direct flexion, we find the exciting cause of the lowering of the neck, which changes a useful exercise into an injurious one.   In it the head is low, the bend of the neck is at the withers instead of at the poll, and the head of the horse is in profile instead of facing one.

Fig. 34.—Incorrect lateral flexion.

A comparison of Fig. 34 (wrong flexion) with Fig. 33 (correct flexion) shows us at a glance the advantages of the lateral flexion which I have described, and the faults of the flexion which is commonly practised.   To complete this criticism, I need only repeat all what I have said about the wrong method of direct flexion and its faults.

We need not be surprised that flexions have been blamed for softening the neck ; that is to say, for rendering it movable, independently of the remainder of the body, which

is precisely the result of lateral flexion at the withers ;
whilst lateral flexion at the poll, on the contrary, stiffens
the neck, and binds all the forehand in such a manner as to
displace it from the whole, which is an indispensable result, as
I have explained, because the rider has no direct action on
the shoulders. Head low and isolated from the body by a
movable neck, which yields of itself without drawing the
shoulders, and allows the horse to oppose every movement of
the neck by a movement of the shoulders in an opposite
direction, with consequent impossibility of directing the forehand, and the results of a lateral flexion at the withers and of
a lowering of the neck which follows it.

Contrary to direct flexion (which I never practise, either
on foot or mounted, except when going forward), lateral
flexion at first is done on foot, when the horse is standing
still, on account of the difficulty of putting the hind quarters
in movement. In mounted work, I practise lateral flexion
only when going forward. I make it an absolute rule, once I
am mounted, never to ask my horse anything except when
he is advancing, and I have consequently avoided making
my school horses inclined to get behind their bit, which is
the usual danger in high school breaking.*

In mounted work, lateral flexion is made by the same
mechanism as on foot. In order to bend the neck to the
right, the near snaffle rein, tightened and drawn to the right,
keeps the head high, and, being pressed against the upper
part of the neck, it pushes the head from left to right, while
the off curb rein, *slightly tightened*, aids this movement, and
loosens the jaw (Fig. 35).

---

* I have already said that a high position of the neck can be obtained only
during forward progression, and that the reason I keep the necks of my horses very
high is because I continue to drive them forward during all the work I give them.
In fact, the greater the forward impulsion, the more do the hind quarters get
under the centre, and the more is the forehand lightened.

As the first care of the rider should be to keep his animal straight, he should use both legs to obtain impulsion, the leg of the side opposite to the bend of the neck being applied more strongly than the other leg.

When the legs act simultaneously, they are agents of propulsion ; but when one acts stronger than the other, it is an

Fig. 35.—Correct lateral flexion when mounted.

agent of direction.   One leg should never act by itself : the simultaneous action of both legs is propulsion ; the predominance of one over the other is direction.   Finally, as the hands are much more effective for guiding than the legs, they should be used in a very light manner.

The fundamental error of Baucher's lateral flexion is as well marked in mounted work as in foot work.   Compare Fig. 36, which I have taken from Baucher's book, with Fig. 35, which represents correct flexion.

Fig. 37, taken from a recent book, shows clearly that many persons of the present day who claim to practise lateral flexion have no idea of its mechanism or object.

Fig. 36.—Baucher's lateral flexion when mounted.

The lateral flexion I have described is a suppling exercise, whether it is done on foot or when mounted, and is of great importance. Equilibrium, lightness and mobility depend on the flexions and on getting the horse in hand, and until he has learned all this, it would be folly to ask for more. It is therefore of the highest importance to make the lateral flexion complete, so as to obtain extreme obedience from the horse.

Fig. 37.—Incorrect lateral flexion.

But when we practise lateral flexion in later work (changes of direction, work on two tracks, etc.), we ought to content ourselves with a very slight lateral flexion of the neck,* which, like the head, should always be well placed. We can understand that a too strongly accentuated flexion checks the effect of propulsion by throwing all the weight on the outward shoulder.

* As long as the jaws work we have lightness, and the slightest indication is sufficient for changes of direction.

The suppling exercise, which we term lateral flexion, is not the less necessary, because it demands much in order to obtain little.   But we must recognise the fact that in later work it is enough to obtain a slight bend of the neck, provided that the head and neck are always well placed, and above all things that the jaw is loose.

Fig. 38.—Lateral effects in rotation of croup and shoulders.

ROTATION OF THE CROUP AND SHOULDERS.

When I have successively made the horse readily yield to the whip, and to perform the lateral flexions with equal facility, I have then to combine both these movements into a single movement.

I have at first taught him to yield to the whip from left to right, while helping the movement with the near snaffle rein, which draws the head to the left, so as to carry the croup to the right.   This work is called "lateral effects" (Fig. 38); because the two effects are produced on the same side (left rein and whip to the left).   Having done this, I succeed, little by little, in making the horse give way, by holding the head straight (Fig. 39), which is called a "direct effect." Now it is necessary for him to yield, by adopting "diagonal effects" in the same way, namely, with the whip on the left and the flexion on the right (Fig. 40).*   For that purpose, without using the snaffle rein, the end of which is in my left

Fig. 39.—Direct effects in rotation of croup and shoulders.

hand,† I catch hold of the near curb rein, quite close to the mouth, with the left hand, while the right hand, at the height

* I have already explained that *lateral equitation* is only a preparation for *diagonal equitation*, which is the only rational method, and by which alone we can obtain combined effects. Everyone understands that the action of the rider should be effected diagonally, for the simple reason that the movements of the horse are produced diagonally.

† For the better explanation of the action of the reins, I have omitted the snaffle in Fig. 40.

I may remind my readers that the proper way to hold the ends of the snaffle reins is to have the buckle in the hollow of the hand (Figs. 38 and 39).

of the horse's breast, holds both the whip and the off rein, for
which the withers act as a pulley (Fig. 40). The horse will
then make the direct flexion. I then try to obtain the
beginning of the right lateral flexion by raising the head by
means of slight upward jerks on the curb, and by pressing
the head to the right, while at the same time I make the
croup give way by working the whip from left to right.

Fig. 40.—Diagonal effects in rotation of croup and shoulders.

Finally, I increase these effects, until the yielding of the neck,
jaw and croup is complete.

I thus succeed in making the horse *pivot*, while I do the
complete lateral flexion.

I purposely use the word "pivot," which expresses my idea
in an incomplete manner, but which accurately discribes
Baucher's method of doing this rotation. In fact, during the
rotation of the croup, according to his plan, the forehand

remains stationary and serves as a pivot, which I have found to be a mistake. During breaking, none of the parts of the horse should be stationary, because immobility often degenerates into a means of defence. Therefore, instead of making the horse pivot, I try to make him describe a very small circle with the forehand round the centre, and a large concentric circle round it with the hind quarters.

Of course, I do not pass abruptly from lateral effects to direct effects, or from direct effects to diagonal effects. On the contrary, I go imperceptibly from one to the other, so that the horse may well understand what I want him to do, and that he may not evince any surprise or confusion. The employment of lateral effects has been a preparatory step towards the execution of the movement by direct effects. In the same way, direct effects are only a preparatory measure for diagonal effects.

This work would be of no use if its only object was to make the horse give way to the whip. Its great end is, without frightening the horse, to prepare him to obey the legs at first, and the spurs subsequently and by degrees.

We now come to mounted work, which I do by again passing from lateral effects to direct effects, and from direct effects to diagonal effects, as during work on foot.

If, when in the middle of the school, I wish to obtain the rotation of the croup (*reversed pirouette*) from the left to the right, I bring my left heel close to the animal's side. As a green horse does not know what I wish him to do, his first movement will be to lean against my leg, at which movement the good effect of the preceding work will come to my aid. I touch him lightly with my whip on the left side, as near as possible to my heel, and I avoid above all things touching him too far back, which would be almost certain to make him kick. At the same time I use the left snaffle rein to make him carry his croup to the right. I can assure my readers that no horse will resist these indications, if they are gently employed.

I use the near snaffle rein according to the amount of resistance which the horse often makes at first. I draw the head a little more to the left, while continuing to touch the animal's side with the heel and whip if the resistance is great. The horse is forced to yield to these three forces acting on the same side.

As soon as the horse takes a step to the right, I stop him and pat him on the neck. I then let him go quietly round the school, in order that he may think over what he has just done. It is most important always to let a horse be free and quiet after he has obeyed. A horse will accept this as a reward, which we should not be chary in giving him. Stoppage of work and pats on the neck are the only means to make him understand that he has done well. We are so often obliged to have recourse to punishment during breaking, that we ought to eagerly seize the opportunity of patting him on the neck, when he shows the slightest sign of obedience. The more we pat him on the neck, the less will we be forced to punish him.*

As I have just said, by letting the horse walk at ease for a few moments, we give him time to understand the movement which he has just done and the indications which cause him to do it. Apparently the horse yields only physically, but in reality it is his intelligence, or, to speak more correctly, his memory to which we appeal. We must therefore work on his memory, and for that reason I allow him the necessary time to permanently remember this fact.

Having let the horse go quietly round the school, I do the

---

* The great art in breaking is to reward and punish in an appropriate manner in order to do which we must seize the exact moment of obedience or resistance. Here we must bear in mind the fundamental principle of breaking, namely, that reward should follow obedience as quickly as punishment follows disobedience.

same exercise over again, twenty or thirty times, without changing the side, until he obeys the moment I close my heel to his side. I then give him similar work with the right leg.

When the horse accurately obeys both legs, I put on dummy spurs (stump spurs), in order to accustom him to obey something more severe than the heel. Then, each day I increase the effect of the leg, while diminishing that of the whip, which I gradually discard.* Later on I come to the spur.

I use the whip, only to aid the memory of the horse, and to induce him to obey the spur without frightening him. We should not forget that the effect of a touch of the spur on a green horse at the beginning of the breaking, is exactly similar to that of the sting of a fly, which he at first tries to drive away with his tail. If he does not succeed in this, he will cow-kick on the side he is pricked. If the insect does not fly away, he will look out for some object, such as a wall or tree, upon which to lean or lie, in order to crush the author of his sufferings, the fly. Therefore, when we give him the first touch of the spur, how can we expect that his first movement will not be to cow-kick or to lean against a wall?

We may see that it is a grave mistake to use the spur without having prepared the horse for it, by making him successively obey the whip, leg, heel and dummy spur.

If we spur a horse which is neither prepared for nor accustomed to it, he will not understand its meaning, and will not obey. If we try to force him to do so, he, not knowing what we want him to do, and feeling the pain which we inflict on him, will instinctively defend himself. The more severe the attack, the more stubborn will be the resistance at first, and

---

* I have already said that I discard the whip when mounted, and I take it up again only to make the horse obey the leg and to obtain the first extension of the legs in the Spanish trot. In both cases I continue the use of the whip for only two or three lessons.

8

the more energetic the subsequent defence.   If the horse is
soft, he will lean against the spur ; but if he is impetuous, he
will immediately make a most violent defence, and the breaking will have failed in every way.   Some animals will become
restive, others will become maddened at the mere approach of
the leg, and the breaker, instead of having taught anything,
will have rendered education impossible.

It is always thus in breaking, the great difficulty being to
make the horse understand what we want him to do.   As we
can appeal only to his memory,* the means which we employ
with him should be simple, and should be invariably the
same.

In riding, the horse ought to be taught to understand that
the spur is simply an " aid," and that it becomes a punishment only when he plays up.†

Many persons who have only a superficial knowledge of
equitation imagine that, instead of touching the horse behind
the girths with the spur, it is more rational to keep the knee
tightly pressed against the flap of the saddle, and by drawing
back the heel to spur the horse on the side.   Nothing can be
more faulty than this method, by which the spur slides along
a large extent of the side.   By it we succeed only in tickling
the animal and provoking him to defend himself, and we
are unable to spur him with sufficient power to drive him
forward and to paralyse his defence.   The further back the

* For this reason, I have already said that in the same lesson we must carefully avoid requiring the horse to do two or more things which might confuse
him.   As his comprehension is very slow, we ought to guard against perplexing
him.

† It often happens that the horse throws himself on the spur, sometimes to one
side and sometimes to the other.   In this case we ought to effectively correct
him with the spur, for which object I place him in the middle of the school, and
drive my heel and spur into his rebellious side, so as to make him bring it round.
When he has thus made two or three pirouettes, I stop and begin again the work
I left off.   If he again resists, I recommence the work, until he has thoroughly
given in.

spur is drawn away from the girths, the nearer it approaches the most ticklish spot. In fact, horses are not ticklish near the girths, but all of them are ticklish further back.

Besides, in this kind of attack, the lower part of the leg cannot remain close to the animal's side, because the foot swings backwards and forwards ; the result being that the attack is sudden, instead of the horse being prepared for it by a gradual pressure of the leg. It should, on the contrary, be capable of being regulated with precision, so that it can be light, well-marked, or extremely severe, according to the resistance offered by the horse to the indications given by the rider's legs.

When spurring a horse just behind the girths, the knee should be turned a little outwards, so that the spur, like a sword, may be brought at right angles to the side, progressively and with certainty. The scratching and fraying form of attack is made without precision and by jerks.

Those who believe that the fact of the knee being slightly turned outwards diminishes the firmness of the rider's seat, should be taught that the rider gets his strongest grip by means of the upper and back part of the calf of the leg. Therefore the position which the leg occupies when it spurs the horse just behind the girths, is the one which is most favourable to the rider's firmness of seat.*

Gripping too tightly with the knees pushes the thighs upwards, and causes the rider to be more or less raised out of the saddle.

By gripping with the hollow of the leg just behind the knee, we have, on the contrary, perfect adherence from the buttock to the heel. Besides, we can do fine work with the horse only

---

* The fact that all beginners and bad riders instinctively assume this position, in order to get the greatest possible firmness of seat, prevents them from being able to use the spurs. Besides, every rider instinctively adopts this position when his horse plays up.

by always keeping the heels close to his sides. With the knees and toes turned inwards, the heels are too far from the sides, and can work only by jerks. Good horsemanship cannot be practised without progressive and delicately effected transitions.

When the horse readily yields to the legs, I change the feeling on the reins by degrees. It is always necessary to finally place the head of the horse on the side to which it is directed. Nevertheless, the change should be made so gradually that the animal will not notice it.

At first he will yield to my leg only when I use it, while feeling the rein of the same side—a lateral effect. I gradually diminish the tension of the rein, until he will obey the leg by itself, and I then employ both snaffle reins to keep his head straight—direct effect. Finally, I succeed little by little in using the opposite rein—diagonal effect.

Here progress will be similar to that which was obtained when doing the same movement on foot; solely by the aid of the whip, that is to say, the horse will finish by rotating his croup to the right, while keeping his muzzle to the right; and *vice versâ*. At this work I never require complete lateral flexion when mounted. A very slight bend towards the side to which we are going is sufficient.*

Having obtained this result, I teach the horse to do the *simple pirouette*, in which he turns his shoulders round his hind quarters.†

We should not only supple the hind quarters, but should

---

* When the horse readily yields to the action of the legs, it is well to use them alternately ; but only as an indication, to make the hind quarters slightly yield, in which case a step or two will be sufficient. The rider will thus succeed in sending the hind quarters from one leg to the other leg, and to measure this action. This is the beginning of "equestrian tact."

† This work can be properly done only when mounted, on account of the necessity of supporting the hind quarters and of pressing the horse forward.

also give to the shoulders the greatest possible mobility, which is an indispensable quality for every kind of work.

We can exert no direct action on the shoulders, as we can on the mouth and hind quarters. The impulsion to put them in movement is given by the hind quarters, which are put in action by our legs ; and the direction is given by the mouth, which receives the indication of the reins.

I shall now describe how I make the shoulders rotate, namely, how I do the pirouette from left to right.

Having halted the horse in the middle of the school, I carry both hands to the right and close the legs, in order to prevent a retrograde movement ; the left leg being pressed more strongly to the side than the right leg, so as to prevent the horse from bringing his hind quarters round to the left. I work the snaffle reins simultaneously with the legs, the off rein being lightly drawn to the right, but not backwards, while the near rein pushes the shoulders to the right. The near rein performs another office, as follows : If the horse, having carried his shoulders to the right, wishes to throw his hind quarters to the left, a slight pull of the near rein gives immediate help to the left leg to keep the croup in its place, by carrying the head more or less to the left, according to the extent the hind quarters have swung round to the left.

At the beginning we should make a large circle rather than a small one, which would be a true pirouette. In this way we keep the horse in hand, and we easily prevent him getting behind the bit, which we should always take the utmost care to do.

The absolute necessity of avoiding any tendency in the horse to get behind his bit, makes it dangerous during the first period of breaking to teach simple or reversed pirouettes, which are excellent exercises for both man and horse, when they are sufficiently advanced in their education.

The reversed pirouette has the great fault of leaving the

shoulders inert; and the ordinary pirouette, that of fixing the hind quarters on the ground.

We cannot get a horse to do a pirouette, if we drive him forward.

At the beginning of breaking we should not employ any movement which will leave one part of the horse stationary, for the great point is to make the horse move with his whole body.

Instead of pirouettes, it is better to do ordinary and reversed *voltes*, in which we can always press the horse up to his bridle. The volte is, in fact, only a pirouette described on a large circle.

In the *reversed volte*, the croup describes the great circumference. A horse which enlarges the circle has a tendency to get behind his bit. In the ordinary volte the shoulders describe the great circumference. Then, if the horse diminishes the size of the circle, he has a tendency to get behind his bit, to avoid which fault he should be kept between the legs. We should ask him to do only movements which bring his whole body into play, and we should keep pressing him forward.

SCHOOL WALK.

When the horse is well in hand at the walk, we can make him do the "school walk," which is a shorter, lighter, and more cadenced pace than the ordinary walk. In it, the feet are put down in the same succession as in the trot, from which it differs only by the fact that its steps are shorter.

To obtain the school walk, we should use the legs energetically and the hands moderately; should make numerous movements with the horse's whole body by means of these aids;* and should cover as little ground as possible, by

---

* By this I mean the movements of the horse as a whole which bring him into hand, namely, to send him by the legs on the hand and to send a part of the impulsion from the hand to our legs. ;

shortening the steps. Too long steps show that the horse has not begun to collect himself, without doing which his steps cannot be in cadence.

The school walk is an excellent form of gymnastics, in which the combined " aids " of the rider bring all the powers of the horse into play. It makes him supple, graceful, light and well posed ; in other words, it puts him into perfect equilibrium, and it prepares him finally for the artificial paces, and especially for the *rassembler*, which of itself brings him to the *passage* and *piaffer*.

I teach the horse to do all the changes of direction at this school walk ; but only when he can do them easily at an ordinary walk.

THE REIN-BACK.

People generally, when trying on foot to make a horse rein back, commit the great fault of holding his head as high as possible while pushing him back. The exact opposite of this should be done ; because, by raising the head while pushing the horse back, we overload the hind quarters, which require to be light in order to perform this movement.

In fact, the hind quarters are the first to move, which they cannot do freely if they are overloaded. Even if we try to push back the horse only a little, we will make him get behind his bit and rear, which is a most serious vice.

To make a horse rein back properly, we should, on the contrary, put the preponderance of weight on his shoulders. In order to do this, I slightly lower the head of the animal * by light, downward pressures on the snaffle reins.

I stand directly facing the horse, and seize with each hand,

---

* Reining back is the only work during which I put extra weight on the shoulders.

close to the mouth, a snaffle rein, with which I push him
back. I need hardly say that in this position the rein-back
is very easy, the horse being on his forehand and his loins
and hocks relieved. The hind feet, like those in front, will be
easily raised instead of being dragged, and when the animal
is pushed back by the snaffle he will not be able to arch
himself.

We ought to be contented with two first steps to the rear,
and should then pat him on the neck and bring him forward.
We should frequently recommence this work, which is better
than prolonging the rein-back, which at first will fatigue the
horse, who, not having his loins and hocks suppled, will have
his joints more or less stiff at this new work. The more we
prolong the work, the less will we impress the memory of the
horse ; because we do not stop to pat him on the neck and to
make him understand that he has done well. Finally, we
must bear in mind that all work which fatigues the horse
discourages him, if he is not brought up to it by degrees and
prepared by successive suppling lessons.

I never require from a horse more than ten or twelve steps
when reining back, and I then bring him forward the same
distance, while keeping him continually in hand. I never
make him do this movement more than three or four times
consecutively.

We rarely fail to obtain the rein-back by the means which
I have described, and which should be invariably combined
with great gentleness.

It sometimes happens that the horse refuses to rein back,
either from stubbornness or from pain. I have seen horses
resist all known means, even the most violent ones, which,
unfortunately, are nearly always employed with these
animals.

In such cases I stand directly facing the horse. I hold in
each hand a snaffle rein close to the mouth, and I simply step

on his feet while pressing him backwards. I have never met a horse which would not yield to this method.

When the horse reins back without stiffness, and with the head lowered, I try to make him do the same movement with the head more and more raised, for which object I place myself at his shoulder, and I do the direct flexion in reining back. I thus endeavour to obtain a very free rein-back with the horse well in hand.

If the horse reins back too quickly, in order to escape from the bit, I draw the snaffle reins forward so as to make his retrograde movement more slow. This is the normal rein-back, for which the preceding work is only the preparation. It is evident that if the horse is ready to rein back at the very first sign of the direct flexion, there will be no necessity to lower his head, and still less to tread on his feet. The lowering of the head is useful only to prevent him getting behind his bit. I therefore do not practise it unless the animal shows signs of wanting to rein back.

When the horse readily reins back by means of direct flexion when held by the hand, I begin to put him through the same work while on his back.

In mounted work I do not force the forehand. In fact, it is dangerous to pull on the mouth, which action throws too much weight on the hind quarters, and may consequently lead to his getting behind his bit and rearing. Also, I never attempt the mounted rein-back unless I am certain that my horse will go freely forward by a pressure of the legs, which, in my opinion, is the best means of mobilising the hind quarters, and with which I always begin the rein-back. I feel the bit reins only lightly, in order to make the horse lower his head after I have halted him. I then close my left heel, and the horse, being already obedient to the legs, raises his near hind as if he was going to take a step to one side, because he was taught to give way to the spur. At this instant I gently feel the off snaffle rein in a backward direction, but not to one side, which would have the effect of turning his head. The near hind foot, which is in the air, places itself firmly down on the ground behind the off hind, at the moment when the off snaffle rein makes the off shoulder go back. I then close my right heel. At the instant the horse obeys the indication I give him—namely, when he raises his off hind, as if to take a step to one side—I utilise this moment to give a backward pull on the near snaffle rein, the off hind being of necessity placed in rear of the near hind at the instant the near snaffle rein brings the left shoulder back.

Having obtained two steps of the rein back, I am content, and I hasten to pat the horse on the neck to show him that he has done well.

When the horse has often done two steps, and then four, he will be able to rein back easily.

I do not use spurs at the beginning of the rein-back, so as to avoid exciting the animal unless he is very sluggish and does not answer readily to the legs.

I have just shown the way to proceed at the beginning, when teaching a horse to rein back. But we must not conclude that we should always continue the same effects of the legs separately. That would, in fact, make the horse sway his body from right to left, which would be wrong, because, when he reins back, he should always remain as straight as he does when he goes forward. When the horse understands the movement, and when he can easily take his first steps backwards, we should use both reins and both legs. The rein-back will then be correct ; and if the haunches have a tendency to deviate out of the straight line, we can easily straighten them by pressing a little more strongly with the leg of the side towards which the croup deviates, than with the other leg.

When I say that I use a certain rein or a certain leg, I mean the leg or rein which ought to have the stronger action. During the entire work both reins should be lightly felt, and both legs ought to be kept close to the side. Continual co-operation ought always to exist between the hands and legs.

It is certain that a horse can rein back without the help of the diagonal aids, and that a rider who knows nothing about the principles which I have just enunciated, can make him do so. But he will never succeed in having his horse in hand, with the head high, as if he were going forward, the hind legs being raised as high as the fore ones, and, above all things, with the points of the buttocks not further to the rear than the hocks.* We should thoroughly understand that these conditions are essential in retrograde movements.

THE "RAMENER," COLLECTION, "RASSEMBLER," AND EQUESTRIAN TACT.

Before going further, we may recapitulate as follows the results we have obtained : The horse carries himself very freely forward on the legs being brought close to his sides ; he correctly does the direct and lateral flexions of the jaw ; is well in hand ; yields immediately to the action of each leg ; easily executes the respective rotations of the haunches and shoulders ; and performs all the changes of direction with facility.

It must be well understood that during all the time my horse does these suppling exercises while I am on foot, I had also given him the same work mounted, and that I only seek by general effects to confirm and improve the results obtained on foot.

Respecting flexions and collection when mounted, I ought to remark that it is more easy to profit by acquired propulsion than to create it. By this I mean that, if I am at

* If this condition is not fulfilled the horse will be behind the bit.

the walk, I have two things to do, namely, first, to create impulsion by the legs; and, second, to make the horse do direct or lateral flexion. At the end of a turn at the trot and canter I am, on the contrary, full of impulsion, and to get the horse in hand I need only a fingering of the reins (in direct or lateral flexion), while keeping the legs close to the sides. Under these conditions there is no risk of the horse getting behind his bit, and he then comes most easily to hand.*

We now come to the *ramener, collection,* and *rassembler.*

If the *ramener* and *collection* belong to ordinary riding, the *rassembler* pertains only to scientific equitation. I therefore crave the forbearance of my readers for discussing at present the *rassembler,* which is the last stage of the general effects, of which the *ramener* at first, and subsequently the collection, are only the beginning.

The word *ramener,* which is borrowed from Baucher, means nothing else than direct flexion.

The *ramener* is only the first part of getting the horse in hand, and signifies that the horse's head is high, his head perpendicular, and that he champs and plays with his bit, when the rider feels it by means of the reins; but owing to deficient impulsion he is not light in hand. The effect obtained is localised in the jaw and in the upper part of the neck. It is therefore only partial and leaves the general equilibrium incomplete. It is the first step towards perfect distribution of weight; collecting the horse is the second, as I have just said; and the *rassembler* is the last. I mention the *ramener* only out of respect for the authority of Baucher, who, working on the horse while standing still, brought him

---

* When the horse will not obey the diagonal effects, it is an excellent lesson for him to finish the trot or canter by a well-marked lateral flexion, with the opposite leg very close and with great impulsion. The direct flexion is made naturally, if the time of halting is correct; because we ought to stop the horse between the legs and hands (with both legs close) when he is full of forward movement.

back (*ramener*); but I try to obtain direct flexion only during forward movement, which at once enables me to get the horse in hand. I therefore exclude from my vocabulary the word *ramener*, which indicates a backward action, and is therefore entirely opposed to my system of riding.*

Direct flexion should always be preceded, sustained, and completed by the action of the legs pressing the hind quarters on the forehand.

The legs ought to *take and give* like the hands, and with the hands, that is to say, simultaneously and in the same proportion. This constitutes general movement. If the hands give and the legs continue their action, the horse will be *out of hand*, because the propulsion developed by the legs will no longer be received by the hands. If the hands act without the legs sending them any impulsion, the horse will bring his chin into his breast or will get behind his bit; because his hocks have been left too far behind him. The expression " take and give," as I have explained it when speaking of direct flexion, therefore applies as well to the action of the legs as to that of the hands. Legs and hands should always act in harmony, according to the desired result. We get the horse in hand by this combination of the alternate actions of the legs and hands acting on the whole.

Getting the horse in hand, which is an excellent term of the old school, is the result of equilibrium during propulsion, obtained and preserved by direct flexion, resulting from the action of the legs impelling the hind quarters on to the forehand. Here we are in the best conditions of good horsemanship. The hind legs, being well under the body, drive it forward and maintain equilibrium by the high position of the

* A sluggish horse which does not go up to his bridle, and which answers badly to the action of the legs, would be *ramené'*d if his neck was bent at the withers according to the system of Baucher. The *ramener* never conduces to good equilibrium, but on the contrary destroys it, and does not help to get the horse in hand.

neck.* The momentum of the mass ends at the bit, namely, at the end of the arm of the lever (of which the flexibility from front to rear increases from rear to front), whence the hand of the rider sends back, in its turn, the amount necessary to maintain equilibrium,† towards the hind quarters, which by a fresh spring again impels all the mass forward ; and so on· This horse is thus truly in hand.‡   In my opinion, he ought at the same time be *on the hand*. The horse is *on the hand* when, being in direct flexion, he closes his jaw on the bit from time to time, so as to remain in constant communication with the hand of the rider. ‖

* When the hind legs are well under the body, the croup is low, and consequently the forehand is high.

† Naturally, the greater part of the force of propulsion is employed to send the horse forward.

‡ People often make the mistake of saying that a horse which " cracks nuts " is well in hand.

A horse that " cracks nuts," continually snaps with his teeth, whatever may be the position of the neck, but more often when it is high. It is true that this horse is light, but he is not in hand. For a horse to be in hand he should obey the indications of the hands on the reins, which he cannot do unless he lets go the bit. A horse which " cracks nuts " gives himself up to this trick, but he never releases the bit. Nevertheless, the mobility of the jaw caused by this habit is a proof that the horse does not stiffen his jaw, and he is therefore always light. From which we can conclude that the horse which " cracks nuts " is generally well balanced. For all ordinary riding he has a sufficiently delicate mouth, but if we want to do high-school work with him, it is indispensable that he should champ and yield to the bit each time the rider requires him to do so, that is to say, he should be in hand. For that object it is absolutely necessary that he should be made to give up his nut-cracking trick, by progressive and rigidly correct flexions. We will thus succeed little by little in making him release the bit and get into hand.

I wish to draw my readers' particular attention to the following important distinction : When the horse " cracks nuts " he retains command of his lower jaw ; but when he is in hand, the rider has control over it.

‖ The horse which pulls at the hand is not *on the hand* ; he is *beyond* it. When a horse which is *on the hand* seeks to force it and go beyond it, we should, according to Baucher's teaching, pull him up, put him into flexion, and set off again. My advice is to press him up to the hand by an energetic use of the legs, at the risk of upsetting him, and I thus succeed in getting him into hand by impulsion.

Finally, the horse comes up again on the hand when the impulsion communicated by the legs brings the hocks strongly under the animal's body and sends him freely on the bit, which is possible only when the horse is in hand to a maximum extent, which form of control is the *rassembler*. It is necessary that the tension of the reins is light enough to allow the propulsion to pass, but great enough to establish contact between the bit and the hand, and to give us the feeling that as the impulsion comes freely on the hand, we can dispose of it as we like.

As the neck in this case is necessarily high, and as the action of the horse is lofty, the meaning of the expression, " the horse comes up to the hand," is perfectly clear.

We can now understand what is meant by the horse being *between the hands and legs*, both of which send back impulsion to each other, so as to preserve equilibrium while going forward.

The school horse should be completely *enclosed between the hands and legs* ; and the hack should be in front of the legs and on the hands, so that he can lean a little with the bars of his mouth at fast paces. The horse which does not answer to the legs is *behind the legs*. He has too much weight on his haunches ; in other words, he is behind the bit.

Every horse is not capable of being perfectly *rassemblé*'d, which is the extreme limit of *being in hand*; but every horse ought to be trained to get into hand with good equilibrium, no matter what may be the work for which he is required.

The hack, hunter, charger, and even the carriage horse, acquires a good position only by being got into hand, in which case the equilibrium is straight or horizontal.*

It is generally thought that the object of getting a horse

---

* Straight or horizontal equilibrium is the distribution of weight for a hack, and is between that of the race-horse, which is too much on his forehand, and that of the school horse, which is too much on his haunches.

in hand is to give him a fine carriage, which no doubt is valuable, but is its smallest advantage. Equilibrium, which is the result of getting the horse in hand, gives mobility, namely, the facility of instantly doing, without effort or fatigue, every required movement at all paces. Also, this equilibrium keeps the horse sound during severe work ; because it requires from each part of the horse only those efforts which come naturally to him. We thus avoid wearing the animal out prematurely ; because no special strain is put on any particular organ.

If army horses were sufficiently suppled by a first course of breaking, and if the soldiers who ride them understood equestrian equilibrium, and knew how to take advantage of opportunities, our cavalry would gain in appearance, firmness of seat, and staying power. The men would have more confidence in themselves and their horses, and they would be more active, more skilful and more energetic. The horses would stand more work, and they and the government budget would be relieved from needless expense.

We must not think that the horse should be always kept in hand. I certainly do not advise that this should be done the whole time one is hacking, hunting, foraging or charging. So far from that, I am the resolute enemy of keeping the horse always collected. We should know how to be able to get the horse in hand, whenever we wish to do so, and at all paces ; but only from time to time, and when occasion demands. It is of the utmost necessity at certain moments of difficulty, as, for instance, when we think the horse is going to play up, and when the animal, from fatigue, softness of constitution, or some other cause, goes in a lumbering, unconnected manner. Getting him into hand restores his balance and is of great use in every respect.

As I have already said, all horses can be got into hand, but only some are sufficiently well shaped to be *rassemblé*'d.

The *rassembler*, which is the act of getting a horse into hand to a maximum extent, is the complete equilibrium of the animal in all his movements. It is the perfect form of collecting the well-suppled horse. In it the loins, hind-quarters and hocks are flexible ; the hocks stoutly press the mass forward ; the shoulders are free and movable ; the neck is high and the jaw readily obeys the feeling of the rider's hands on the reins, and all the parts of the horse being in action and equally enterprising, combine to form an energetic, harmonious and light whole. The equilibrium is so perfect and so unstable, that the rider feels that he can make his horse do whatever he desires by the slightest indication of his wishes. Both of them, so to speak, are in the air. They are ready to fly !

How can we succeed in bringing to perfection and in refining the art of getting a horse into hand, so as to obtain this ideal of equilibrium ?

If we have well understood the action of collecting a horse, and the coming and going of the forces of the legs to the hands, and of the hands to the legs, we will remember that the hands allow the amount of impulsion necessary to the forward progress of the mass to pass, and throw back towards the hind quarters only the amount of impulsion required to preserve balance. This is obtained by the delicate and constant play of the fingers, which may be compared to the fingering of a piano as regards delicacy and speed.

The question is : what proportion of the force ought the hand allow to pass through it, and what proportion ought it retain ? We should measure this proportion with absolute precision at each stride, by the correct combination of the " aids," so as to send to the hind quarters only the amount of force necessary to maintain equilibrium with a maximum of propulsion. *Equestrian tact* consists in doing this. If the fingers do not work with enough decision, the centre of gravity will be carried to the front a little too much, and the horse will be ready to go beyond the hand. If they act too strongly, too much weight will be put on the hind quarters, and the hocks will be brought too far back. In both cases there will be no *rassembler*. The fingering of the reins should regulate with absolute precision the distribution of the propulsion.* We have to solve this problem at each stride, which is not identical to the preceding one or to the following one. Here is the end we have sought.

We can succeed by work and perseverance to get the horse in hand in a manner which approaches the *rassembler*, and even to occasionally obtain the *rassembler* ; but very few riders can keep up the *rassembler* by a scientific fingering of the reins.†

* In order that the rider may properly feel his horse—that is to say, when the *rassembler* is perfect—the harmony and union between him and his animal should be such that the force of propulsion and the effects of the whole should be transmitted without intermission or interruption.

The propulsion and the effects which the whole sends from the rider to the horse, and from the horse to the rider, are like an elastic ball. The spur, so to speak, goes to seek for this ball in the hind legs of the horse, and makes it come up close to the heels of the rider, whence, passing by the seat, it ascends to the withers, follows the upper part of the neck to the poll, falls into the mouth, where the hands receive it, and, following the lower part of the neck, it returns to its starting point, where it is picked up and sent on again by the legs. Therefore, this ball continually goes round a circuit when the horse is *rassemblé*'d. To make this comparison perfectly exact, we should say that it is a football which leaves the legs and arrives at the mouth, and a billiard ball which comes back.

† It is impossible to obtain and preserve a good *rassembler* unless the horse has been kept perfectly straight during his course of breaking. If we do not succeed in holding the animal in this straight line, which begins at the poll and finishes at the tail, the horse will escape being *rassemblé*'d. If any part deviates —haunches, shoulders, or jaw yielding laterally, instead of yielding in a straight line—the result will be spoiled propulsion, and without complete propulsion there can be no *rassembler*.

♭ Being able to feel that the horse is straight is the first manifestation of equestrian tact. The moment the slightest deviation is perceived, the legs send the hind-quarters to each other, whilst the effects of the hand, which combine with the effects of the legs, straighten the forehand. At this moment the rider succeeds in getting the *equestrian feeling* (*equestrian tact*) by the more or less fine perception of the successive positions of the forehand and hind quarters, until the animal is perfectly straight.

Although I have ridden horses for fifty years, I did not obtain perfect *rassembler* until the last ten years. It is true that I worked for a long time according to the somewhat inexact data of Baucher. But the fact is that for many years I continually felt the *rassembler* escape me, by the displacement of the centre of gravity, whether to the front or to the rear. I had to greatly refine my tact and consequently my " aids " to obtain the complete *rassembler*, and to preserve it with a maximum amount of propulsion.

But this is not all. There are not only direct movements, but also those to the side and when turning. In these movements one leg always predominates, in which case the impulsion which comes on the bit is not equally distributed between the two hands. The right leg throws more impulsion on the left hand, and *vice versâ*. It is therefore necessary, in order to preserve equilibrium in turning to the left, that the left hand, while remaining bound to the right hand, sends back to the centre a larger amount of force, which is all the more diff:cult to measure ; because this hand, while keeping up the *rassembler*, has to regulate the change of direction.*

If we now reflect that in all work of equitation, the horse, whether going forward or keeping himself back, constantly tries to escape to the right or to the left, by his haunches or shoulders, we will see that in order to maintain perfect equilibrium we have to simultaneously perceive all the actions of the horse and all those which are being prepared, so as to combine them by opposing them, by the simultaneous action of the " aids," and to produce from them the desired ideal of equilibrium.

I said a short time ago that the *rassembler* in direct move-

---

* The difficulty is so great that Baucher acknowledges that the " lightness " (read *rassembler*) escaped him in changes of direction. The fault was less his, than that of the bad position of the neck which I have pointed out.

ment is the end of equitation. The continual *rassembler*, not only in side movements and turning, but in all movements, whatever may be their combinations, is the supreme refinement of riding—the full possession of the ideal. Thus the two organisms are so combined that *the man is one with his horse ;* the former perceives the efforts of the latter so directly and rapidly that each action of the man responds so surely and rapidly to a corresponding action of the horse, that the animal expects it, and lends himself to it instantaneously. Then the horse has only reflex actions. The only brain he has is that of his rider. I am right in saying that it is the ideal of which we dream.

How can we obtain this tact, this keenness of perception, this refined and rapid feeling of all the efforts of the horse in every degree, preparing the efforts which are going to follow ? This cannot be taught in a book. For these faculties we require practice, work, and, above all things, natural aptitude and love for horses.

By his seat and legs the rider ought to feel with absolute certainty everything that goes on under him, as for instance, if the hocks are brought more or less under the centre, or if they remain behind ; what legs are raised, and to what height, and if the croup is going to deviate from the straight line.

By his hands and legs, helped by his eyes, the rider ought to be able to feel the actions and above all things the tendencies of the jaw, head, neck, and shoulders. As the forehand begins the movements desired by the animal, we can say that " the hand ought to feel *the ideas of the horse.*"*

* High school work naturally demands very complicated efforts which the rider ought to feel on account of the precision which it requires.

The most difficult effort to perceive is that which is called "the magpie jump," which the horse makes by simultaneously placing his two hind feet on the ground, so as to relieve himself. When the movement is softly made and the pasterns bend, it is difficult to catch. However, if we allow a horse to contract this habit, he will lose all regularity of action.

Thus the rider will have the feeling of the complete equilibrium of the horse, and the free disposal of his forces at any moment.

I cannot say more on this subject, except to advise my readers to devote themselves to practice.*

SIDE STEPS AND TWO TRACKS.

I was obliged to discuss the *rassembler*, which belongs to scientific riding, when referring to collecting a horse, which subject leads up to the *rassembler*. I have even to speak at the same time of the side step and the "two tracks," because these two movements are closely connected ; although the former pertains to ordinary riding,† the latter belongs exclusively to high school riding.

The first remark to make, is that in side steps—and still more in the "two tracks," because the speed is faster—the rider ought to freely carry his weight to the side towards which the horse is proceeding. The necessity of this is emphasised by the fact that the side movement of the horse naturally displaces the rider towards the side away from which the animal is going. Consequently, when the side movement is rapid, the rider can be very easily thrown off to the side away from which the movement is made. Therefore the rider ought to lean to the left, on the saddle and stirrup, during side steps from right to left. This position, which unites the rider to the horse, by giving them the same impulse, has the further advantage of relieving the right

* Pictures of a *rassemblé*'d horse can be seen in photographs in this book. I attach great importance to these photographs, because they are free from all trickery. If we study them with attention, we will see even in the most energetic school work, that my horse maintains straight or horizontal equilibrium. In ordinary school equilibrium, the horse is often too much on his haunches. The great impulsion which I try to obtain always keeps my horse in horizontal equilibrium, however high the action of his fore legs may be.

† The great utility of this movement is that it enables us to place our horses where we like, and at all paces, when riding in the open.

shoulder, which has more ground to cover than the left one.
We require a certain amount of practice to attain this result;
because, as I have already said, the side movement of the
horse naturally puts the rider into the opposite position.
I never begin to teach the side steps when the horse is going
along the wall, which would uselessly increase the difficulty,
by the want of impulse resulting from the change in direction.
By removing the horse from the wall, I forcibly stop his
forward movement,

I make the horse do the first side steps at the end of a
change of hand, from right to left for instance. I am on the
track, going to the left, with the wall to the right. On
arriving near to the wall which, at the end of the change
of hand, will be to my left, I carry both hands to the left,
while closing the legs and acting vigorously with the right
leg. The near snaffle rein draws to the left, and the off rein
applied against the neck, presses the shoulders equally to the
left. We can see that these are absolutely the same "aids"
as those for the rotation of the shoulders, although the movement is made while gaining more ground to the front. If
the horse resists the right leg, I have recourse to the off rein,
to make him carry his haunches to the left.* Even if the
animal makes only two or three side steps, I am content with
his progress, I pat him on the neck, and slacken the reins.

After that, I make the horse do a change of hand from left
to right when leaving the wall, which is on my left. While
thus going obliquely, I hold him as straight as possible, and
when I arrive near to the wall, which will be on my right,
I carry my hand to the right and I apply the left leg, while
pressing him up to the hand by means of both legs. I may
add that the hand ought to profit by the supplemental

* In other words, I have recourse, as I always do, to lateral equitation, in case
of resistance proceeding from the incomplete education of the horse. But at the
stage of breaking to which we have arrived, his education ought to be sufficiently
advanced for diagonal equitation to give us all its results.

impulse, to transform the forward movement into a movement from left to right, with the least possible resistance *

I continue this work for a sufficiently long time, and accentuate it according to the progress obtained, by which I wish to say, that at first I am content to make the horse take two or three side paces.   Later on, when he gets more expert, I require more from him, always at the moment when we arrive close to the wall, so as to obtain five or six side steps.   Further on, I begin the side steps at the middle of the school, so that I can make him do twelve or fifteen steps. I finally make him do the shoulder-in.†

* Energetic impulse is the first condition of correctly executed work on two tracks.   It results from the firm support of the inward leg, providing that the outward leg has a predominant action.

If, during work on two tracks, the inward hind leg of the horse is carried away from the body instead of being brought under its centre—as would be the case if there was sufficient impulsion—the horse will be inclined to get behind his bit ; the cause of this fault being the insufficient energy of the inward leg of the rider, the action of which ought to be supplemented by a corresponding action of the outward leg.

† I do not put the horse's shoulder to the wall until he has been well trained. A horse has only too great a tendency to allow himself to be guided by the wall, instead of giving himself up exclusively to the "aids."   I greatly dislike continual work close to the wall.   If the horse is straight and limits himself to following the wall, whatever the pace may be, he will let himself be guided by this permanent obstacle, much more than by the rider's "aids."   He will even take a kind of moral support from it, and his natural tendency will always be to slightly carry away his croup, and to get the shoulder close to the wall ; hence the difficulty of holding him straight, and of keeping him well between the legs.

In movements on two tracks, the wall leads the horse so well and helps him so much in keeping his shoulders in the proper direction, that he quickly begins to shave the wall too closely, which often becomes a "defence" on his part.

If we remove the horse from the wall, we will be obliged to direct the shoulders with the hand, which ought to be the only guide.   If the horse, when doing the shoulder-in, gets behind the bit, and brings his hind quarters too close to the wall, we should stop the movement on two tracks without changing the position of the horse, should push him forward with the legs, and make him go down the centre of the school.   No exercise is better than this to give impulse in the movement on two tracks, and to make the horse independent of the wall.

The number of side steps which we succeed in obtaining is of little consequence.   The essential thing is to
see that the horse is well placed—the shoulders being always
more advanced than the croup—which is the only position
that facilitates the side movement.   Position is everything.

At the beginning of the work I try to give cadence to the
horse, but only at the moment I am going to get him to do
side steps.   By the expression " to give cadence to the horse,"
I mean the school walk.   At this pace a horse has great mobility,
and the side movement is made more easy, because the fore
legs and hind legs can move more readily, without touching
each other, which is impossible at the ordinary walk.*

Up to this, I have purposely used the expression "side

We are never completely master of a horse which we have allowed to contract
the habit of always keeping close to the wall, which is a bad preparation for
riding in the open, and also for high school work, the first condition of which is
that the horse should be always *between the legs* of the rider, or, to speak more
precisely, should be solely guarded by the " aids."   It is therefore well to work
the horse at a distance of one or two yards from the wall.

When the horse has got into the habit of pressing his shoulder into the wall,
how are we to put him straight ?   And if we wish to take him away from the
wall, to go down the centre, to do a demi-volte, or to set off on " two tracks,"
what " aids " should we use ?

Let us suppose that the rider is on the right hand.   He will then instinctively
feel the off snaffle rein to bring the left shoulder away from the wall, which is a
mistake, because in pulling the off rein he will bring the head and neck to the
right, but the more he draws them to the right, the more will the lateral flexion
of the neck push the left shoulder to the left.   The proper way to bring the left
shoulder away from the wall is to draw the near snaffle rein rather high and
forward on the neck, then carry it to the right, while lightly feeling the
off rein, and we will then bring the whole neck along with the shoulders to the
right.

* To make side steps from left to right, the horse should pass his near fore and
the near hind, one after the other, over their respective off legs, in order to gain
ground to the right.   When the horse is at the ordinary walk, the pace is too
slow and two low for the legs to pass over their fellows without touching them.
In the side step, at the school walk, each of the near legs passes successively its
corresponding off leg, and (this is the important point and results solely from the
cadence) is put on the ground only at the moment when the off leg is just raised.
They therefore cannot hit each other.

step," and not "two tracks," because we always begin by
going to one side, which is far from the two tracks.

When a horse does the work I have just described, it is
said that he *goes sideways*, no matter how bad may be the
position of his head and neck.   But for this work to merit
being called " work on two tracks," the position should
be correct.   Yet the position is correct, and a horse moves
truly on *two tracks* when he goes *obliquely forward* on two
parallel lines, the one made by the forehand, the other by
the hind quarters.   He thus advances from the side, *with the
head and forehand always leading the hind quarters.*   The
head and neck ought to be kept high and slightly bent to the
side towards which the horse is going.   Above all things,
he should be well in hand, light, and in a cadenced pace.

In my opinion, this is the longest and most difficult work.
If we seek to obtain it complete and correct from the
beginning, we will either get no good result, or we will cause
the horse to at once resist, because he had not passed
through the " mill " of lateral, direct and diagonal efforts
which I have described.*

My reason for laying considerable stress on the subject of
" two tracks," is that this work has a great influence on all
the subsequent breaking, where we always meet during propulsion the same combined action of the diagonal " aids."

When the horse knows how to go on two tracks, he will
seek every means to escape from the *rassembler.*   At first,
he refuses to yield to the direct leg ; he then yields too much

---

* A horse which his rider persists in working only by means of lateral effects,
can never become a good school horse : he is ungraceful, and his work is disunited.   In fact, in lateral equitation, he carries his head and neck to the opposite
side to which he is moving ; and further it is impossible for him to do the *rassembler*, because, when we work with the two "aids" of one side we have nothing
to support the other side, which consequently escapes us.

We should therefore continually work both reins and both legs ; but it is
principally the double action of the opposite rein and leg which should play the
chief part in all movements.

and forces the opposite leg.   *He escapes by going too quickly to one side.*

I will suppose that the rider is placed with his shoulder to the wall and is going to the right.   The horse which tries to checkmate all the efforts the rider makes to keep him in hand and in good position, begins for instance, to lean against the rider's left leg (*outward leg* or *direct leg*).   The spur pricks him and forces him to give way.   He then tries to get behind his bit.   In order to drive him forward, it is necessary to employ the right leg (*outward leg* or *opposite leg*).   As we hardly ever use the spur of the opposite leg, from fear of straightening him, the horse will finish by pressing against this leg and by saving himself by running to one side, which will prevent us getting him in hand and regulating his work on " two tracks."

.   The remedy is simple.   It is sufficient, when the horse throws himself on the opposite leg, to attack him vigorously with the spur of that side, in order to make him straighten himself.   We must adopt this plan each time the horse throws himself to one side, which he will soon give up doing.

As we may see, the best system is to throw into disorder, in order to establish order.   This procedure, which is criticised by all those who have not the audacity to practise it, is the only one which incontestably establishes the power of the breaker over the animal.   By it, the horse learns that there are insurmountable obstacles to the carrying out of his wishes.   That point being settled, if we keep him balancing between reward and punishment, he is ours.*

---

* Every horse which knows how to go on " two tracks " makes an abuse of it. When horses are accustomed to do demi-voltes and changes of hand on " two tracks," they often put themselves sideways when their rider wishes them to do these movements while holding them straight, and by this defence they escape being *rassemblé*'d.   By holding the horse straight, we make him bring his hocks under his body, which is the very thing he tries to avoid doing by placing himself sideways.   The remedy is in the legs of the rider.   Later on, when the breaking has been finished—the horse being kept at the *rassembler* in all the school movements—he will not be able to obtain help from this defence.

According as we quicken the pace at the work on "two tracks," in order to pass from the school walk to the ordinary trot, or even to the fast trot, it becomes more and more difficult to employ the "aids" in an appropriate manner. We should, in fact, hold the horse very straight in the hand, because every effort to straighten the hind quarters, or to support the forehand, diminishes the propulsion, which ought to be extremely energetic.   To obtain a maximum of impulse at the quickest pace, we must keep the forehand and hind quarters absolutely on their own respective tracks, and must combine the energy of our legs, which give the impulse, with the delicacy of the constant action of the diagonal effects,* which enable us to keep the horse in position, without diminishing the impulse in any way.

This movement is perhaps the most inconvenient one, on account of the extreme difficulty of correctly combining the effects of the "aids" with great propulsion.   Not the least difficulty is to hold the horse always straight.   The direction of the impulse, even in work on two tracks, will always pass between the two ears, if the head is well placed.

The correct position during work on two tracks at a fast trot, is very difficult to keep.   In fact, the energy of the pace increases the natural disposition of the rider to carry his body to the side opposite to that to which he is going.   Hence the necessity of continual watchfulness on his part.

The great difficulty as regards the horse, is to make him quicken the trot without breaking into the canter.   This is the touchstone of impulse, and the proof that the animal answers freely to the "aids."

Work on two tracks, as I do it, in no way resembles the

* The delicacy of the diagonal effect combines admirably with the energy of the legs, because it results from the preponderance of one "aid" over the other. Besides, the true action of the "aids" is: legs energetic, heels delicate, and hands light.

sleepy work on two tracks which we generally see in riding
schools. I pay particular attention to demanding energetic
work, and I keep my horse full of enterprise, which is the
exact opposite of what is usually done. If my mount is enterprising, he becomes so on account of my legs having been
enterprising in the first instance.

In sleepy work the horse obeys conditionally ; in energetic
work he obeys without conditions ; he keeps nothing in re-
. serve and he gives himself up to his rider, which is the first
condition of equitation.

Figs. 41 and 42 show Germinal (a thorough-bred by Flavio
out of Pascale) at work on " two tracks " at the school walk.

In Fig. 41, the horse begins by putting himself into position,
at which he is perfect in Fig. 42. We can see how far the
correct position is from the crossed position, which many
riding masters adopt in work on " two tracks " ; the result
being that they stop all impulse.

The impulse appears greater in Fig. 42 than in Fig. 41, because
the horse, which is going on two tracks from left to right, was
photographed at the moment when he rested his right hind
foot on the ground, the right being the side to which he was
going. In Fig. 41 (two tracks from right to left), the near fore
foot, which forms the support, belongs to the side (the left) to
which the horse is going.

A comparison of these two illustrations enables us to thoroughly understand the movements of the horse's legs during
work on two tracks.

THE TROT.

To make a horse trot, we must begin by slackening the
reins, and increasing the pressure of the legs a little. We
ought to avoid striking him with our heels, which might upset
him. But if he is sluggish, we may at first make him feel
the heels, and afterwards the spurs, but only after a pressure

Fig. 41.—On "two tracks" at the school walk, from right to left.

Fig. 42.—On "two tracks" at the school walk, from left to right.

of the legs. At first we must limit ourselves to the short trot, and, above all things, we should make the animal do it in a correct and cadenced manner, that is to say, the foot-falls should be equal as regards time. As the horse is supple, and has been trained to obey the " aids," he will soon do what we require.

At first it is well to allow the horse to be as free as possible, in order that we may see if he trots level naturally. If at first we keep him in hand when trotting, he will not go freely, and if there is an inequality in his gait, it will be difficult to judge whether it is due to a fault of conformation, unsoundness, or bad horsemanship, namely, erroneous effects produced by the " aids." The reins, especially those of the curb, ought to be only very slightly felt. If the horse carries his head too high, we should use the curb reins. The fact of the head being carried too high and in a backward direction, crushes the hind quarters. If, on the contrary, the head is too low, we should use the snaffle reins ; but should not draw them to the rear, because that would stop the propulsion. We should give light quick pulls to these reins alternately, without jerking them, while taking care always to keep the hands high. We had best trot the horse only twice round the school, stop him, bring him into hand, and do the same things over again several times.

When we have got the horse into a good position at the trot, with his neck high,* and the line of his face nearly perpendicular, but a little farther advanced than the vertical line, we can keep up this pace for a longer time. We should gradually work up to this, because the more tired a horse becomes, the lower will he carry his head. If we prolong the work, he will become heavy in hand, in which case we should stop him by strongly closing the legs, and, having got him completely in hand, should set off again.

* This naturally increases the height of his action.

10

When we have succeeded in trotting for five minutes to each hand without fatigue, and, above all things, without the horse "breaking," we can make him go faster. We should, however, avoid abruptly passing from the short cadenced trot to the fast long trot, which would upset his balance, and would un-expectedly throw a considerable weight on his shoulders. At first we should increase the speed of the pace only towards the end of a turn at the trot. During the last couple of turns round the school, for example, we may act vigorously with the legs, while taking only a light support on the snaffle reins, the action of which should be limited simply to keeping the head in place.

By practising these exercises we shall succeed in making the horse do all he can at the trot, as regards high action and speed.

Above all things, we ought to avoid trying to make the horse trot faster than he can do ; for such an attempt will probably teach him the false and ugly gait of trotting in front and cantering behind.

There are two ways of riding at the trot, namely, the French (bumping in the saddle) and English (rising in the saddle). The former is of no practical use, although it is an absolutely indispensable school exercise,* for giving a good seat to beginners when they trot without stirrups ; but I disapprove of it for all other purposes. It is fatiguing to the rider, and still more to the horse. I cannot understand why it has been used for such a long time in the army.

When we rise at the trot there are neither jerks nor reactions. The rider should have his loins slightly bent, and con-sequently the upper part of his body should be inclined a little forward. He should not try by rising to follow or to anticipate the movements of the horse, but should let himself be raised. His ankle joints and knees acting together will

---

* It is the foundation of all good riding.   Without it there would be no seat.

sustain his movement, and will make him descend softly into the saddle, and into the cadence marked by the pace of the horse. He should always rise from *under* himself, that is to say, he should let the horse raise him, while helping the movement with the knees and ankle joints ; but the upper part of the body should do nothing. Otherwise, the muscles of the loins and shoulders will be contracted, the rider will become stiff, and will not be firmly united to his horse. The body ought to rise and fall as a whole.

The rider who hollows out his back, in place of using only his legs, necessarily carries his abdomen forward when he rises, and backward when he descends into the saddle, than which nothing can be more ungraceful.

Only one-third (the ball) of the foot should be placed in the stirrup. If the foot is "home," the ankle will lose all its elasticity, and consequently the trot will become stiff and painful.

The natural trot of a horse which is not upset or suffering, is an alternate and absolutely identical movement of the two diagonals.

At the rising trot, the rider can trot either on the left or right diagonal biped.*

The rider is said to trot on the left diagonal biped, when he rises at the same moment that the horse raises his left fore foot, and comes down on the saddle, when the horse puts that foot on the ground.

In the well-executed English trot, the rider rises and comes down only once during the succession of the two bipeds. He rises and descends along with the left biped, for instance, without the right biped having any influence on his move-

---

* In equestrian language, the diagonal always takes its name from front to rear. Thus, the right rein and left leg is the right diagonal, and the left rein and right leg is the left diagonal. It is the same with the legs of the horse, the right fore and left hind forming the right diagonal, and the left fore and right hind the left diagonal.

ments.   But if he is not in rhythm, he will come down too soon on the saddle, and will receive a shock from the right biped, as the result of the straightening of the left hock.   He will come twice in the saddle and will ride incorrectly.

The rider ought to be able to ride at the trot equally well on one biped, as on the other biped, and should be able to change from one to the other, so as to relieve himself, and especially the horse, during a long journey, but this requires a certain amount of practice to do.   A rider ought to learn how to know on what biped he is, which is difficult at first.   It is best to begin a preliminary study at the walk, while raising ourselves in the stirrups at each step the horse takes, as if he were trotting.   We have thus time to see what movement of the horse we are following.   After a little practice at this exercise, we can start again into the trot.

It is worthy of note that each rider naturally adopts one particular biped, and almost always without knowing that he does so, and he becomes so habituated to it that he feels ill at ease when he changes to the other biped.

If we wish to have a fine trotter, we should complete his education in the open, after having made him do in the school the exercises I have just described.   On a road a horse lends himself more readily to the work, and goes freer than in a school.   As we have space in front of us in the open, we are able to keep up the speed of the pace for a longer time ; but in a school the corners oblige us to slacken a little at frequent intervals.

All horses do not trot in an equally free manner.   Certain animals readily maintain this pace, if the speed is moderate ; but if the speed is increased, they will break into a short canter. It is correctly said that such horses *keep themselves back*.   It is very important not to allow a horse to change his pace without giving him the indications to do so, but it is not less important to make the horse, whenever we like, exert himself to the utmost at his trot.

If a horse starts into the canter when we want him to do the fast trot, we can at first try gentleness in order to correct this habit, which is only idleness. We can stop him and pat him on the neck, to reassure and calm him, and then put him again into the trot. This plan generally succeeds with impetuous horses, but it has no good effect on lazy ones, with which we should do just the contrary. When an animal breaks into the canter to avoid the fast trot, we should vigorously push him forward into the gallop, and should keep him at it for a certain distance, say for 500 or 600 yards, which is to be the punishment of his resistance and laziness. After a few experiences of this kind he will perceive that, so far from obtaining relief by breaking into the canter from the trot, he lets himself in for a severe and trying pace. This plan is within the reach of everyone. There is another which I can recommend, but which requires a greater knowledge of riding.

When the horse of his own accord breaks into the canter, in order to escape from the fast trot which his rider wants him to do, he naturally leads with the easier leg of the two. I have already said that every horse has one side more easy than the other. We can therefore thwart him in the pace he has taken by pressing him forward at the canter, while making the other leg lead ; for instance, with the right leg if he has of his own accord struck off with the left leg. We will then employ the near snaffle rein, in order to keep back the left shoulder, which takes the lead, and the left leg to press the haunches to the right.*

We should apply the opposite "aids" if the horse leads with the right fore leg. It is self-evident that this plan, like the

---

* It will be noted that I am doing lateral equitation here ; my reason being that I take for granted that the horse is either imperfectly broken or unbroken.

preceding one, is applicable only to horses which are imperfectly broken. When a horse is well broken, he never breaks into a pace which we do not want him to adopt.

If a horse does not readily take to the trot, we should not be too ready to think he is lazy or bad-tempered. The fault is often due to the fact that the rider's hands are bad for a sensitive mouth, because they are either too heavy or they move about too much. It may happen that the bit is too severe,* or that the horse's mouth is sore, from having been bruised. Also, the horse may be suffering in his loins or other parts, and his reason for changing the pace may be only to relieve himself. In all these frequently occurring cases, the best remedy is to remove the cause.

In place of first putting the blame on the horse, which is only natural, the rider ought perhaps begin by trying to find out if he himself is not the culprit.

The following is an excellent means of finding out if soreness of the mouth is the cause of the horse not trotting true. Instead of allowing him to bear on the snaffle, leave its reins perfectly loose and catch hold of a good-sized handful of the mane near the middle of the neck, and draw it towards you. Horse dealers use this plan every day.

The trainers of trotters, whose only object is a maximum of speed, generally let their horses take a very strong bearing on the hand. The regularity of the pace and lightness of mouth are of little matter to them. Their horses, being impetuous, always pull very hard, and the rider, on his part, pulls no less vigorously on the mouth ; because he thinks that the more he pulls, the faster will the horse go. This is a great error ; because, by pulling too strongly on the mouth, we throw the weight of the body on the hind quarters, and we

---

* Thin mouth-piece, long cheeks, high port, each one of which conditions will of itself make the bit severe ; and combined, they will convert it into an instrument of torture.

thus fatigue the loins and hocks. To make a horse trot well, we should simply try to get him to lean on the hand. No doubt, in a flat race, as at the trot, the rider to some extent *carries* the head and neck of his horse ; but he should take care to carry it *upwards* and not *backwards*, by doing which he would infallibly check the power of the loins and hocks.

To study the exact conditions of trotting races, I once went and lived at Dozulé, which is a small village in Normandy. I had previously ridden on the flat and across country, and as I had also broken three or four school horses, I thought I was going to astonish the Norman lads by my science. I admit, in all humility, that the most surprised one was your humble servant.

At Dozulé there was a brave boy called Pascal, who was very well up in everything about horses, and especially about trotters. I had known him for a long time, and we had previously arranged together the plan of my sojourn at Dozulé.

Pascal had charge of the training of two remarkable trotters, which belonged, if I remember rightly, to the Marquis of Croix. This was about the end of 1864.

On the morning after my arrival, we were in the saddle, and at first we walked on the trotting track, which was a mile and a quarter in length. Then we began to trot, and Pascal beat me easily. I took my defeat with a smile, because I thought that his horse was faster than mine. On the following day we changed horses, and Pascal again beat me. I admit that I was all the more annoyed, because the same result was reproduced the following fifteen days, on each one of which Pascal rode the horse on which I was beaten by him the previous day.

He pulled with all his might at the reins and jerked them, which he called " ringing " his horse. I told him that his way of riding was not rational ; but he replied that it was the only

way to get all the speed out of a horse, and apparently he
was right.   I then asked him to let me ride the same horse
for a fortnight, during which time we ran no races together.
During this period, I succeeded in making the horse take only
a light bearing on the hand, and to hold his head steady,
and finally I beat Pascal four times running.   I afterwards
obtained, in an equally short time, the same result with
the other horse.

The two horses having been placed with confidence on the
hand, and having the free play of their hind quarters, trotted
as a whole without breaking and almost without fatigue.
According to the system of Pascal, on the contrary, they
broke, trotted almost always disunited, and also were soon
knocked up.   I was also *closer to the horse* than he was;
he made violent movements, while I made none; and finally,
having succeeded more rapidly than he could in getting my
horse at full speed, I was able to maintain it longer.

I do not claim that I gave more speed to my horses, but
with my handling they did their work with confidence and
ease, whilst he hurt their mouths and fatigued them, which
fact was to be seen at the winning post.   Not having to make
the same efforts when I rode them, they were neither blow-
ing nor sweating after the trot.

Trotters which are trained according to Pascal's method,
are generally unpleasant and sometimes dangerous to ride.
In fact it is difficult, when they have once started, to stop
them quickly.   Nevertheless, if taken out of training and
given suppling exercises, they will very often do excellent
service.

Pascal had the great advantage over me of knowing his
horses, and he knew—at least, I like to think he did—when
they were at their top speed.   This knowledge is much more
important than is generally thought.   If a jockey who has
not a knowledge of pace, is riding a trotter which is going at

full speed, he will probably try to make him go faster, and by pressing him on, will make him break into a gallop.

The feeling which makes us press on a horse under all conditions is very natural. Nothing unnerves us more than to ride a race alongside a horse which keeps a neck in front of us. Nevertheless, if the trotter we are riding is at the top of his speed, we should take care not to force him beyond it, which would cause him to gallop. In order to put him back into the trot, we would have to slacken speed, and would consequently lose several lengths.

Finally, when we ride a trotting race, we should know the moment the horse has attained his highest speed, which we should keep up as long as possible. The result of the race will then become a question of staying power; because the animal which can keep up his highest speed for the longest time, will have the best chance.

We should note that in a trotting race a rider should keep his mount at the top of its speed from the start. We will see further on that this is not the case in flat-race riding.

THE CANTER.

Of all paces, the canter is the most difficult and complicated. Few riding masters succeed in making a horse do the movements they require at the canter.

I never begin the canter before getting the horse thoroughly under control, by which I mean that he should be physically, and, if I may say, morally obedient to me in all his paces; that he should be supple, well in hand, and should readily yield to the legs.

I expect, above all things, the loins, haunches and hocks to be perfectly supple, and the horse to obey the effects of the whole without hesitation, in order that I may be able to utilize the resulting forces as I wish.

Having obtained these conditions, I am certain to presently
succeed in placing my horse in a proper position for the canter,
and to immediately get the canter which I wish the horse to
do, and not the one he desires to perform.

If the horse obeys the legs, I shall be able to prevent him
from going *sideways*, which is an extremely bad habit, and
which is better to prevent than to punish.　It is much more
difficult to straighten a horse which is accustomed to throw
his hind quarters to the right or left, than to teach him to
canter straight from the beginning.*

At the canter, the rider ought to keep his body straight.
If he leans too much forward, each stride of the canter will
throw him on to the animal's neck.　If he is too far back, the
loins will become hollow, and the body will consequently
become stiff.

The horse canters either on the near fore or off fore.　He is
said to lead with the off leg, when the right legs are in

* In the school, when a pupil wishes to make his horse strike off into the canter
with the outside leg, he generally puts him too much sideways.　I take for granted
that he is going to the left, and wishes his horse to strike off with the off fore.
He will then carry his hands to the left, which will be all right, if he does it
only just enough to put the weight on the left shoulder.　But if he does not succeed,
he will probably carry his hands more and more to the left and he will turn his
horse into the position of shoulder-in.　The horse at this period of breaking
does not know how to do the shoulder-in at a canter ; because his teacher should
have begun by making him canter straight on the inward and outward legs before
doing that.　The pupil thus succeeds only in destroying all impulse, and in
making the canter impossible, by causing the horse to get behind his bit.　He
should, therefore, carry the hands to the left only just enough to put the weight
on the left shoulder, but not sufficient to place the animal sideways.　If the horse
puts himself in an oblique position, he should not insist on making him canter,
but should straighten him, and should begin starting him off again, while
holding him straight.

Starting well is not everything.　We should keep the horse straight.

When the horse canters with the outward leg leading, the rider, at starting, and
also to keep up the pace, has always a great tendency to place the horse sideways
by bringing the shoulders in, and by placing the horse on two tracks.　If we
persist in this fault, all progress will be impossible ; because the horse can never
canter correctly on two tracks, if he has not learned at first to canter straight on
the outward leg.

advance at the moment they come on the ground. In the canter to the left, the left legs do this.

To teach a horse to canter on the off fore, we ought to close both legs, carry both hands to the left, and feel the off reins a little stronger than the near reins.* In this way we put the weight on the near shoulder, without bringing to the left the head, which should always remain straight, with the end of the muzzle slightly inclined to the right.

As soon as a horse has learned to keep in a good position, he should be put into movement. The hind quarters, which act the part of a propeller, ought to push and carry the fore hand forward. To bring the hocks under the body, I increase the effect of the legs, while pressing equally with them, Finally, I use a stronger pressure with my left leg, and I carry it a little further back than my right one.†

If the horse has some "go" in him, the effect of the legs will be sufficient to send him up to the hands (bridle). At this moment, I raise my hands while feeling the reins, and I profit by the impulse given by the legs, to raise the horse, while preventing him extending himself and breaking into a trot. If the horse is sluggish, we should prolong and increase the action of the legs, and if need be, we should use the spurs.

Under these conditions, it is difficult for the horse not to lead off with the off fore. It may however happen that he leads off with the near fore, or trots. In either case, I stop him as quickly as possible, and I replace him in the position I have previously described. I then begin again, and continue

* I always begin by using the snaffle, whatever may be the pace I am teaching.

† By means of the left leg, the rider throws, so to speak, the weight of the horse's body on his right leg, which sends it to the hands.

to do so, until he leads with the off fore.*   As soon as he has
done three or four strides on this leg, I stop him, pat him on
the neck and let him walk round the school in perfect freedom.
After that I do the same exercise three or four times.†

Baucher, by a singular error, recommended lateral equitation
for starting at the canter.   In his edition of 1846, page 219,
he advised for starting with the off fore leading, to carry the
hands to the left—which would put tension on the right rein
—and to apply the right leg.   I attribute this error to the bad
flexion of the neck which he practised.   The neck being low
and bent at the withers to the right, causes the left shoulder
to be rounded, and the effect of the left leg would bend the
two ends of the horse towards the inside, that is to say, to bring
his head and croup towards each other.   The effect of the
right leg, on the contrary, is to partly remedy a bad equilibrium resulting from the faulty flexion of the neck.   How could
Baucher reconcile this practice with his great principle—in
turning—of "applying the leg of the side opposite to which
the turn is made" (Edition of 1846, page 189)?

* If the horse starts disunited, that is to say, if the forehand canters to the
right, and the hind quarters to the left, we should increase the action of the
" aids " to obtain the canter which we require, and if the hind quarters in this case
are disunited, we should use the left leg energetically.

I advise beginners who find some difficulty in understanding the canter, to
exercise prudence, for there is nothing worse than to try to remedy a fault which
does not exist.   At first, lean forward a little, so as to see with which leg the
horse canters.   If the right shoulder is in advance when the fore feet come down,
we may be certain that he is leading with his off fore.   We should now *feel our
seat*, and the regularity and suppleness (ease) of the displacement of the body
will tell us if the canter is well united, in which case the horse will be leading
with the off hind as well as with the off fore.   But if the displacement of the
seat is done in a jolting manner and with a double shock, the canter will be disunited, and the near hind will be leading.

We can then, but only if we are absolutely certain, use the left spur to drive
the hind quarters to the right, and keep the left leg close to the animal's side, in
order to force him to remain united.

† I have already said that we should always finish with the new work, so as to
impress it on the memory of the horse.

According to this system, it is necessary when turning to the right at the canter to use a stronger pressure of the right leg, in order for the horse to lead with his off fore ; and the left leg, in order to turn to the right. The inconsistency is so evident, that it is sufficient to merely point it out. Everyone knows that if a horse has learned to canter with the near fore leading, by means of the support of the left leg, the effect will be to make him change his leg, and not to turn to the right.

I think it is useless to describe the means by which we make a horse lead with his near fore, because they are naturally the opposite ones to those which we have just described. We ought always to begin the canter with the off fore * leading, and for this object we ought to make the horse circle to the right in the riding school. I never ask the horse to lead with the near fore until I can readily make him canter freely with the off fore leading. This is a matter of a few days, the number of which we cannot exactly fix. Some horses easily lead with the off fore, but others find this difficult to do, although they may be very clever at starting with the near fore leading.

Horses are like men—some are naturally and by habit right-handed, and others are left-handed. It seems probable that some horses are naturally right-footed ; because, if we did not take account of contracted habits, all horses would be left-footed.

In fact, when we lead a horse by the bridle on foot, we always keep on his left side, which is also the side on which we feed, saddle, and bridle him. As the horse likes to take notice of what goes on around him, the left is the side towards which he constantly turns his head, and consequently he ought to be more supple to the left than to the right ; but he

---

* The rule in riding is to begin all movements to the right. On a straight line in the open we generally canter with the off fore leading, which is the style adopted by ladies. For all reasons it is best to begin the canter in this way.

is not so. I have met as many right-footed horses as left-footed ones. We can find out which he is by working him; for there is nothing in his conformation that would enable us to decide that question.*

As a right-footed horse will remain all his life much more supple and easy to the right; the left side will naturally be the one to which we should work him in flexions, side steps, voltes, canter, etc.; and *vice versâ.*

Before requiring the horse to do more, I wait till he can canter as readily with one leg as with the other, while keeping him straight all the time. I then try to get him completely in hand, which I certainly will not be able to do at the canter, if I have not first made his mouth supple and light at all paces and during all the preceding exercises.

The best definition of the action of the "aids" in the present case, is that the hands make the walk and the legs the canter—namely, that whilst the legs press the horse with energy, the hands lightly restrain him. He then finds himself controlled by two opposing actions; propulsion being the dominating one. They oblige him to raise himself and canter.

The riding master will find that he has attained his object when the horse canters slowly without effort, and, above all things, without trying to escape from the hand.†

* All Arab horses are left-footed, with respect to the fact that they always turn to the left and never to the right, which peculiarity is simply the result of education. If we place ourselves on the right of an Arab horseman, he cannot touch us. He must turn to the left-about in order to reach us.

† Almost all authors advise that when a horse pulls at the canter, he should be stopped and made to rein back, than which nothing is less rational. A horse pulls because his hocks are far from the centre of the body. In making him rein back we push the hocks still further to the rear, and we directly counteract the object we desire to attain. On the contrary, without stopping the horse, we should press him well up to the bridle with the legs, should keep him in hand while he is moving forward, should make him do movements as a whole, and take and give with the hands and legs in order to collect him, which is the only means for

There are three ways of seeing that a horse canters with the off fore leading :

First, it is sufficient to look at his shoulders or feet. If he canters with the off fore leading, the off shoulder, and especially the off fore foot, will respectively be in advance of the near shoulder and near fore foot.

Second, the horse has always his croup a little turned to the side of the leading fore leg.

Third, when the off fore leads, the right leg of the rider is more shaken than the left leg,* and consequently it is more difficult to keep that knee close to the flap of the saddle than the other knee.

After a series of attentive observations, we ought to be able to tell with what leg a horse leads, even with our eyes shut.

Before going further in the teaching of breaking, it is important to explain the movements of the canter.†

The canter of the school horse and hack ought to be in well-marked three time. ‡

Three times (beats) are, therefore, necessary to form a stride of the canter. Let us take, for example, the canter with the off fore leading.

bringing his hocks under his body. Thus the forehand will be lightened in proportion as the hind quarters drive the body forward.

At this time, half-turns on the haunches will be very useful, provided that the rider has enough *tact* to keep the haunches well engaged and the horse well up to his bit.

* The right hock, placed under the body gives more impulse in the canter to the right than the left hock, and it is the one which displaces the right knee of the rider. The action of the left hock, which is much more to the rear, and is consequently a less powerful propelling agent, has necessarily a much less displacing effect on the left knee.

† This study is necessary for the changes of leg.

‡ The long-striding gallop, like that of the racecourse, is in four time. The very short canter of a *rassemblé*'d horse, of which pace I shall speak later on, is also in four time.

First time.—Near hind in support (Fig. 43).

Second time.—Left diagonal support, the near hind and off fore having just quitted the ground (Fig. 44).

Third time.—Off fore in support (Fig. 45).

I will now indicate the action of the "aids" which the rider should employ during this stride.

First time.—Strong support from the left leg. The horse finds himself resting for a moment only on his near hind, but the period is so short that it cannot be seen without great practice.

Fig. 43.—First time of the canter ; near hind in support.

Second time.—Left diagonal. The two legs of the rider ought to exert their pressure to try to get the horse in hand.

Third time.—The horse's off fore is in support. The rider ought to receive the horse lightly on his hands ; at first to support him, and immediately afterwards to complete the task of getting him in hand, which work was initiated by the legs during the second time.

I will now explain the effects of the "aids" during the three times which make a stride.

First time.—The rider's left leg ought to be strongly pressed against the horse's side, because the horse is standing, so to speak, on his near hind, while his body is inclined forward and his other limbs are not much raised from the ground. The entire weight of the horse and rider are, therefore, carried on this leg, and if the rider does not support the left side of the horse, it is certain that this leg will give way under the excess of weight, and that the croup will swerve to the left.

SECOND TIME.—The two legs of the rider exert their pressure in order to press the horse up to the hand. This is

Fig. 44.—Second time of the canter ; left diagonal in support.

the only moment of the canter when the horse has two supports, and we ought to profit by the impulse he has just received, to get him into hand at the following time.

THIRD TIME.—The rider receives the horse on the hand. This is the easiest moment at which to get the horse completely in hand ; because, at the second period, the right hock being under the body, gives the greater part of the propulsion, which our hands should utilise to *rassembler* the horse.

The hands ought also to support the horse a little during the third period ; because the animal's off fore is then his

11

only support.   At this moment horses usually make mistakes, and are apt to fall if they are not supported.

Of course I point out only the chief "aids." We understand that the hands and legs should always co-operate with each other.

It might appear, after what I have just said, that the near hind is the leg which becomes most fatigued at a canter to the right.   In fact, this is the usual opinion of many of those who have written on this subject.   Nothing could be more

Fig. 45.—Third time of the canter ; off fore in support.

erroneous ; because the off hock, being under the body and having to raise all the weight, does the most work during each stride, which is a fact beyond dispute.   I am aware that the near hock, being placed at the end of the arm of the lever, is under a much less favourable condition for action.   But precisely because the position which the off hock occupies under the body, is more favourable to the complete utilisation of its force, it makes a greater effort than the near hock, and consequently it becomes more fatigued.   If we attentively watch a horse which is cantering with his off fore leading, we will quickly see that the off hock and fetlock become much more bent than the near ones, and consequently their upward action is better marked and their spring more energetic.*

If we canter to the right, a horse which has an unsound off hock, caused, for instance, by a spavin or curb, he will immediately become disunited, on account of the movement causing him pain. But if we make him canter with the near fore leading, he will not change his hind legs.

The off hock therefore exerts more force in the canter to the right, and the near hock in the canter to the left. On this account, the rider ought to keep his legs firmly closed, especially during the second period of the canter. By doing this, the hock which is under the body, is quickened in its action, the horse is pressed forward, and is prevented, at the second period of the canter, from remaining longer on the ground than at the first or third period. If we do not act thus, the second period will be slower and heavier than the other two.

VOLTES AND DEMI-VOLTES AT THE CANTER.

When I have taught a horse to canter in a light and easy way, I make him do great voltes. It is best to describe large circles at first, because it is more difficult to keep a horse straight in small ones.

Horses generally carry their haunches either to the outside or to the inside ; the former fault being more easy to remedy than the latter.

Let us suppose that the horse is cantering with the off fore leading and is turning to the right. After having closed the legs, I carry the hands forward and to the right,—forward to prevent him stopping, and to the right to bring his shoulders

---

* Among ladies' horses which always canter with the off fore leading, the off hock always becomes prematurely worn out. Ladies do not like to canter to the left, because it displaces their seat too much. As they are seated on the near side of the horse, the propulsion given by the off hock is not made exactly under their seat, hence the displacement is less than in the canter to the left.

away from the wall. The off snaffle * rein should be pulled to the right, while the near rein presses the neck and consequently the shoulders to the right, and at the same time it helps the left leg to support the haunches, and thus assists to hold the horse straight. If the horse tries to throw his croup to the left, my two legs ought to increase their action to push him forward, the left leg acting a little more vigorously than the right, to keep his right leg leading. The right leg pushes the body forward and forces the haunches to follow the same line as the shoulders.

It is very easy to understand why I prefer a horse which carries his quarters to the outside, to one which carries them to the inside. In the former case, the animal presses on my left leg, and I then use the spur, which has two objects. First, to prevent the croup deviating to the left; and, second, to force the animal to keep cantering with the off fore leading. But if he carries his quarters to the inside of the circle, I am obliged to use my right leg, and sometimes the spur, with more or less force, and I thus run the risk of making the animal change behind. Also, the horse which carries his haunches towards the inside of the circle, is behind his bit. These faults seldom appear, if we begin on large circles, which we should only gradually make smaller, and in proportion to the ease with which the horse does the work. I may add that even in small circles we should keep the horse very straight.

Immediately after, I begin demi-voltes, which present no difficulty if executed without precision, but which are very hard to do in an absolutely correct manner. I have rarely seen them thus done.

---

* I have already said that I always work with the snaffle when beginning any new exercise. It is the means for direction; and the curb, for getting the horse in hand. In proportion as the snaffle is brought into play, the curb aids more and more in getting the animal into hand. This continual action of the curb is found in all exercises to be associated with the action of the snaffle in giving direction.

The horse being placed straight and in hand, as in the voltes, ought to leave the wall. When he has made three strides, he ought to cover the rest of the ground on two tracks, while coming up to the wall.

To go on two tracks, while the horse is cantering with the off fore leading, the off snaffle rein pulls the head and neck a little to the right, whilst the near rein, being applied against the neck, presses the shoulders to the right. The left leg causes the haunches to move to the right, and the right leg helps to press the horse forward and to keep him in hand, which is important, because he has to advance while going to the side.

On arriving at the wall, which is on the right of the rider, we should straighten the horse,* stop him, get him into hand at the walk, and start him into the canter with the near fore leading. We can do the same work on the other foot.

When the horse can do demi-voltes well, I prolong them for some strides at the canter, without changing the leg. Thus, I begin the demi-volte at the wall, which is on my left. While cantering the horse with the off fore leading, I turn to the right, and continue to keep up the canter on the off fore, even after the demi-volte, but only during two or three strides at the first attempt. I increase the number of these strides only little by little, according to the lightness and cleverness of the horse. This is the most simple way to teach a horse to canter with the right leg when turning to the left; and *vice versâ*. This exercise is indispensable if we wish to readily obtain changes of leg when cantering round to the right or left.

When the horse goes round the school correctly on the leg which is next to the wall, we should start several times with the off fore leading, and also with the near fore leading, both

---

* The shoulders should arrive first at the wall, so that the movement may be correct.

to the right and to the left, while always keeping him along the wall.

CHANGES OF LEG.

When a horse at the canter leads equally well with both legs, it is necessary that the rider should make him strike off with whichever leg he likes. He should also know how to make the horse *change his leg*, namely, to pass from one canter into the other canter without stopping. This is not high school work, but belongs to ordinary riding, whether practised in the school or outside.

If, for example, we are at the canter with the horse's near fore leading, and we wish to turn to the right, it is impossible to make this change of direction without danger. In fact, the near leg, which is in advance, will cross the off leg, and the horse will probably fall, in which case the rider will be almost certain to blame the horse; but the fault is his own.*

If, when cantering with the near fore leading, we wish to turn to the right, while maintaining the same pace, we should first of all make the horse change his leg, in which case the turning movement will be made easily and without danger. In fact, the horse will have his head and body bent towards the side to which he is turning. Further, it is the forward leg which covers the ground of the side to which the change of direction is being made.†

* A horse which crosses his legs may escape falling, but only if he is lucky.

If a horse which is cantering with the near fore, falls on being turned to the right, he does so because he is abruptly put into the position for the canter to the right. In high school riding we succeed very well in turning to the right, while our horse canters with the near fore. To do this we should make a large circle when turning, should always keep the horse in the position of the canter to the left, and should even exaggerate this position, by using the right leg to push the croup a little more to the left. It is easier to change the leg.

† With respect to changes of direction, I give the following advice : always enlarge the circle as much as possible ; slacken the speed a little when turning ; and if not quite certain of the change of leg—which is difficult in proportion to the speed—it is best before turning to make the horse change into the trot and not to put him into the canter again until he has completed the turn.

We should exercise great care in teaching the horse to change his leg.

It is very difficult to lay down in a book the exact time when a horse is ready to learn changes of leg. I can only say, in a general way, that the proper time is when he has become free, supple, light, and well balanced in all his paces, obedient, and above all things, attentive to the "aids," by means of the exercises we have described.

We have now arrived at the point when the horse will start freely into the canter with the off fore leading when going to the right, and with the near fore when going to the left, and that he will do so with equal freedom on both legs.

To obtain a change of leg, I proceed in the following manner:* I start the horse into the canter on the off fore while going to the right. When he has gone some strides on this leg, I stop him and make him start off on the near fore while circling to the right, and taking care to hold him as straight as possible. I repeat this work several times, and continue it until I feel that the horse is perfectly light in hand, and that he will start off into the canter at the slightest pressure of the legs, without hurrying himself and without trying to carry his haunches out of the straight line.

To make sure that the horse does not carry himself sideways, we should start him at about a yard away from the wall, although it is difficult to do so.† The result of this is to make the rider keep the horse very straight, without the help of the wall, and, at the same time, to make him more precise in his work.

We should not try to get the horse to change his leg away from the wall, before making him do so, while going along it. The horse should also very readily start into the canter on the

---

* I again repeat that I always begin a new work at the end of a lesson.

† The difficulty is not in starting, but in keeping the horse at a uniform distance from the wall while holding him straight.

leg we wish, when we have placed him in the position to do so, and have given him the proper indication with the legs.* I then start him into the canter on the off fore, and keep him at it until he becomes quiet. I then walk him for a minute or two, and put him into the canter on the near fore, and keep him at it, the same as before, until he is light and quiet, after which I again walk him for some moments. Finally, I start him into the canter on the off fore, and so on. I therefore make successive starts at the canter, each one being on a different leg. Little by little I shorten the periods during which I let the horse walk between the starts at the canter, in such a way that he does not take, for instance, more than five, four, three, two, and finally, one step between the respective starts. At last he learns to start into the canter alternately from the stationary foot to the other foot, the starts being interrupted only by the halt.

Thus, the horse having been started into the canter on the off fore, is stopped, and is immediately started again into the canter on the near fore, this change of leg being helped by the halt. As the true change of leg is done without halting, it is called a change of leg in the air.

At this period of his training the horse is ready for the change of leg, which I ought to be able to make him do without upsetting him in the least. I start him into the canter on the near fore, while going to the right. He therefore canters on the outward leg,† and I support him at that time with the near rein and right leg, which gives a stronger pressure than the left leg. When I come to a corner of the school I completely change my "aids," and use the off rein and left leg. This

---

* Position by legs and hands and stimulation by the legs are two most important principles in riding.

† In this case he is cantering "false," which is the term used by English cavalrymen.

change of " aids " ought to be done with great decision and perfect combination. In order for the movement to be well done, it should be executed with extreme quickness, and without the slightest jerk. This quickness and smoothness are possible only if the rider has constantly taken the precaution of lightly feeling the off rein, and of keeping the left leg very close to the animal's side, so that he need only feel this rein a little stronger and press the leg a little more. As the horse has already lightly felt the off rein, and as the left leg has been kept very close to his side, there will be neither jerk nor irritation to the horse when this hand and this leg predominate in their turn.

Finally, as we have practised our horse to start on the off leg, by the action of the off rein and left leg, and as we ask him to do this first change of leg when turning to the right, which will be easier for him to do than when turning to the left, he will very rarely refuse to do so, even at the first time. If, however, he does not obey, we must not persist in roughly forcing him, because that would cause him to throw his haunches to the right, and make him afraid of the change of leg, which he would not understand. He should be stopped, brought into hand at the walk, made to start on the near fore, and then asked to change his leg. But before doing this we should wait until he has got quiet.

The fact of the horse failing to do a change of leg several times, is a proof that his preparation is insufficient; that being surprised by the " aids " he tried to escape or throw himself to one side ; or that he did not understand what we wanted. In all these cases we should begin starting him afresh. Any failure in this respect will be extremely rare if the horse has been properly prepared.

Whenever we meet with a difficulty we should go back to the start, with the near fore leading, or with the off fore leading. By these repeated starts with a halt, we shall succeed in

making the change of leg so easy, that the horse will often do
it on his own account, when prompted merely by the pre-
parations to which he has been submitted.   In fact, when we
stop him on one leg, the "aids" ought to slightly prepare him
to start off on the other leg.

Whenever I have had time to prepare a horse, I have never
failed to make him change his leg at the first attempt.   Whatever kind of horse he may be, he will always do one change
correctly, after having failed to do several.   We should then
get off, pat him on the neck, and send him back to his stable.
At the following lesson we ought to repeat and prolong the
same lesson, until the animal changes easily from the near fore
to the off fore.   Having then turned round, so as to go to the
left, we should, in the same way, make him change from the
off fore to the near fore.

We should always avoid making him change at the same
place, as that would always make him want to change
when he passes it.   It would therefore become impossible to
make him change as we wish, because our will would be
subordinated to his.*

When I have got the horse to readily change from the outward to the inward leg in the corners, I put him to do the
same work on a straight line.

The change of leg should be required only at a certain
period of the stride, when it is easiest for the horse to do.   As

* I have said that in all things horses acquire habits with great facility.
Therefore, during breaking, we should most carefully avoid giving him bench-
marks (if I may use the term), whether by putting him to the same work at the
same place, or by repeating different exercises in the same order.   This advice is,
I think, all the more important, because the majority of riding masters persistently
give bench-marks to their horses, which makes the breaking apparently more
easy.   Although the horse by routine does his work at a given moment, at certain
spots, and according to a prearranged programme, he is not properly trained,
because, so far from being submissive to the will of his rider, the rider has to
accommodate himself to the habits of the animal.   Consequently the horse is
habituated, or, as we may say, "routined," but he is not broken in.

I have already said, each stride is composed of three distinct periods, which are marked by the feet of the horse coming down on the ground. In reality there is a fourth, namely, the period of suspension, which is not marked.

The canter to the right may be divided as follows: 1st period, near hind; 2nd period, off hind and near fore; and 3rd period, off fore. The fourth period begins at the moment the off fore leaves the ground, and ends when the near hind is placed on the ground. At this moment the horse is in the air, between the third period of one stride and the first period of the next stride.

The best time to obtain the change of leg is at the fourth period, because the horse is then in the air.*

---

* Baucher gives no explanation of this subject. The majority of riding masters make this change of leg during support, and not when the horse is in the air, as I have advised. Their plan gives rise to an inevitable halt, which destroys the rhythm of the canter, and consequently alters the canter. My method, on the contrary, maintains the canter with all its impulse, and allows the rider to lengthen or shorten the stride, as he may wish, in all the changes of leg.

A correctly executed change of leg at each stride thus forms a true pace, at which I obtain so much impulse that I am ready, without false modesty, to challenge anyone to have a race at it.

On this subject I sent the following letter to the editor of *Gil Blas*, who declined to publish it. I fortunately got it inserted in the *Echo de Paris*, but it received no answer :—

" Paris, 27th August, 1890.
" To the Editor *Gil Blas*.
" Sir,—

" Baron de Vaux has severely criticised my book and my riding in a long article which recently appeared in *Gil Blas*. It has in no way annoyed me, and I, being a horseman, have not the rashness to find fault with the criticism of a penman.

" There is, however, one point which I think is worthy of notice, because it can be submitted to practical proof.

" The writer of the article tries to make out that I do not hold my horses straight in the changes of leg. If this be true, I must necessarily lose ground in forward progression. That being the case, I propose a race of changes of leg at each stride, which I believe is an original idea that has never been tried. The winner will, of course, be he whose horse is the straighter of the two.

To obtain the change of leg during the fourth period, we should give the signal to the horse during the second period, when the diagonal is in support. When cantering to the right, the effect of the spur, at the moment when the left diagonal is in support, will be a vigorous straightening of the off hock, which will forcibly send the near shoulder in advance of the off shoulder when the horse is in the air.

The near hind leg will go in advance of the off hind leg all the more easily, because it is off the ground when the off hock gives its push. Under these conditions, after the spur has touched the horse during the second period, the third period (support by the off fore) loses the greater part of its impulse in the stride, and will be accentuated only as much as the equilibrium may require, because it is the off hock which has given the increased propulsion necessary for a change of leg.

Everyone can now understand the meaning of change of leg in the air.

The reversed indications are used for changing from the near fore to the off fore.

In this chapter I have spoken of changes of leg only from an ordinary point of view. Later on I will discuss this subject with respect to high school work.

THE HACK.

I will not try to describe the proper type of hack, because every riding man or woman has his or her own ideal, which

"As Baron de Vaux knows many riding masters whom he favourably criticises, I would like to get one of them to accept my challenge.

"I am ready to accept my adversary's conditions as regards ground and length of course. He can also fix the stake, which should go to a public charity.

"This will be a good business for the poor, if not for riding. Ten thousand francs, for instance, will give them a great deal of pleasure.

"I am, Sir,

"Your most obedient servant,

"JAMES FILLIS."

the riders choose according to their habits, temperament, and style of riding. Horses have certain innate qualities which cannot be given or replaced by breeding, rearing, or breaking.

The first thing to require is surefootedness, which is a *sine quâ non.* It is absolutely necessary that the animal will make no mistake at any of his paces. Hence we like our horses to raise their feet freely and to place them in a well-balanced manner on the ground. A horse which drags his legs, or "daisy cuts," is apt to make a false step by striking a stone or other inequality on the ground, and may consequently fall down.

A horse which brings his toe first on the ground will be very apt to stumble, which is a fault we find among animals which "daisy cut." A horse which raises his feet properly, cannot dig his toes into the ground, and must necessarily place them flat.

A hack should have pluck. That is to say, he should not be restless or nervous. No amount of training can cure a horse of stumbling, or give pluck to an animal which is always ready to shy or spin round.

As long as a good rider holds his horse between his hands and knees, and is on the alert,* he will save him from break-

* We should not only watch a skittish horse, but should also engage his attention as soon as he shows any signs of nervousness. In such cases many riders will not use their legs for fear of exciting the animal, and they continually hang on to the reins, especially those of the snaffle. By allowing him to be a prey to his fear, the rider does the very thing to increase it. By giving the animal a support on the bit, he is placed in the most favourable condition to play up.

We should act in an entirely different manner, and, by the energetic use of the legs, should drive the horse forward ; because, at the first show of uneasiness, his tendency will necessarily be to get behind his bit, which is a preparation for shying, spinning round, and rearing. We should at the same time profit by the impulse given, in order to place the horse vigorously but lightly in hand, by means of the alternate effects of the curb and snaffle. Having got him in hand, we should give him a lateral flexion to the side opposite to which his object of terror is on. Finally, while keeping him well in hand, we should press him boldly forward, which is, in every case, the least dangerous thing to

ing his knees or from meeting with any other accident. But, if he relaxes his attention, he will run a good chance of bringing back a blemished horse to his stable. Under these conditions, hacking ceases to be a pleasure and becomes a labour, a continual preoccupation, and an *ennui* which soon makes one hate riding.

We see that the two first good qualities of a hack are surefootedness and pluck.

In my opinion there is a third quality which excels the first two, because it includes them and everything else which we desire from a horse. This supreme quality in every horse is impetuosity, namely, energy, fire, courage, and constant readiness to go forward.

A horse which is not surefooted knows his defect, will always be hesitating, and will not dare to rush forward. A horse which is not plucky is always ready to get behind his bit. A horse which is a free goer is confident in being able to keep his feet, and, though glad to go forward, he does not get disturbed by the things which he passes. No matter what may be the breed or shape, a horse, like a man, takes his value from his mental qualities. Energy and heart make the horse. What use is the most beautiful railway engine, if it has no steam to drive it along the rails?

Above all theories, there is the fact that the only good horse for every kind of work, whether for high school equitation or outside, is the horse which will go forward: that is to say, an impetuous horse. By this, I of course do not mean an animal which has irregular paces, is restless, vicious, apt to "play up" on no provocation, and is ready to run away.

do. These manœuvres will turn the attention of the startled animal from his cause of fear, and will place him in the most favourable position to avoid violence or disorder. It is evident that we should use these means in proportion to the skittishness shown by the animal. As a general rule, when a horse becomes impatient, we should send him up to his bit by the vigorous application of the legs, and he will instantly become quiet.

The impetuous horse is one which wishes only to go forward, and in consequence of his being well balanced and having plenty of natural energy, he goes freely up to his bridle. True balance and natural energy are innate qualities in him, because they are conditions of his being: this includes everything. Equitation cannot exist without energy. In the horse I speak of, the energy is already made, and he gives it to his rider. It is easier, as I have said, to profit by impulse than to create it. The fault of being behind the bit is the stumbling block in every kind of riding, and the natural disposition of an impetuous horse is directly opposed to this tendency.

In every case, no matter what happens, a forward movement is the least displacing one for the rider. The fact of Arab horses being hot, generally makes them easy and agreeable to ride. These animals canter high, and always bring the hocks well under the body.

For the above reasons I am right in saying that every horse which is not hot is fit only to be put between the shafts.

As a rule, people are afraid of an impetuous horse, and they are wrong; because he is the only one which will be faithful, and will not do them a bad turn. He is the only animal which, by reason of his constant desire to go forward, is plucky even in his defences.

The sluggish horse, which is generally preferred, can neither be reliable nor plucky. In every case, so far from giving himself up to his rider, he continually restrains himself, and is always ready to keep behind the bit, which, in my eyes, is the worst of all faults. He thinks only of returning to his stable,* and tries to take advantage of every chance to

---

* The tendency of every horse, no matter how impetuous he may be, is to return to the stable quicker than he left it.

In order that the rider may not be obliged to come back quicker than he went out, I advise him to begin his ride at a fast pace, so as to quieten the animal down, which is most important later on for preventing him jibbing, shying,

gratify this caprice. If we wish to go fast, and quiet means
are not sufficient, we should use the spurs or whip. When
the sluggish horse defends himself, he does so with all the
more spite, because he has kept back all his energy to oppose
the will of the rider. There is a great difference between the
two, because the impetuous animal gives all his strength for
the advantage of the rider ; and the sluggish horse, for the
detriment of the man in the saddle.*

A *cold* horse does not take us into his confidence, because
when riding him we are obliged to vigorously use the " aids,"
which are a punishment to him.

A *hot* horse which gives himself up wholly to his rider, gets
only pats on the neck, and appreciates all the slight differences in the indications of the "aids."   There is neither fear
nor distrust between the two.

Many riders find fault with hot horses, because they are
impatient, and start off at a quick pace immediately the
reins are touched.   The fault is on their side.   In fact, whenever we wish to go rather fast, we begin by shortening the

kicking, etc.   If we take the trouble to make the horse return at a slow pace,
during a certain time, we shall succeed in being able to regulate his paces as we
wish for the entire period of the ride, and we shall thus prevent him pulling or
starting off at a canter the moment his head is turned home.

I also advise that the horse should not be turned sharply round to come back
to his stable by the road he came out.   Such a habit would prompt him to pull
immediately he was turned.

* In 1857, at Chalon-sur-Saône, two horses were brought into the riding school
to be broken.   One was so skittish and lively that I found it extremely difficult
to put my foot into the stirrup.   After having made several unsuccessful attempts,
they took me by the seat of the trousers and threw me into the saddle.   When I
got there, the horse did nothing wrong, and went forward well in hand as soon as
I stopped holding him back.

As the other horse held his head down, did not move, and looked like a sheep,
the master of the riding school thought he was quiet, and mounted him without
any trouble, but he did not remain in the saddle long, because this supposed *cold*-
tempered horse bucked him off at the first attempt, but the *hot* horse carried
me gaily round the school.   The conclusion which I draw from this, is that we
should distrust a horse which looks too quiet, and that we should not be afraid of
an impetuous animal.

reins, and the horse quickly establishes a connection between these two acts. But if, in place of starting off the moment we adjust the reins, we keep the horse at the walk, he will not contract this bad habit, or he will give it up if he has acquired it. The signal for a fast pace should be given only with the heels.

With respect to breed, we find in the first line in this book, the cry of my heart: "I break only thorough-breds."* I unhesitatingly put thorough-breds above all others, whether for hacking or for high school riding. They are pre-eminently the best for all kinds of work. Besides, a man who has got into the habit of riding thorough-breds, will not care to ride any other horses.

For me the ruling qualities of the thorough-bred are the lightness, the elasticity of the fine steel spring which puts them into action, and the suppleness which will be developed by breaking. If we listen from afar off, for the sound of his foot-falls, we shall hardly hear them on account of the light-

---

* I wrote this book at the time when I made my *début* at the Hippodrome with Germinal and Markir. Remarks were made on the apparent contradiction between my statement that I broke only thorough-breds and the fact that I had carried the breaking of the half-bred Markir as far as with any other horse, no matter what his breed might be.

The truth is that I bought Markir, not only on account of his good points, but also for his strength and activity, which I greatly admired. While breaking him, I often asked myself if he would do all I expected, and I frequently feared that his abilities would not come up to my requirements, which he amply fulfilled to my great surprise, and to such an extent that I determined to find out if the pedigree he had been given was correct. I therefore wrote to my friend Lenoble du Theil at the Haras du Pin, and told him that Markir had been sold to me as being out of the thorough-bred mare Thérésine by the Norfolk half-bred Weighton Merrylegs, and I begged him to see if this was right. Imagine my surprise and joy on receiving the following answer : " The thorough-bred mare Thérésine was put to Merrylegs, but did not hold, and was covered two months later by Cyrus, which is a thorough-bred Anglo-Arab, and the sire of Markir."

Markir is therefore thorough-bred. The curious thing about this matter is that it was proved by practical experiment before any investigations had been made.

ness with which he puts his feet on the ground. He skims the ground, which he treads with a delicacy full of energy. The feet of other horses, compared to his, clatter and hammer the ground, and their paces are much heavier.

On the other hand, there are many excellent half-breds. We sometimes meet with horses which show no signs of breeding, but which develop marvellous qualities in the same way that certain thorough-breds of illustrious pedigrees are mere garrons.* This prompts me to again say that a horse should above all things be *hot*. I may add that the thorough-bred is incomparable in courage and energy.

As the thorough-bred has the reputation of being *cold*, I shall no doubt be asked how I can reconcile my love for him with the superiority which I claim for the *hot* horse? This contradiction is only apparent, and I find that I have already explained it. There are *cold* horses and *hot* horses among thorough-breds, as there are among other breeds. I will even say that the innate energy of a thorough-bred will more easily make him generous, if he is ridden as he

---

* Nothing is more deceptive, even for speed, than pedigrees. Paternal and maternal atavism jumble up everything. Nevertheless, certain sires transmit characteristic points to the majority of their progeny.

I have ridden four horses sired by Vermouth and broken two of them. All four were sulky and required punishment to make them pass their stable. As long as they were ridden vigorously they went on a little, but no one could make them move freely except when they were playing up. I kept my eye on them for a long time, and found that they all turned jibbers.

The progeny of Zut are nervous, ticklish and restive.

The stock of Parmesan and Gantelet are excellent horses, supple, energetic and good-tempered.

The stock of Clocher are good, but not handsome; they can stay and carry weight. The same can be said of the sons and daughters of Braconnier, which are not so good-tempered as those of Clocher.

Horses got by Castillon are slugs.

Flavio sires good, supple and very wiry, though hot-tempered horses. It is clear that observations of this kind, which could be multiplied to infinity, are all the less exact, because the influence of the dam has not been taken into consideration. Nevertheless, they are partly true, and are consequently worthy of mention.

ought to be, and if he is asked to do what may be expected from his conformation and propelling power.

The fact is that the horses which are selected for the turf are long-striding animals, which consequently " daisy cut."* A horse which has high action is not admitted into a training stable, which fact enables me to obtain in him all the generosity and heat which I value above all things, whether for hacking or for high school riding.

People say that the thorough-bred does not make a good trotter ; but the reason for this statement would be difficult to give. On the contrary, the make and shape of the thorough-bred are admirably suited for all three paces. It is merely a question of education. We can train thorough-breds to the trot, as well as to the canter, and I have known thorough-breds which were wonderfully good trotters.

Breaking will develop in a sound well-built horse all his innate qualities, and by its course of rational gymnastics, will partly replace absent qualities. It will make him clever, light, and well-balanced.

A horse which can walk, trot, canter, turn easily, rein back and move from one side to the other, is sufficiently broken for work in the open ; but he should first be made quiet to mount, at which he should not require to be held. He should have a free long-striding walk. The trot and canter should be lengthened and shortened, according to the wish of the rider ; this is a question of breaking.

At the walk a horse should be allowed to have his head free, so that he may get confidence and may be able to lengthen his stride at his ease, and his neck should be nearly horizontal. Above all things, he should not be allowed to jog.

---

* My answer to the objection that many thorough-breds are " daisy cutters," is that such animals will not make good hacks ; but this fault in a hack is a good quality in a race-horse. Although a horse which gallops high will be turned out of a training stable, he will be gladly bought by a man who wants a nice hack.

At an ordinary trot, a horse should be let as free as possible. We should keep him well in hand, with his head and neck high, so that he may be light by being well-balanced.

In the fast trot, the head and neck should be nearly horizontal, so as to allow the animal to reach forward as far as possible. The horse ought to go freely up to the bridle, and the rider ought to keep only a light feeling on the snaffle.

There are three kinds of canter,* namely, the *well-collected canter*, the *hand gallop*, and the *full-speed gallop*.

In the *well-collected canter* (strong action of the legs and slight action of the hands : taking and giving), while gaining but little ground, he should carry his head and neck high.

The *hand gallop* is a shortened gallop, which should be well-collected, if the rider is worthy of that name ; but in it the horse is almost always behind his bit and extended. If we go to the Bois any morning, we shall see many of these unfortunate thorough-breds, which are worthy of a better fate, fully extended, with their hind legs dragging behind, head and neck low, and going stiffly in a mechanical style of gallop. Such horses caricature the movements of a gallop, while having a man on their back ; but this inelegant combination has nothing to do with equitation. In the hand gallop we should give some liberty to the horse, and as we press him up to the hand, we should proportionately support him. Although the collection is not full, our legs should bring his hocks well under the body.

In the *full-speed* or *race-course gallop*, the horse should lean well on the hands, and should stretch out his head and neck. Although he is not collected, the hocks are not less energetically brought under his body ; for speed could not be obtained without their action.

* In French, the same word is used for " canter " and " gallop "—Translator.

The rider ought to be able to easily make his horse go from one of these paces into another.

The horse ought to be able to lead equally well with either fore leg. Ability to change the leg is of great use, when riding in the open, so as to be able to readily turn to either side. It is not, however, indispensable if the rider takes care to stop at the moment of turning, and to start off on the leg of the side to which the turn is made.

It is of the utmost necessity that the horse readily yields to the legs, so that we can place his haunches as we like at all paces. When a rider passes or crosses another rider, he should be able to direct the movements of the hind quarters with his legs at the same time as he does those of the fore hand with his hands, so that he may guide the horse as a whole and not in parts. If, for instance, the hands pull the forehand to the right, and the haunches are allowed to swing round to the left, the horse will be put crossways, which is just the thing he ought not to be made to do. In this way the rider may get thrown off, or the man who passes by him may get kicked.

If a horse obeys the legs properly, we can easily, at all three paces, approach or leave one or more riders. When we are all together, obedience to both legs will enable us to leave the others, and, keeping the horse in hand, to let them pass us, if such is our wish.

There is extreme pleasure in riding a well-broken *hot* horse.*

Nothing is more agreeable than to work a horse in the open. Flexions, diagonal effects, two tracks, the *rassembler*, starting into the canter with the off fore and near fore leading, and other fine points of horsemanship, keep us on the alert, and make the time pass quickly when hacking.

---

* A horse that stumbles, shies, pulls, or won't go on unless spurred, soon disgusts us with riding.

The weather is always good for riding, except when there is snow and frost.*

In cold weather there is extreme pleasure in hearing the quick foot-falls on the hard ground, of a horse which is excited by keen air.

If it is raining or misty, the damp ground will be excellent for the horse, who will bravely plunge his feet into puddles and mud, and will joyously splash everything in his road.

When it blows hard, how pleasant it is to feel the wind striking our face, while we dash along at full speed!

Behold the sun! Let us go to the woods to enjoy the freshness and deadened brilliancy of the soft light.

The walk is the pace for reverie. The land spreads out its panorama, of which we are a living, moving part, because we are carried away by the country in the cadence of a continual movement to the long striding walk of a thorough-bred. What pedestrian will believe that the walk of a horse can inspire his rider with the feeling of speed? Nevertheless, that is the pleasure which is reserved for us.

The trot and hacking canter give us the pleasure of travelling without fatigue, of enjoying a harmonious movement produced by a reaction as free as it is elastic, with an energy increased a hundredfold by the generous ardour of the noble animal which is at our disposal, and which will give us all that is in it. Where does man end; where does the horse begin? We know not. The two make the most intimate, supple, living and vigorous whole which forms all the joy of life and action.

What intoxication of happiness to rush at full speed into space towards the unknown! If fences come in our way, what excitement there is in flying over them! What quiet daring fills our heart!

---

* When the ground is slippery, we should take our feet out of the stirrups, so that one of our legs may not get under the horse, in case of a fall.

We cannot express the infinite joy there is in the full speed of a thoroughbred. It is like the rocking of a wave, but it is so soft, so refined, that the air which we cleave annuls the feeling of weight. It is a mighty, intoxicating flight, without effort and without fatigue ; a physical joy which puts the mind to sleep, and leaves nothing living in us, except the maddening pleasure of flying through space.

I consider that the thorough-bred horse makes man perfect.

CHAPTER III.

HORSES WITH VICES.

Nervous Horses — Horses which throw their heads about — Horses which run away.

NERVOUS HORSES.

IT is usually said that a horse which is nervous will jump to one side or spin round, when the sight of some object or some noise makes him stop.

Any horse can be more or less surprised, according to its degree of impressionability. Happily all horses are not timid.

The impressionability of a horse can be greatly diminished and modified by breaking. Custom establishes mutual confidence between horse and rider. If the animal has not been beaten, or violently forced up to the object of his alarm, and if the presence of his rider reassures him, instead of frightening him, he will soon become steady.

It is a sound principle never to flog a horse which is frightened by some external object. We should, on the contrary, try to anticipate or remove the impression by "making much" of the animal.

I have already said that a horse has but little intelligence. He cannot reason, and has only memory. If he is beaten when an object suddenly comes before him and startles him, he will connect in his mind the object and the punishment.

If he again sees the same object, he will expect the same punishment, his fear will become increased, and he will naturally try to escape all the more violently.

All horses are not equally timid. Some are more impressionable on one side than on the other, whether accidentally or naturally, which fact gives rise to the saying that some horses are nervous on the near side, and others on the off.

We may note that wall-eyed horses are always nervous.

It is often wrongly said of a horse that he is nervous, when he is only fresh or green. It would be more correct to say that he is *in the air*, that he wants to use his muscles and extend himself, or, in other words, that he is in the position of a child who, having been for a long time quiet, begins to play and frisk about. In such cases punishment and caresses are equally useless. What we ought to do is to give him what he wants, namely, plenty of exercise. Send him along for two or three miles, and after that he will be perfectly quiet.

There are certain horses which are restless by nature, and are constantly on the alert to notice anything they may see or hear. They are afraid of all sorts of imaginary things, they make sudden starts at every moment, and are consequently very disagreeable to ride. Give them lots of work to cool them down and pats on the neck to give them confidence.

The number of the different kinds of nervous horses is so large, that it is impossible to enumerate them all. There are, however, certain ones which I would like to particularise. Some are afraid of everything which goes past their head, or everything which overlooks them, such as a carriage, omnibus, a low bridge, or carriage entrance. All things of that kind frighten them. People say that these horses are afraid of their heads being hurt. They are, however, absolutely indifferent to things which are low.

Other horses are afraid only of things on the ground, such

as shadows, rays of the sun, puddles, streams, and heaps
of stones.   They pay no heed to things which are above
them.

There are also horses which are afraid only of things which
come behind them, such as children, dogs, horses, and
carriages.   They seem afraid only of things which they do
not see.

My only advice about the management of nervous horses
is to give them confidence by " making much of them."   If
we see in front of us an object which we know our horse will
be afraid of, we should not force him to go up to it.   Better
let him at first go away from it, and then gently induce him
to approach it, without bullying him too much.   Work him in
this way for several days, as long as may be necessary.
Never bring him so close up to the object in question that he
will escape or spin round ; because in this case we will be
obliged to punish him ; not for his fear, but on account of his
spinning round, which we should not tolerate at any time.
In punishing him, we will confuse in his mind the fear of
punishment and the fear caused by the object.   In a word,
with nervous horses we should use much gentleness, great
patience, and no violence.

It now remains only to speak of horses which are wrongly
classed as nervous, which have all the appearance of fear, but
which are only vicious.

All horses are very fond of their stable, and are more lively
and impetuous when they are returning to it than when
leaving it.   Those of whom I speak seem to have only the
idea of returning to their stable, and of seeking every occasion of making a move to the rear, in the form of a spin
round.   We see them stop at the most trifling object which
they meet, and then they wheel round sharply if the rider
shows the slightest hesitation.   These horses, I repeat, are
not afraid ; they are vicious, and nothing I have said about

nervous horses applies to them. They have to be promptly brought back, and severely punished.

The proof that they are actuated only by vice is that, when returning to their stable, they will treat with absolute indifference the objects which caused them to spin round, when going out.

If under these or any other conditions the horse shies, we ought to steady him and bring him back by lateral effects. If he shies to the right, the right snaffle rein ought to be strongly carried to the left, and the right leg should be vigorously applied. In other words, to correct a shy to the right, we should apply two effects from right to left. By using the left rein—which people usually have the bad habit of doing—the rider will help the horse to throw to the right his haunches, which his right leg will not be able to keep straight. Further, if there is danger to the right, the horse may throw himself unwittingly into it, because, having his head turned to the left, he will not be able to see where it is. But the right rein, when applied strongly to the neck, presses him to the left, and aids the effect produced by the right leg, which prevents the haunches from being carried to the right.

If the horse shies to the right, the rider is shifted to the left. In such cases he keeps his seat in the saddle by the strong pressure of the right leg, from which he obtains safety.

Horses which spin round, almost always do so to one particular side. If we have a mount which uses this mode of defence, we should begin by finding out the side he turns to, and by holding on that side a stick about eighteen inches long. I do not like a whip for this purpose, for it is too flexible ; and if, for instance, we use it on the left, its end may bend and strike the right side, or, what is worse, may injure the animal's eyes.

Immediately the horse turns his head to spin round, but

before he can do so, strike him sharply with the stick on that side of the nose. I have never met a horse which has not been quickly made obedient by this method of correction when it has been applied with severity and precision. After a few times the mere sight of the stick will be enough.*

I like to work alone without any help, not even that of a groom. Those who do not believe this can easily verify my statement. I have kept my horses at livery in several schools and I have always broken them in these places. I have never asked the help of any one at the *manèges* of Latry, Vincent, Quartero, or l'Etoile.

HORSES WHICH THROW THEIR HEADS ABOUT.

There are very few horsemen who have not had the trouble and even the danger of riding animals which threw their heads about. Some forcibly lower the head, and thus, so to speak,

* The most disagreeable animal I ever met was a stallion which was very restive and a fiend to bite.

As it is impossible to break a horse without the help of the legs and spurs, it was necessary to find a means to make this horse bear their touch. The first six weeks passed off fairly well, because I did not ask him to do much, but as soon as I tried to get him in hand by means of the spurs, he tried to bite my legs, threw himself violently on his knees, and in this position made desperate efforts to catch hold of my feet ; and he had the best of the struggle, because I was not able to use the spurs, on account of having to draw back my feet out of the way of his teeth.

I then put on the snaffle reins two iron rods, fifteen or sixteen inches long. Having thus put the animal in such position that he could not turn his head round, and as my legs were then safe from his teeth, I felt sure of victory. But this demon of a horse, being rendered furious by his feeling of powerlessness, continued to throw himself on his knees, and being unable to bite my feet, bit his own breast, which I thought he would stop doing on account of the pain. So far from that, he tore away strips of flesh from his breast, and I have no doubt that if he had unseated me, he would have devoured me. I then put on him a very thick leather apron, which was in shreds in three days.

I succeeded, however, in mastering him by placing under his chin a kind of half funnel made out of white metal. Being unable to bite, he soon dropped that detestable habit, and I completed his education at No. 78 Avenue Malakoff, in a place kept by the son of Mr. Gost, who was a horse dealer, and who more than once was present at these equine battles, which I fought singly as a rule.

take a spring to raise it with greater violence.   Others content themselves with throwing the head sharply back, without lowering it in the first instance.   In the former case we should catch the horse with the snaffle reins (which are held in the right hand) at the exact moment when he begins to lower it. On account of the shock he will quickly raise his head, at which instant we should drive him forward by a strong pressure of the legs.   The curb reins are loose, but are firmly held in the left hand in such a way that the moment when the horse, by raising his head, tightens the curb reins, he will receive a severe blow on the bars of the mouth.   Therefore he has been stopped by the snaffle when he wished to lower his head in order to get his impulse, and has been punished by the curb when, in throwing up his head, he brought it too far back.   When he thus throws back his head without obtaining an impulse, we should drive him forward with a pressure of the legs the moment he raises his head, and should receive him on the curb, under the same conditions as those first mentioned.

To sum up, we make in the first case three movements of the snaffle, legs and curb.   In the second, we use only the legs and the curb.   Although these movements are successive, they follow each other so closely that they almost unite into a single one.   In both cases, if the action of the legs does not precede by ever so little that of the curb, we shall run the risk of making the horse rear, or at least by crushing the hind quarters we make him get behind his bit.

HORSES WHICH RUN AWAY.

I have always been fairly lucky, both as regards my pupils and myself, in avoiding accidents from run-aways.   My good luck was not altogether a matter of chance.

When a horse is running away, he will not listen to reason, and I do not think any one rider would be able to stop him much better than another ; but we can do a good deal to stop him from running away. Here the real knack consists in prevention, and therefore the watchful horseman will never let his animal get out of hand. Immediately he feels that the horse is ready to break away, he will steady him and calm him down by the voice and pats on the neck.

A horse often runs away because the bars of his mouth have become insensible on account of the rider pulling at him, which in this case is like pulling at a wall, and consequently the horse can bolt when he likes.

To keep the mouth fresh, the rider ought to use the snaffle and curb alternately ; that is to say, he should not let the animal take a bearing on either reins.

Some horses run away with their heads high, others bring the chin into the breast. We should always try to lower the heads of the former with the curb, and to raise those of the latter with the snaffle.

If the horse succeeds in bringing the head so low down and in rounding the neck so much that the cheeks of the curb are in contact with the breast, the more the rider pulls at the curb reins, the less will the bit act on the mouth,* and the more will he maintain the wrong position of his head and neck. The only thing he has to do in this case is to saw the snaffle.

With horses which get the chin into the chest it is well to use a gag snaffle, which acts upwards instead of backwards. It is also useful with a horse that has a heavy head and neck, which such an animal always tries to make his rider carry. Of course I offer this advice only to those who do not know how to balance their horses.

A horse is often said to run away when in reality he is only carrying away his rider.

---

* By pulling on the cheeks of the curb, we fix them against the breast and cause the mouthpiece to shift upwards in the mouth, which action relieves the bars.

A horse that runs away is a maddened horse which does not answer to the aids, and which cannot be guided.

A horse that carries away his rider is an old rascal who gets excited by a gallop, and who bolts whenever he gets out of hand.   Although we cannot stop him, we can guide him. He takes care to avoid obstacles that are in his path ; but the run-away gallops with his head down, his eyes are injected with blood, and he will dash himself to pieces against anything he meets.

A horse can carry his man away at all paces.   I have seen an animal do it even at a walk.   Such horses pull without ceasing, they make a half rear when the rider tries to stop them, and when they have completely tired him out, they carry him off.   We should therefore take care never to allow them to get out of hand.   If they succeed in catching the rider unawares and carrying him off, he should simply guide them into some open space.

The first thing which the rider should do, is to separate his reins.   By sawing the snaffle, by the alternative effects of the snaffle and curb, and by loosening the jaw, he can succeed little by little in changing the pace, putting the horse on his hind quarters, and consequently mastering him.

Above all things we should take care to manipulate the reins in a uniform manner.   Giving and taking is the invariable principle, and the legs ought always to remain close to the sides of the animal.   On these occasions the majority of riders think that they gain strength by making a " triangle " with their legs stuck out in front, in which case the horse will always be stronger than the man.

Many horses which have been raced, try to go off * with their rider, either at the trot or canter.   To accomplish this

* Many old race horses try to carry off their rider when he turns them round, because on race courses, horses start on being turned round.   We should be on the look out with such animals.

they stretch out the neck and forcibly lower the head.   If the rider pulls sharply at the reins, the horse will probably drag him out of the saddle on to his neck by throwing his head down.   We should "give" to the horse by bringing the hands forward without letting the reins slip through the fingers, then rather vigorously raise the neck, take up the snaffle and curb, and use the legs as soon as the neck has been straightened.

When a horse is really running away, the reins should be used in the same manner as when he is carrying off his rider, but the difficulty is much greater, because it is almost impossible to guide him.   If we have a plain in front of us we may succeed, even in this case, in turning the horse to the right or to the left.   To do this, supposing the reins are separated, as they ought to be, we should let go one of the reins, take hold of the other with both hands, pull with all the weight of the body, so as to produce a more or less decided lateral flexion, which will certainly turn the horse out of his course.

If the rider of a run-away horse finds himself alongside a stream, he ought to force the animal into it.   There is danger in everything on land, whether we meet a fence or get a fall on level ground ; but in water there is no danger, and a bath makes us quits.   The only thing to avoid is a perpendicular bank.   The majority of horses will stop as soon as the water comes up to their breast, and they will become perfectly quiet. Others strike the water with their fore feet, give themselves up to disordered movements, but always finish by becoming quiet in a short time.

In order to correct run-aways, I have often let them gallop as fast as they could along the low banks of a river, and when they were in full swing I sent them into the water, which I was able to do very easily.

Any horse which has been properly *rassemblé*'d can neither run away nor carry his rider away, because the use of the spurs, by bringing the hocks under the body, raises and lightens the forehand, and consequently the animal can be easily stopped.

While riding with my pupils I have often asked them what would they do if a run-away horse came up to them either from the front or the rear? I have also often asked persons who have ridden horses all their lives the same question, but I have rarely received a satisfactory answer, although this contingency ought always to be provided against. We should bear in mind that a man on a run-away horse generally runs less danger than the riders who are in his road. We often see a run-away animal dash into a group of horses with his head down. To avoid him we must get behind the first obstacle. If we are in a forest we should get into some bushes, and will then escape with a few scratches. If we are on a road we should get behind a tree ; if in a street, behind a lamp post. In fact, anything will serve to shield us from the terrible shock. Above all things we should move as quickly as we can.

If in place of getting out of the way, we wish to help a man on a run-away horse, which is a praiseworthy but very difficult attempt, we should gallop at full speed in the direction he is going, while keeping a few yards in front of him. We ought to speak in a loud tone of voice and try to give the rider confidence. We should then slightly slacken speed, and as the run-away passes alongside of us, we should try to catch hold of his curb reins as near as possible to the mouth, and endeavour to stop him little by little.

If we do not gallop in front of the run-away nearly as fast as he is going, the jerk we will receive at the moment we catch the reins may throw us out of the saddle. As we ought to have one hand free, we should hold our reins in the other hand, so as to be able to control and guide our mount.

I may add that it is almost impossible to stop a run-away

13

while going on a straight line.   I have never succeeded in this.
If the amount of open space and the nature of the ground
allows us to do so, we should at first take a very large circle,
and should decrease it little by little.   We should of
course place ourselves on the inside of the circle, so as to be
able to pull the run-away in the direction we are taking.
If we are on the outside we will not be able to make him
turn.   It is evident that we cannot employ this means of
stopping a run-away unless we are sure of our horse and
ourselves.

I was lucky to stop two mad run-aways in the manner I
have just described.   The first one was at Havre, and his rider
had let go the reins and had caught hold of the pommel of the
saddle with both hands.   The second was in the Bois at Paris,
and was ridden by a young girl.   In both cases, it took me
from fifteen to twenty minutes to stop the horses.   As I was
on thoroughbreds, I had strength and speed at my disposal.
With respect to the lady, I took the precaution to place
myself on her off side, for her legs would have been in the
way on the other side.

CHAPTER IV.

JUMPING.

IT is generally said that to make a horse jump, the hands should be raised the moment he comes to the fence; but in acting thus his natural powers are hampered and he is prevented from jumping freely.

In order to jump, he should have his head and neck perfectly free, because if they are raised by the hands their freedom and spring will be spoiled, and the weight will be thrown on the hind quarters. Consequently, if he has a light mouth he will pull up in front of the fence, and if he has a hard mouth he will get the better of his rider, in which case he can only make a half-rear, and consequently his fore legs will clear the obstacle and his hind legs will catch in it. Hence, while driving him forward with the legs, we pull him back with the reins. The forehand can get the better of the curb, but only by an effort which will considerably tire the horse.

There is a general theory for making horses jump, but we can quickly see that, in practice, each horse has his own particular way of leaping. In my opinion, the best way to teach a horse to jump is at first to place a log of wood on the ground, and lead him over it at the walk. When he obeys, he should be patted on the neck and have some carrots, so as to gain his confidence. This will be an affair of only two or

13*

three lessons of about ten minutes' duration.   When he has
full confidence, we may lunge him over the log, while
gradually getting further and further away from him.   As
soon as he will walk over the bar, while the breaker stands in
the middle of the school, the bar can be raised from 12 to 16
inches, and the horse left to jump it in his own way.   The
chief thing is that he clears it.   This plan of accustoming a
horse to a fence, has been practised in circuses from time
immemorial.

A horse which likes jumping will generally rush, and
should be calmed down, so that he may take the leap quietly.
If, on the contrary, he stops or hesitates, he should be
encouraged by the voice and should be shown the driving
whip, but should not be struck with it, or frightened at
starting.   We should, however, make him go over the bar,
and should carefully note how he jumps.   The best fencers
jump straight, freely, and without pausing.   Some leap
" stickily," and others jump sideways.   Horses which jump
freely and of their own accord need only be taught to
clear the fence, successively, at the walk, trot and canter.

Horses which make a half halt when coming up to the
obstacle, should be stimulated by the driving whip until they
have lost the habit of stopping.   Consequently, we should not
let them jump at the walk and trot, until they will freely do
so, at the canter.

Things are not much more complicated with horses that
jump sideways, and we have only to oppose their shoulders to
their haunches.   If, for instance, we are on the left hand, and
the horse throws his hind quarters to the left, and consequently to the inside, we should pull the lunging rein, in
order to bring his shoulders to the left, and at the same time
we should touch the left haunch with the lash of the whip, to
send the hind quarters to the right.   If, on the contrary, the
horse brings his haunches to the right, that is to say, to the

outside, we should let out the lunging rein, and at the moment the animal is taking off, we should make him carry his shoulders to the right, by threatening him with the whip under the muzzle.

The bar should be kept very low for this work, and should be raised only little by little, according to the strength and cleverness of the horse.

We should take great care never to raise the bar so high as to require the animal to make a great effort to clear it, especially if he is young. Although this would not be so bad with old horses, we should do all we can not to discourage them.

As soon as the horse jumps freely with the lunge, he can be mounted, and made to follow the same programme, while beginning with the bar on the ground.

At first, we should not trouble about the animal's style of jumping, but should let him fence in his own way, and should study it.

In leaping, as in every other exercise which demands great energy on the part of the horse, the rider should take account of the natural capabilities of his mount, and should adapt himself to them. If they require to be set right, he should gradually do it later on.

I have said that the hands should make no effort to raise the horse when taking off. I repeat that the head and neck should be perfectly free, but I do not say that the reins should be let go ; because the horse, when he is jumping, ought to maintain on the hands a light bearing,* which he does not take at the moment of raising himself, because he has had it when coming up to the fence ; in fact, he merely preserves it. The elasticity of the hands and even of the arms of the rider allows him to keep up this bearing on the bit, without

---

* It is an absolute rule in riding that the hands ought always to remain in communication with the mouth.

increasing it. It is better for him to diminish it a little, when
the horse extends his head and neck to jump. In other words,
the horse, not the rider, takes this bearing.

Some horses jump best if they have a good hold of the bit,
when coming up to the fence, especially if they are going fast.
Others require to be ridden with a slack rein, so that they may
take the necessary spring. Nevertheless, in order to be certain
that a horse will jump, we should firmly close our legs and feel
his mouth, for otherwise he can very easily refuse. It is of
course understood that the reins should be slackened a little,
the moment he is taking off. If the reins are slackened too
much, he will often jump stickily or refuse, and if we slacken
the reins too late, we will prevent him jumping, or will hamper
his movements.

The hands, therefore, ought to do three things:—1. Support
the horse up to the moment he takes off. 2. Give him his
head during the time he is clearing the obstacle. 3. Feel the
snaffle,* so that we may lightly get him into hand the
moment he lands.

The legs of the rider ought to support the horse during the
whole time—namely : 1. Before leaping, so as to press him
up and make him jump. 2. During the leap, in order to
make him get his hind legs under him, so that he may not
hit the fence. 3. After the leap, in order to support the hind
legs when they come down and relieve the fore legs. Finally,
when the legs are thus supported they will keep the rider in a
good position.

The pluck and confidence of the rider plays a large part
in jumping. If he comes up to the fence without having
decided to clear it, the chances are that he will remain on
this side of it.

It is said that the horse understands the feelings of the

* I use only the snaffle when jumping, and I employ this curb only to
regulate the speed between the fences.

rider. This is not quite true, because it is evident that the animal cannot know what is in the mind of the man on his back; but he can feel that the "aids," like the will of the rider, are hesitating.

To make the horse resolute we should, in the first instance, be resolute ourselves. If our pluck gives way, our "aids" will be vacillating; but if we harden our heart, we will transmit

Fig. 46.—Clearing a fence.

confidence to the horse by means of the "aids," which, in this case, should act with vigour and precision.

The rider who goes up to a fence for the first time, usually imagines that he will receive a terrible shock. As a rule, he instinctively stiffens himself so as not to be displaced, and when he falls off, the accident is generally due to this stiffness.

As I have already said, we should give with the hands at

the exact moment when the horse raises himself, and should preserve his suppleness by a stronger pressure of the legs. In this way the shock and displacement of the seat are only trifling.

I have said that all horses do not jump in the same way. With those which raise themselves well with all four feet, and

Fig. 47.—Horse raising his forehand a good deal when jumping.

clear the fence while keeping the body nearly horizontal, the rider has only to keep his body in a perpendicular position (Fig. 46).

If the horse, when jumping, raises his forehand a great deal, as in a half-rear (Fig. 47), the rider ought to proportionately lean forward at the moment when the horse raises himself; but as the horse comes down, he should bring his body back, for three reasons: First, not to be thrown forward by the propulsion given by the horse; second, to lighten the forehand, which, on coming to the ground, will have to bear all the weight of both horse and rider; and, third, to keep his seat and support his horse in case the animal's forelegs give way.

When a horse brushes a fence with his forelegs, and raises

Fig. 48.—Horse raising his croup when clearing a fence.

his croup as if he were kicking,* we should carry the body back the moment the forehand is raised as high as the fence, so as to avoid putting weight on the forehand. When the fence has been cleared, the body will be put back in its place by the force of propulsion.

I cannot too strongly impress on my readers that in all the

---

* See Fig. 48 :—If the reins were drawn tighter, this illustration would serve equally well to show the position of a rider who is about to receive his horse after a jump.

backward movements of the body during the leap, the arms should preserve the greatest possible elasticity, so that the tension of the reins may be in no way increased, and that the horse may jump freely. If the reins are too short, we should let them slip through the fingers, and should take them up again as soon as the animal lands.

I am naturally led to say a word about steeplechases and hurdle races. The ignorance on the part of jockeys about the paces of horses is inconceivable. Very few of them can tell with which leg a horse is leading in the gallop. Baron Finot, who is a master, astonished me one day by saying: " Jockeys ride by instinct, and do not take the trouble to think."

In hurdle racing a horse clears the hurdles, thanks to his enormous momentum, and the harder he pulls the better pleased is his jockey. In France, steeplechases are ridden at the same speed as hurdle races, which at first sight appears dangerous. I have spoken to many jockeys on this subject, and they have all told me that the faster the speed the less danger there is for them. This seems a paradox, but it is really true. Their reason is that if a horse which is going at a moderate speed strikes a fence and comes down, the horse will nearly always fall on the jockey, in which case the result will be very serious, if not actually fatal. But if a similar fall occurs when the horse is at full speed, the jockey is thrown a few yards to the front, and generally escapes being hurt. In such a case the jockey rolls like a ball, huddles himself up, takes care not to stretch out an arm or leg, and thus nearly always gets off with only a few bruises.

In England, a steeplechase jockey slackens his pace when he gets near a fence, and thus husbands the horse's strength, and allows him to more accurately measure his distance. Horse and man thus act in harmony.

The French system is more break-neck, and requires less

knowledge, but it can help to win a race. The English system is a matter of good horsemanship, but we must admit that the French system has more chances of success if the horse does not fall.

In my opinion, the jockeys Hatchet and H. Andrews are brilliant exceptions respecting the way steeplechases are generally ridden. Hatchet has a very remarkable method of riding over fences, and I always follow him with great pleasure, because his style bears out the theory which I am never tired of maintaining—namely, that there is only one way of riding. There is only one kind which is always good on the racecourse as well as for hacking, and without it success is either pure luck or mere knack.

To see Hatchet ride a steeplechase is a great treat for a connoisseur. He remains glued to the saddle, and daylight is never seen between him and it. On coming up to a fence he does not lean back, for he knows that the impetus of the hind quarters would throw him forward. He gets well down into the saddle and rounds his back so as to keep his seat and suppleness. He holds his hands low, his arms half-extended, and the reins just sufficiently felt to keep him in constant communication with the mouth of the horse. He evidently yields his fingers at the same time as he does his arms, because he is never pulled forward at the moment when the horse stretches out his head and neck to jump. He keeps a nice feeling on the reins—more by the play of the fingers than by that of the arms—even during the wild speed of a race, which is a fact that few sportsmen will admit. Also, he keeps his position before, during, and after a jump. With him there is not the slightest shock; everything is smooth and perfect.

I often hear people say on racecourses that if a horse is going to fall, nothing will prevent him, but we can deceive ourselves. It is evident that if an animal makes a mistake and fails, he will fall ; but what I want to say is that a mistake

which will not happen with one jockey will occur with another
jockey. A horse's fall is very often due to the man who rides
him. I mention the following instance of this because it is
conclusive :—

In one season at Auteuil, Hatchet won nine races out of
eleven on Baudres, and the horse fell in the two races he lost.
For personal motives, another jockey of very high reputation
was put on Baudres, who, in seven races, fell four times and
lost each of these four events. After that Hatchet won ten
consecutive races on Baudres without a fall. Thus, Baudres
fell four times out of seven with a good jockey, and fell only
twice out of twenty-one races with a jockey whom I consider to be exceptionally good. A remarkable fact which
perhaps will help the reader to remember what I have said,
is that all these falls occurred at the brook in front of the
stands.*

Hatchet has a particular way of his own in taking the last
turn on the Auteuil racecourse, which is on the left of the
stands, and is very sharp. He takes it very short, and
slackens his speed to a marked extent. The others keep up
the speed, and are consequently obliged to take a wide turn.
Although the difference between the two methods may appear
to be of no matter, it is of great importance. As Hatchet
turns very short, he loses no ground, although he slackens
speed, because he has less space to cover; and as he thus
allows his horse to recover his wind, he is able, in the straight
run home, to get out of his animal a last and supreme effort,
which the others cannot obtain, because they kept up full
speed the whole time.

We should not forget that in such cases, horses win races

* In that fence there was nothing to catch a horse's legs. To clear it, like all
other wide jumps, the only thing that was required was plenty of impulse.
Seeing Baudres change his leg a few yards from this fence on account of the
jockey trying to raise his head, I said to his owner : "Your horse is going to
fall." In fact, the impulse was stopped and the fall came off.

not with their legs but with their lungs, namely, by being able
to stay.

I have lately mentioned the name of H. Andrews, which
was a pleasure I could not resist, when finishing the description of the particular qualities which make him unrivalled.
Any one who has not seen Andrews finishing, can have no
idea of the enormous energy he possesses. I have seen him,
on losing his whip, take his cap to flog his horse ; and then
losing his cap, he used his right arm and hand with the utmost
vigour and perseverance. It is no exaggeration to say that when
coming up to the winning-post, he communicates energy to
his horse, and shoves him in front in a particular way of his
own, without the slightest slackening off.

CHAPTER V.

FLAT RACING.

I HAD occasion to say, that in all exercises, the ordinary horseman, riding master or jockey should know what he ought to require from his horse. It is generally but wrongly thought that this rule does not hold good with respect to flat racing, at which the most successful jockeys are those who best conform to it.

In a flat race, when all the horses are on about the same level, as regards speed and staying power, the jockey who can set the pace in his own way will have the best chance, and consequently his success will depend on his knowledge of his animal's capabilities. He will give him the exact support which is necessary, and will put him at the speed to which he has been accustomed towards the end of his training ; will maintain it during the race, and will reserve his supreme effort for the finish.

As the horse has not been over-ridden during the race, he can easily, at the finish, make the last rush, upon which success almost always depends. I can easily prove this fact by the case of Archiduc, whom everyone remembers. On three consecutive occasions, Archiduc took the lead at a pace which suited him, and no horse was able to get near him. In the Chantilly Derby, however, Fra Diavolo tried to take the lead. These two struggled for supremacy, and were at the top of their speed before a quarter of the distance had been covered. The jockey of Little Duck, who was behind, did not trouble about the others, but judged his own pace for three-quarters of the course, and thus saved his animal's powers for the last moment, at which time he suddenly sat down and rode, passed the others, who had not an effort left in them, and won easily. The jockey of Little Duck simply put into practice the rule which I have specified. In a word, he knew how to keep something for a rainy day, which in this case was a reserve of energy to be used at the finish.

The greatest difficulty for a jockey who is leading, is to judge the pace, and to know how fast his horse ought to go.* If he goes beyond this speed, he will take the wind out of his horse, and will be unable to make a last rush. If he keeps back, he will necessarily do so by taking too strong a hold of the reins, and will consequently tire the horse's loins and hocks. But it is the loins and hocks which win a race at the finish.

The best jockeys win at the last moment, and as near the winning-post as possible. Their perfect knowledge of pace enables them to judge if their opponents can keep up the speed at which they are going, and to feel if they can increase their own speed. At Chantilly, I saw Watts on Louis d'Or apply this principle in a very clever and lucky manner. It was a welter race, and all of them carried 12st. 8lb. Atalante was the favourite, and was certainly the best made to carry weight.

In this two-mile race, Watts let Louis d'Or go his own pace, and did not try to catch up the others. Although he was two hundred yards behind at the beginning, he did not increase his speed. The others having gone too fast, were obliged to

---

* Such judgment is extremely difficult with a speed of about eleven hundred yards in a minute.

slacken speed, but he maintained the same pace and beat the favourite by a few yards. We can say with confidence that he won this race by his knowledge of pace.

Fred. Archer gave a grand performance by winning the Grand Prix of Paris on Paradox. He did not fail for an instant in fine horsemanship, coolness and cleverness. At first he remained behind his field, but towards the end he drew up alongside Reluisant, who had won the Chantilly Derby, and was his only formidable opponent. He stuck close to him, and although he saw that Reluisant could go no faster, he kept with him until close to the winning-post, and then won by a neck. This victory shows us only a part of Archer's talent. The thing which was best about him and which made him a great master, was his seat. He sat well into the saddle, and rode with long stirrups. When he raised himself on his stirrups, his seat grazed the saddle.

His seat had no resemblance to the strange, if not ridiculous position which many jockeys adopt, and which some of them exaggerate to such a degree that we could place a hat between them and the saddle.* Archer always sat like a horseman, with his horse enclosed between his hands and legs.

In short distance races, he was unjustly said to be tricky at getting off first. At the moment when the starter lowers his flag, the majority of jockeys are content to slacken the reins and let the horses go off as they like or as they can. Archer left nothing to chance, and he ruled his horse like the true horseman that he was. Having always his legs close to the horse's sides, he surprised the animal at the moment of starting by a vigorous pressure of the legs, and instantly put

---

* Jockeys, of whom the majority sit badly, do not now ride in a "triangle," as people formerly said, with the reins, saddle and stirrups as their three points of support. If this style has left the turf, it is still unfortunately employed in hacking.

him on his feet before the others could get on theirs. He was therefore going fast before his opponents were out of a canter.

We see by these examples that all kinds of riding resemble each other. The science of equitation is as necessary to a jockey as to any one else, and consists of judgment, hands and legs.

CHAPTER VI.

THE HUNTER.

ALTHOUGH a hunter need not be of any particular breed, he should be chosen from the best horses. My advice to a man who wants to hunt is to select a horse which has been born, reared and trained in the country where the hunting is to take place. Horses, like men, have natural capabilities which correspond to the climate and nature of their native land. If they are sent elsewhere they will lose these qualities, without being able to acquire those of the animals which were born in the place.

Let us take for instance the small horse of the Pyrennees, which has marvellous qualities. In his own country he is clever, active, very sure-footed and temperate, and in the country about Pau he makes a first-rate hunter; but if he is taken to Rome or Vendée he will lose some of his good qualities. It is the same with all other breeds of horses. Therefore, for hunting, take a horse of the country. The English hunter is the only animal which is good in all countries, and which preserves his good qualities, no matter what is the nature of the sport. He combines almost all the desirable points. He is nearly thorough-bred, although his shape and make are not what we would look for in a race horse, which has plenty of daylight under him. The hunter is closer to the ground, and should be particularly good about the loins and hocks.*

His breaking begins later than that of the thorough-bred. He is taken up at about three-and-a-half years old, and requires a year or eighteen months to learn his work.†

In judging him, we should specially consider his style of jumping different fences, and the pace at which he takes them. If the obstacle is a hedge, he should take it quietly, on account of the small effort required to clear it. If it is high and stiff he should collect himself for a big effort, and should go very straight and steadily at it. If it is a fairly wide stream, the pace should be quite different, and the head and neck, which should not be hampered by the hands, should be extended. The horse should stretch himself out, should take a light but very free bearing on the hands, and jump at full speed with freedom and pleasure.

The only fault an English hunter has, is that he costs a great deal of money. Usually one pays about three hundred pounds for a good animal of this sort; but in exceptional cases, the price may be five or six hundred. I repeat that this kind of horse is the only animal which is fit to hunt anywhere.

In every country, except in England, it is generally thought that as accidents are very common in hunting, only cheap horses should be used for this work. All my readers know from experience that in buying a horse, they cannot be sure of getting value for their money. Therefore I think it very foolish to practise economy when buying a hunter. The English, who are very practical, and who know the value of

---

* The hunter is the only horse they have not tried to produce in France. This is to be regretted, because breeders would have succeeded with him, as with other horses. Frenchmen make the mistake of wanting cheap hunters.

† His work is simply jumping, and he never fetches a high price, unless he is a free goer, very sure-footed and a big jumper. The long training which he requires is the cause of his high market value. Ordinary jumpers are ready at from three-and-a-half to four years old.

14*

money, are economical in the purchase of harness horses ; but price does not stop them when buying a hunter, to whom they will have to trust their life.

We often hear it said that Mr. X is fortunate with all his horses, and that Mr. Y, being out of luck, cannot place his hand on a good animal. We may be certain that chance has not much to say in this matter. The fact that Mr. X has often good horses is perhaps due to his understanding their powers and working them with good judgment. If Mr. Y has only bad horses, notwithstanding the long prices he gives, it is perhaps because he is an indifferent rider who does not understand horses, and is ignorant of what he ought to require from a horse and of the manner he ought to require it,

I do not hesitate to recommend those who will take my humble advice, to get the best and strongest horse they can for hunting.

The English say that hacking is an art,* and hunting is pluck. In my opinion this proverb is absolutely correct. Without doubt pluck is required more with hounds than when hacking, because the speed is greater, and the fences are unknown. Nevertheless, pluck cannot replace the science of riding, which is even more necessary when crossing a country than when hacking, because the risks are greater and more frequent.

To hunt, as well as to hack or ride races, it is necessary to know how to ride.

* I must say that I have always seen more hacking than art in Rotten Row.

CHAPTER VII.

THE ARMY HORSE.*

My intention was to discuss in this book all kinds of riding, but up to the present I have spoken only of hacking, riding for sport, and breaking,

The saddle horse is not only destined for sport, and riding is not merely a luxury. At the present time the horse is an essential element of the military power of a country. He is a warlike arm which it is necessary to choose, prepare, and manage.

Late wars have proved that cavalry are required to play a decisive part in military operations. In every country, this branch of the service has been increased in number and strength. Recently pamphlets, leading articles of newspapers, and reviews have shown the great attention with which the public has studied the subject.

I trust I may be permitted, or at least pardoned for saying a few words about the war horse.†

* I hope that my readers will excuse the liberty and freedom of my criticisms, on account of my absolute conviction that they are only too well founded. Besides, I believe that many persons who have special knowledge about these things, would willingly agree with the majority of my observations, if they had liberty of speech.

† In my opinion, the half bred is the best animal for war. In this I am not contradicting myself, although I said at the beginning of this book, that I preferred the thorough-bred to all others. He has energy and cleverness which is rarely found to the same extent in other horses ; but these qualities are not the only desirable ones in an army horse. The thorough-bred will perhaps stand

The troop horse, which is the constitutive element of the cavalry, ought to have certain qualities, of which the principal are soundness and hardiness. With him it is not a question of fine handling or scientific movements. He has to carry his man safely and for a long distance, and by the strength of his constitution he has to bear fatigue and all the miseries of a campaign.

Also, he must not cost too much, because money is the chief sinew of war, despite progress and innovations.

A horse does not cost merely the sum paid to his owner, to which has to be added all the money spent on him from the day of his purchase to the time he is really fit for work. A horse bought for forty pounds, which has to be looked after and fed for a year at a remount depot, before being sent to his regiment, will really cost eighty pounds up to the day he takes his place in the ranks.

I have not the presumption to discuss financial and military questions, which are entirely beyond my province. I reason only as a horseman. I say with respect to remounts, that we should consider their necessary qualifications and net cost at the same time. If I occupied myself with their qualifications without touching on the subject of price, my theory might appear useless, but I have the one firm ambition to give only practical advice.

We all know how horses are bought for the army. Remount

fatigue better than any other. In a charge he has marvellous and incomparable dash ; but how will he bear all the privations and miseries of a campaign ?

In the Crimea, the English lost the majority of their thorough-breds, but the Normans, Percherons, Bretons and Auvergnans held out admirably. The war horse ought to remain serviceable under conditions of hunger, cold, rain, snow and nights without shelter or covering. I do not think that the thorough-bred is capable of this form of endurance.

A breed which has not been hardened may yield capital horses for ordinary work, but they will not be hardy and enduring enough for warfare.

To make use of a thoroughbred, one must know more than ordinary cavalry men do about riding.

officers go to the different breeding centres, examine the horses from three to four years' old, and make purchases. These visits are necessarily foreseen. Dealers of all nationalities, and especially foreigners, take the precaution to come prior to the arrival of the remount officers, and buy the best they can find, which is easy for them, because they give a better price. The remount people choose the best of what is left. These horses, which are considered too young for any work, are sent to the remount depots, where they are kept until they are five years old. Sometimes they are put out to grass with farmers at a moderate cost.

I set aside all details to arrive at the principal point, namely, the age at which remounts should be bought; taking for granted that they are not fit for work until five years old.* Only at that age they are begun to be exercised and are put to more or less appropriate regular work, in other words, they are broken in. This system is a tradition and a principle; but at the risk of running against all accepted ideas, I say that the tradition is an error, the principle false and the system bad.

It is a loss of precious time to keep a horse until he is five years old before exercising, breaking and training him for military purposes. Besides, this delay doubles his first cost and deteriorates his physical organs, which suffer atrophy, on account of insufficient feeding and work.

At three years and a half, a well-shaped horse† which has

* Technically, the horses are five years old, because they take their age from the first of January; but really they are only four years and nine months, because they are born in the spring. They go to their regiments in the first half of the October of their fourth year, and are then four years and six months old.

They are put in the squadron of the depot to have the rough edge taken off them, and are accustomed to the stable, saddle, weight of a man, and external objects. In the first half of January, that is to say, when they are four years and nine months old, they are sent to their respective regiments, and their breaking commences.

† I mean a French horse, from whatever part he may come.

been properly fed and exercised, is sufficiently developed and strong to bear the gradual work which precedes and facilitates breaking. By the age of four years he could be properly broken and rendered fit for military service, after a few months of which work, his training is complete, and he has the strength and endurance that are pre-eminently necessary in an army horse.

If we wish to discard routine, and to adopt a system of liberal feeding and rational breaking, we will obtain a troop horse which, at four and a half years, will be worth as much or more than the six-year old horse, after he has been broken.

Whence comes the deeply-rooted idea that a horse cannot be used in the army before he is five years old? How is it that many eminent remount officers have perpetuated this principle? I suppose that, having ascertained that the five-year old horses they procured were weak and undeveloped, they concluded that it would have been impossible to work them earlier. They were content with the fact, but did not try to find out the cause.

Nevertheless it has been long and repeatedly proved that a three-year old horse, which has been well fed and well exercised, can do very hard work, and maintain a high rate of speed.*

* If the objection is made that some (not many) of the animals may suffer, I answer that I propose that only horses three years and six months .and even three years and nine months old should be broken, in which case they will have a preparation of three months. Also, I would not require from them such severe work as similarly bred animals which race, have to do, and which are trained at two-and-a-half years old at the latest.

Another objection it made about the great difference between the weights carried by a race horse and troop horse ; but the latter is a year older than the former, and his stronger build enables him to carry weight better. He is hardier, he carries his full weight only on exceptional occasions, and his work is much slower. If we go on gradually, as is done with race horses, we shall succeed without any difficulty in developing his weight-carrying power.

To the pure theorists who wish to wait for the complete ossification of the

Let us take as an example the numerous half-bred horses of Normandy. They are supposed to be the least precocious of all the horses produced in France, and it is generally admitted that they cannot be got ready much earlier than six years old.

Norman breeders naturally class their colts, at first, according to their origin, and afterwards by their make and shape.

The young animals are put into the three following classes : —

1. Match trotters.

2. Horses for fashionable purposes* and for trade work.

3. Remounts.

Trotters begin to be gradually exercised and trained at two years old, or at two and a half at latest. They are generally full grown at three, are in good form and compete in races. The best trotting prizes are reserved for three-year olds. They can actually trot a distance of two miles and a half in about six minutes and a half. The distance is often over three miles, to successfully cover which the trotter requires speed and staying power. During his training. and during the time he is racing, he has to undergo the severest exertion of which a horse is capable. †

A horse for fashionable purposes, which is intended for a dealer who can pay a good price for him, is almost a foal at

cartilages before putting a horse into work, I reply by advising them to buy five-and-a-half year old horses, so as to have them ready at six. They will tell me that such animals cannot be found. Why ? Because trade gives them to the buyer at a much earlier age. Therefore the universal practice is to work them at an earlier age. Q. E. D. The four year old should, of course, be treated with care. Here the important thing is to prove that at that age he is fit for work.

* This class comprises horses which had been intended to act as stallions in studs, but as they did not fulfil the expectations of their owners, they were cut and used for commercial purposes.

† It is interesting to note that half-bred trotters stand racing better than thorough-breds.

Thorough-breds "click" ("forge") when running or when being trained, far more frequently than half-breds.

three years old.   His growth is incomplete, his body slender, he is soft, and he ought not to be worked.   He approaches his full height, puts on muscle, and becomes capable of moderate work only when he is rising four, or is four off ; and we then find him in the hands of the dealer, fat, glossy, and ready for the purchaser who is in no hurry and who does not want much from him.   The same remarks may be made about the commercial horse, who differs from the fashionable one only as regards price.

The three-year-old *remount* is of no value.   He is generally fat, at from three to four years old, when he is shown to the purchasing officer.   A few feeds of oats at the last moment, the whip, and ginger, give him an appearance of strength ; but in reality his muscles are weak, and he has neither good paces nor staying power.   Left to himself he gives way, goes on his shoulders, and is not fit for any kind of work.

Such are the horses which are nearly of the same breed. Some are fully furnished at three years of age, and can stand training and racing, which are the hardest kind of work. Others at four-and-a-half years old are hardly ready for even very moderate work.   It is therefore necessary to take great care of them, to let them acquire strength, and to give them the muscular development of which they are deficient.

Whence comes this difference ?   Does Nature make some more precocious than others, all being of the same origin ?   Is a horse's muscular development in inverse proportion to his good looks and speed ?   In no way !   This great difference results solely from the method employed in feeding and educating different classes of horses.   If a uniform system were used, all would have similar precocity, development, and power.   Horses differ in shape, action, and usefulness, but if they were all treated properly up to the age of three years, they would all be sufficiently hardy for any kind of work. The half-bred trotter which is trained and run at three years old is a proof of this. His work is extremely hard, and is out of all proportion as compared to that required from a fashionable horse, or from a troop horse, and he can stand it as well or better than any other kind of animal without becoming unsound. He is, however, well fed from the first, and is methodically exercised from an early age. In fact, he is brought up like a thorough-bred.

All race horses are not thorough-breds, but all have been brought up with a view to racing. From their birth they receive the care and feeding which is appropriate to the work they will have to do. They begin to eat a little oats during the first days of their life, and when six or eight months old they get five quarts of oats a day. At eighteen months they are stabled, highly fed, and trained. At two years old they take part in special races.

A similar, though somewhat slower method, is employed with trotters, which do not run until they are three years old. In both cases nature is helped by feeding, and by gradual and constant exercise.

The breeder of other horses hinders nature by insufficient feeding. A horse grows fast, and his skeleton and muscular system are large. In order that he may grow quickly, and acquire the necessary strength, his food should be abundant, and his exercise should be favourable for the development of his strength and speed. The only young horses which are well fed and exercised, are those which are intended for racing or for stud purposes. Other animals are kept at grass, because that is the most economical method of bringing them up. Under the influence of this watery and innutritious food and want of exercise, the horse's development is retarded in every way, his bones ossify slowly, and his muscles do not stand out. The older he grows, the more debilitated does he become. At three years he is only backward, but between four and five years of age he suffers greatly from anæmia, which is a poverty-stricken disease that needs *repair*. I feel certain that success in its treatment can only be incomplete, and that a horse recovering from it can never be as good as he would have been, had he been brought up differently. The longer we wait to restore the young horse, the longer and more unsuccessful will be the treatment. If the animal is only a three-year-old, a few months may be sufficient, but if he is four years, and still more if he is five, he will require a year or longer. This undeniable fact is easily explained, because the longer the animal suffers from anæmia, the more severe does the disease become, and the greater is the general wasting.

The numerous cases of mortality among young horses are to be attributed to this state of impoverishment (anæmia). The debility which results from insufficient food during the period of growth, makes them unable to resist the slightest illness or the most trifling accident. It is also the cause of many diseases, strangles, for instance, and obscure lamenesses which are generally put down to youth. A young horse is vigorous and healthy, if he is brought up under good conditions ; but is weak and sickly if he has a lymphatic temperament, or is anæmic from want of food or exercise.

Norman horses are generally lymphatic, soft and backward, because Normandy produces less oats than other breeding districts, and it is the custom in that country to give it only to trotters. The breed feels the bad effects of this, and soon degenerates, unless the stallions are chosen from trotters which, having been always kept in good condition, are able partly to correct the lymphatic temperament of the dam which has suffered from anæmia in her youth.

It is not correct to say that trotters acquire their magnificent development and strength on account of their being exceptional animals. Besides the brilliant instances which have been mentioned, there are many trotters which compete in local events, and after leaving the racecourse do excellent work. Often they have nothing remarkable about them, except their pace. They are not naturally precocious. and have advanced by care, good feeding, and education, while others have remained behind.

At five years old the French horse could have nearly all his height and strength and be ready for breaking. If he is otherwise, the state of his development will be proportionate to the amount and nature of the food and exercise he has received.

Formerly it was the rule among riding masters not to break-in a horse for high-school work until he was at least seven years old. For many years I thought and acted like the others, and to make my school horses. I took animals of from seven to eight years old ; but little by little, I became impressed by what I saw on racecourses. At Epsom, Chantilly, Auteuil, and Longchamp, the longest and severest races were reserved for three-year olds.* I observed that when breaking-in a school horse I did not require from him a tenth of the exertion which he would have to do, if he was trained or raced. Starting on the principle that if a horse can do much, he can do little, I came to the conclusion that a three-year-old which could stand training and racing, would much more easily stand school breaking. Although this reasoning appears to me to-day to be very simple, I was not able to act on it without extreme timidity, so great is the influence of preconceived ideas. Whenever I spoke about it to horsemen and authorities of that time, they shrugged their shoulders, and regarded it as nonsensical. Since then I have learned

---

* Without doubt the objection will be made that a great number break down in training. To this I reply that they begin their training at the age of eighteen months, which is a very dangerous proceeding. I finally propose to begin breaking at three-and-a-half years ; the amount of exertion which I require being far less than that incurred during training.

that every attempted innovation runs a great chance of being received in this manner.

Nevertheless I decided, not without great apprehension, to make an experiment, and I took in hand a four-year-old which had been well looked after. I found that he had quite as much strength, and much more suppleness, than my other pupils which were seven years old. Encouraged by this result, I tried a three-year-old with the same success. Since then I have broken-in for high-school riding a score of thoroughbreds of this age, and have always obtained better results than with older horses.

Finally, I pushed the experiment further, in order to find out the greatest amount of exertion which could be demanded from a very young horse without distressing him. I broke Viscope, a thoroughbred mare by Vermouth out of Vinaigrette,* when she was two years old. At three years her education was complete as a hack, jumper, and school horse, and she received a medal at the horse show. She is now seven years old, perfectly sound, unblemished, and had not even a windgall when I disposed of her.

I could cite many other examples. I only wished to explain how experience led me to the conclusion that to take a horse at three-and-a-half years old in order to break and train him for any particular work, is to begin at an age when all horses which have been properly brought up and fed, can stand work. Further, it is to take him at an age when progressive muscular exercise is indispensable to him. This exercise, so far from wearing him out and making him unsound, strengthens his limbs and body, and quickly puts him in full possession of all his powers.

* The precocity of the thoroughbred will of course be put forward as an objection to what I say ; but we are not concerned with two-year-olds. Besides this, the precocity of feeding and exercise has always appeared to me to have a more decisive effect than the precocity of breed.

A three-and-a-half year old horse is more supple and can be more easily educated than a five-year-old. He has not been able to acquire the faults of temper which we find in him later on, and which are almost always the result of injudicious or cruel treatment by people about him. He has not the bad habit—which all horses left to themselves contract—of going on his shoulders, on which account the hind quarters become less developed than the forehand. We can then easily make him rely on himself, and put equal weight on all four limbs, which is of great importance; because true equilibrium of the body is the one thing of all others which we should try to obtain in breaking and riding.

The horse ought to be neither on his shoulders nor on his haunches; but should have his own weight and that of his rider equally distributed on both ends. Only on this condition can he be light, active, and sure-footed, and capable of doing long and severe work without injuring himself, When a horse has been addicted for a long time to the habit of standing and moving in a state of bad equilibrium, his conformation becomes distorted and can rarely recover from its effects. If, as is the most frequent instance, the horse is on his shoulders, his hind quarters are soft and drag themselves along the ground, on account of want of exercise and development; but the forehand works too much and becomes fatigued. Being overloaded and heavy, it has difficulty in changing its place, and the slightest mistake or weakness will involve the entire body. The limbs which are overworked become soon worn out. This is the only cause of the premature reductions which each year decimate the effective strength of cavalry squadrons, and put many horses out of work at an age when they ought to be in their prime.

The most essential part of breaking a horse is to teach him to balance himself properly. No one will deny that a horse can be more easily educated at three-and-a-half than at five

years, consequently it is most important to begin with a horse
at the former age.

The entire question is whether a three-and-a-half years
old horse is or is not sufficiently developed and strong to be
broken and worked. In this respect theory and argument
are useless ; for facts are only of value, and in this case are
undeniable and invariable. Half-breds can be broken and
trained for racing at two-and-a-half, and they become so fit
and well, that they can run at three. Their work during the
six months of training and during their races is twenty times,
a hundred times more severe than that which a troop horse
undergoes during his very moderate and restricted course
of breaking. We are therefore right in concluding that
remounts ought to be bought at three years old ; and by
taking this as the average age, we give a chance to backward
breeds, and also to the ordinary methods of breeding, which,
being as economical as possible, have a retarding influence
in spite of everything.

Remounts at four-and-a-half and five years of age are not
really what they appear to be, because they have not been
properly fed and exercised. I am not afraid of adding that
they are worth more at three years, because they have suffered
for a shorter time, and because the watery and debilitating
food which their breeders give them, though insufficient for
their requirements during the first three years, becomes most
detrimental to them during their fourth and fifth year.
Instead of improving from three to five years by means of the
food of his breeder, the young horse deteriorates.

Whatever one does, whatever price or premium one gives to
the breeder, he will not feed his stock properly between the
age of three and five, because it is not his interest to do so.

But we can easily get him to have his animal in good
condition at three years of age. Precisely because breeding
is a trade, the breeder's chief object is to get rid of his stock,

as early as possible. Knowing that every three-year-old which is in good condition and is well developed will be taken, he does his best to promote the development of the animal. With a horse which he sells at three years of age, at a price even lower than what he would obtain for him between four and five, he can defray the cost of feeding, which he could not continue much longer. He is forced to make this expenditure, under pain of not being able to sell his stock, because with a three-year-old there is but little trickery. Above all things the horse must have height, which he will not have unless he has been well fed and well looked after.

Finally, the State by buying young horses would no longer have to compete against dealers of all countries, because it can do what they cannot do. In fact, a dealer buys only to sell again, with the shortest possible delay ; but the three-year old, when he leaves his breeder's hands, is not fit, even for fashionable work. He requires to be fed on corn and broken during a fairly long time, say, for about a year.

When the remount authorities buy a horse between three and four years of age, they put him out to a farmer, whose interest is to have him poorly fed, or he is sent to a remount depot. Either in the former or latter case, the horse is under better conditions than he was when with his breeder, although the conditions are not perfect. He does not improve as much as he ought to do, and he takes eighteen months before he is ready.

I consider that these young horses should be taken in hand at once, and put on food which will complete their development, will give them the desirable strength and docility, and will make them ready for work at the end of six months. In a word, they ought to be fed on corn and broken in, from the first day, but gradually and methodically.

A remount depot, instead of being an equine sheep-fold, as it was recently defined by a general officer, ought to be a true breaking school, strictly supervised and managed by a competent man, who should have well-instructed horsemen under him.

Young horses are not got into condition by stuffing them with oats, nor broken in by giving them lots of exercise and quickening their paces.

When the horse is between three and four,* he leaves his breeder and is put into a stable. I beg my readers to note the progressive conditions of the following programme, which I propose, for feeding and work during the first three months.

FIRST MONTH.

First fortnight. Six litres (5¼ quarts) of oats a day,† 2 in the morning, 2 at noon, and 2 in the evening. Leading by the hand for an hour in the school, or better still, in the open, if the weather is fine.

Second fortnight. Seven litres (6 quarts) of oats ; 2 in the morning, 2 at noon, and 3 in the evening. The same leading by hand.

Lunge the horses for five minutes daily, half at the walk, and half at a slow trot.

SECOND MONTH.

First fortnight. Eight litres (7 quarts) of oats ; 2 in the morning, 3 at noon, and 3 in the evening.

---

* Colts ought to be cut at least six months before any work ; at two-and-a-half years at latest. Horses which are ridden too soon after the operation always become weak in the loins, and exhibit a characteristic rocking of the croup.

† I take for granted that the animal has never eaten oats. If he has been fed on oats, he can get at first, 8 litres (7 quarts) ; 2 in the morning, 3 at noon, and 3 in the evening.

When I speak of oats, I mean French oats, and not that horrible stuff which is given even now in the army, under the name of white Russian oats.

The time for leading by hand can be increased by half an hour.

The lunging should be very gradually increased, up to making the horse trot on each hand for five minutes without stopping. A few minutes' interval should come between the changes of hand.

Second fortnight. Nine litres (8 quarts) of oats ; 3 in the morning, 3 at noon, and 3 in the evening. The same leading and lunging.

Usually, a horse is given three feeds during the twelve hours between six in the morning and six in the evening, and he is therefore left without food for twelve hours, which I think is a bad method of distribution. The first feed ought to be given at five in the morning, and the last at eight in the evening.

THIRD MONTH.

First fortnight. Ten litres (8¾ quarts) of oats ; 3 in the morning, 3 at noon, and 4 in the evening. Twelve litres 10½ quarts) of oats should be given to heavy cavalry horses. This ration and the same leading by hand should be continued. The speed of the trot should be increased during five minutes towards the end of the lunging on each side, and the horses ridden at the walk in clothing in a plain snaffle for five minutes, the men having neither whip nor spurs. The horses should be quietly saddled in the stable, and loosely girthed up. At first the saddles should be left on for only a few minutes, and the time gradually increased.

Second fortnight. The same work, saddling and bridling the horses in the stable and putting them on the pillar reins. Bridling after lunging, and direct flexions of the jaw. Lunging at the trot when saddled and bridled, with the stirrups hanging down. As lunging at a canter puts a horse too much on his shoulders, it should not be practised until the

15*

animal is broken and well balanced. No caveson should be used in lunging, only a snaffle bridle, and any light rope, a forage cord, for instance.

When the horses are ridden, some men should be kept in reserve to catch hold of the bridles of any of them which do not want to follow the track. This is not a matter of mouthing, but is merely to strengthen the animal's loins and to accustom him to carry a man.

After the three months' feeding which I have advised, the horses will have had enough corn put into them to bear more work. As they have developed their muscles at the trot, learned to carry a man, have been bridled and saddled, and have had their jaws loosened by flexions ; they are, I think, ready for mouthing, which is well under way. In fact, only the A, B, C of breaking is required from the troop horse, without any elaboration. It will be well if he needs rather strong indications, for we should take precautions against heavy hands and rough legs. The horse's breaking is finished when he freely goes forward under the action of the legs, while taking hold of the snaffle ; and when he readily jumps, turns, and reins back. Here we require only *horizontal equilibrium.* Without doubt, an attempt should also be made to get the animal in hand, although this condition should not be insisted upon. It will be sufficient if the rider knows when to place his horse's head in the necessary position for obtaining equilibrium.

The horse should be accustomed to objects and noises, so that he may not be afraid of them. An army horse should be bold and ready to pass anything. To teach him to do so, all sorts of objects should be placed under his feet in the school. He can be taught best in the stable, at the time of feeding, to stand the noise of tambours, clarions, clashing of arms firing, etc.

I consider that three months will suffice to properly

finish this elementary and special breaking with any kind of horse.

After these three months of preparatory work, the properly called breaking has to be undertaken.

FIRST MONTH.

First fortnight. Begin by lunging the saddled and bridled horse at a trot. Gradually increase the speed, by means of the driving whip, so as to make him get his hind legs under him. Press him up to his full speed for a few minutes, while *taking great care not to let him over exert himself;* because, in that case, he would put too much weight on his shoulders, or break into a canter. This work should continue for five minutes to each side.

Ride the horse quietly at a walk for a quarter of an hour, so as to accustom his back to the saddle, without hurting it.

Lead the horse for ten minutes ; practise the direct flexion ; make him turn on his forehand ; and rein him back.

Lead him for an hour in the school or, preferably, in the open if the weather is fine.*

Second fortnight. Similar lunging. Begin the changes of direction by voltes, and diagonal changes of hand, and going down the centre.

Teach the horse to yield to the heel. At the beginning, be content with two or three steps.

Finish with work by the hand.

SECOND MONTH.

Lunge at the trot for two minutes on each side. Ride. Repeat the preceding exercises. Divide the horses into twos and fours. Accustom them to cross each other in every direction. Frequently pull them up, so as to teach them

---

* This remark applies to the entire period of breaking.

to stand quietly. Do at a slow trot the same movements which had just been taught at a walk.

Increase the number of side steps in rotation. Rein back mounted. Work with the hand.

Second fortnight. Lunge in a similar manner. Confirm the preceding work. Do the ordinary changes of direction at the trot, with all the horses in twos and fours, and make them cross in every direction. Do the demi-volte and finish it up by a few side steps. Continue the work with the hand, while requiring the direct flexion* with the head high. Begin the lateral flexions, side steps and shoulder in.†

THIRD MONTH.

First fortnight. Similar lunging. Increase the speed of the trot in all the changes of direction, and in all the movements in which all the horses are working together. Lengthen the trot as much as possible in a straight line. "Two tracks." Begin starting into the canter on the right leg, and as soon as the horse will do this readily, make him lead off with the left leg.

When the horse has become proficient at the canter, make him do at this pace all the movements he has learned at the walk and trot. Increase and improve the suppling exercises by the hand.

At the end of the lesson teach the horses to jump (p. 195 *et seq.*).

Second fortnight. Similar exercises. Confirm and improve the preceding ones. Accustom the horses to flags, sabres, lances, firearms, explosions, passing through fire, swimming,‡ etc.

---

* Up to this, it should only be asked for.

† The shoulder to the wall, which is much more easy, should be done only when mounted.

‡ What should a rider do, when he is in water, trying to cross a river ?

We must not think that a horse which is not accustomed to the water will swim with ease the moment he loses his feet. The only idea which such an animal has, is to keep his head out of the water and to raise his neck as high as

By this kind of breaking, which ought to be continued for three months, the horse will have learned enough for all cavalry movements, and will only require to be accustomed to outside work in the manœuvres, and to become hardened, so as to be able to stand long marches and bad weather.

Fig. 49.—Horse and rider being drowned.

To recapitulate : The horse attains three years of age in the spring. If the remount authorities buy between April and September, he will be on an average three-and-a-half when he arrives at the depôt, where he will get three months prepa-

possible. Therefore, the croup will be pushed down, and the position of the horse will be a half-rear ; that is to say, he will be three-quarters upright (Fig. 49). This position will prevent him from advancing, and if his rider is inexperienced, the chances are ten to one that both will be drowned. If the rider pulls ever so little on the snaffle, or simply leans back, when he is in the

ratory work and. three months' breaking. At four years he
will be broken and perfectly ready for work.

Although it may be said that this four-year-old work would
prematurely wear him out, I assert, and experience proves

Fig. 50.—Rider making his horse swim according to Mr. James Fillis's method.

that, under the conditions I have laid down, it will develop
and strengthen him.

position just described, the horse's croup will become depressed more and more,
the animal will become upright, will turn over backwards, while beating the
water with his fore feet, and will end by sinking.

The moment the horse is carried off his feet, the rider should take hold of a
good handful of the mane, and bend forward on the neck; but he should on no
account touch the head of the horse. He should firmly close his knees, for if he
does not do so, the water will instantly separate him from the horse. This is the
only position which enables the man to remain in the saddle and the horse to
swim. The rider ought to hold one of the snaffle reins in each hand, and when
he wishes to change the direction to the right or left, he should, for the moment,
bring his hand away from the shoulder, so as to act on the animal's mouth. But,
as I have just explained, he should, above all things, avoid pulling the reins in a
backward direction (Fig. 50).

I presume that similar instructions are given to the cavalry of all nations.

In reality, an army horse is taken up when he is five years old, and a year is spent at his breaking, which is regarded as imperfect by competent men ; the reason being that he is put into movement before he is given equilibrium, which is the mainspring of correct and useful propulsion. This was the fault that Baucher found with old-time equitation, which knocked up horses by movement, whatever it was. Its teachers tried to obtain equilibrium, whatever it might be worth, by putting the horses into movement, so that they might get it for themselves. The actual change made by Baucher was to secure equilibrium at first, in order to obtain from it correct and useful movements. The only fault of the great riding master was wishing to perfect and refine this equilibrium, by rendering it unstable, before requiring forward movement. Although I disagree with him, in that I work my horses during *propulsion*, I do not the less begin, like he does, by getting my horse into equilibrium before putting him into movement, as previously explained. The difference between us is that, in place of demanding efforts from the horse while he is in a confined equilibrium, which is akin to immobility and getting behind the bit, I try from the first to make him obedient to the aids while he is in an equilibrium which is maintained during propulsion.*

Persons who trot and canter horses before teaching them to start with their weight equally distributed on all four legs, follow antiquated methods which spoil the breaking.

We cannot advantageously modify a horse's equilibrium by keeping up or increasing his speed at fast paces. Such a proceeding would accentuate his defects and would knock him up, without teaching him anything.

The great majority of horses are heavy in front, *particularly*

---

* The horse which is on his shoulders can move forward, but will drag his hind legs ; and he has no power of propulsion, which results from the hind legs being well under the body, in which case the necessary equilibrium is obtained.

when one begins to ride them. By making them go fast,
without having previously balanced them, one succeeds only
in putting their weight more and more forward, and in prematurely spoiling them. Such animals carry the head low
and the neck on a level with the withers, they are ugly, every
effort in turning or stopping is painful to them, and they
readily fall. Being able to place the head and neck as they
like, they can effectively resist the aids. In fact the neck
must be high and the head almost perpendicular, in order that
the curb may act with all its power.

The curb loses the greater part of its action on the bars,
when the head is low, in which case it is not much more severe
than a snaffle, and the horse gets out of hand. It is acknowledged that a very large percentage of troop horses refuse to
leave the ranks, which is a fact that proves that they are
badly broken.

A horse which will not obey is not broken. What a
poor result is obtained by a year or more of irrational
work !

The military regulations ought to insist that the breaking
should be conducted in such a manner that the remounts
would be fit to go into the ranks on the 1st April, in case of
mobilisation, which would entail a breaking of only three
months' duration. But in time of peace this period of breaking is *intentionally* prolonged for an entire year, and the
remounts are not sent into the ranks until the following year.
To justify this practice, it is alleged that those regiments
which put remounts into the ranks after three months'
breaking, are those which use up most horses. This may be
possible ; but I have my doubts.

The truth is that remounts which are badly prepared by
insufficient food and exercise, are prematurely broken down
by the mere breaking. Rational breaking is, on the contrary,
much quicker, and so far from fatiguing them develops them

and gets them into hard condition, which is a truth that I have demonstrated by incontestable facts.

I imagine that men would adapt themselves much more readily to the kind of breaking I have described than to the violent exercises which they have to go through, and which discourages them, because they do not know the reason. Instead of interesting them in riding and inspiring them with love for horses, which should be the master feeling of a rider, they are often made to suffer through the horses, and the horses through them. People may say that my breaking is too elaborate. How is it, then, that it is not found to be too elaborate by Germans, whose dominant quality is certainly not elaboration? Why do they work troop horses *individually* much more than they do in France? Why do they begin by balancing them? Why do they adopt rational breaking, instead of knocking up their horses? Why do their horses last for a long time? Alas! the reason for this is that they have profited by the teaching which has come to them from France; but in this classic country of riding we are kept back by routine.

CHAPTER VIII.

HIGH-SCHOOL RIDING.

The Spanish walk—Reversed pirouette on three legs—Reversed and ordinary
pirouettes with the feet crossed—Reining back without reins—Rocking the
forehand—Rocking the haunches—Spanish trot—Shoulder-in at the canter—
Pirouettes at the canter—Changes of leg at each stride—Changes of leg
without gaining ground—Piaffers and *passages*—Differences between the
passage and Spanish trot—Serpentine at the Trot—Canter on three legs—
Passage to the rear—See-saw piaffer—Canter without gaining ground
and canter to the rear—New school movements—School horse for ladies.

THE exercises which we are going to consider are the sequel
and perfected product of those which have been described.
These high-school exercises, as, for instance, the Spanish trot,
are more difficult, less used, and are artificial; but the others,
like the canter, are natural.

I have often heard it said that high-school work ruins horses
and prematurely makes them unsound.

It is constantly said : " How is it possible for an animal to
do such severe work without knocking himself to pieces ? "
The answer is very simple : Professional gymnasts also go
through extremely severe exertion. Are they in bad condition ? Are their arms, legs and shoulders spoiled ? On the
contrary, they are in a state of grand condition which distin-
guishes them from everyone else. Their muscles stand out
and are as hard as steel, and their general health is perfect.
No doubt, if they began their work abruptly—I speak of

horses as well as of men—they would not be able to stand it, and would break down. But if the effort required for the gradual exercises is proportionate to the increase of muscular power, the work—no matter how severe it may be—will be comparatively easy, and even healthy.*

It is true that many horses have been ruined by high-school work; but only because the work was badly carried out, or because the preliminary training was insufficient. Riding, like other sciences, has its charlatans and its empirics. When a horse has been methodically broken, the practice of all the exercises through which he has gone, so far from ruining him, will only strengthen him.

With respect to horsemen who turn up their noses at high-school riding, and speak of it with contempt, I content myself with reminding them of the fable of the fox and the grapes.

THE SPANISH WALK.

A horse is said to do the Spanish walk,† when he raises his fore legs one after another, by carrying them forward and extending them.

The principal thing to observe is the way in which a horse puts his foot on the ground; for although it is easy to make him raise his legs, it is very difficult to make him put them down properly.

The breaker ought to begin this work on foot, while standing at the left shoulder of the horse and on the left track, in which

* My horses never get even the slightest blemish from my breaking, although I begin to break them much earlier than any of my predecessors have done.

† It has never been known why this movement is called the Spanish walk. There is nothing Spanish in it, except the name, and it by no means resembles the walk of the Andalusian animal. When the Spanish horse walks, he bends his knees and brings the lower part of the legs inwards, which peculiarity is called *el pasode campaña* (the walk of the bell) on the other side of the Pyrenees. It would be more appropriately termed the "recruits' balance step," because there is a great similarity between the two.

case the wall will prevent him escaping to the right. He
should hold the head of the animal rather high, while pushing
him to the right, in order to throw the greater part of the
weight of the forehand on the right foreleg, and thus to allow
the left leg to be easily raised.

He should then very lightly touch the left fore leg of the
horse with the end of the cutting whip ; but it is somewhat
difficult to determine the exact spot where the leg should be
touched. The sensitive spot, which varies in each horse, lies
somewhere between the elbow and the pastern.

The horse's first impression is one of surprise, because he
does not understand what is required of him, and he generally
tries to escape. Nevertheless, he cannot go to the right, on
account of the wall, and if he swerves to the left, he ought at
once be straightened by the whip. If he runs back, the
breaker ought to immediately bring him forward by touching
him with the whip behind the girths. After a moment, he
almost always shows his impatience, by pawing the ground with
the leg which has been touched. As soon as he raises this leg,
he ought to be patted on the neck, in order to make him understand that he has done what was required. After repeating
this exercise for several days, the horse, in order to avoid being
touched, raises his leg the moment he sees the whip approaching
it. When he well understands, and does this work with the
left leg, the right leg should be submitted to the same practice,
by placing him to the right hand, and taking care to raise his
head and carry it to the left.

As the repeated touching of the whip irritates a horse, we
should at first be satisfied with the slightest sign of obedience,
and will thus take the best means of not disgusting the animal.
He will usually raise his legs during the first lesson ; but the
way in which he raises them will be far from satisfactory,
because he does not extend them, and contents himself by
making impatient movements, pawing the ground, etc. Never-

theless, as I have just said, we ought to be satisfied, at the beginning, by the semblance which he makes of raising his legs. It would be wrong to insist, or even to strike the animal, when we can do nothing with him, beyond astonishing him.

Nevertheless we should gradually obtain the extension of the legs, which will not be satisfactory, unless the legs are completely and horizontally extended at the height of the shoulders. In my opinion, it cannot be said that a horse does the Spanish walk, unless this height and extension are obtained.

As soon as the horse understands what he is required to do, and performs it correctly, that is to say, when he fully extends his legs horizontally, he ought to be taught to place them on the ground without the slightest bending of the knees, which is the most important condition in this movement. To succeed in this, we should, as soon as the legs are fully extended, draw the horse forward by the snaffle, so that he will place the foot well in front, the leg remaining straight until the foot touches the ground. If he bends the knee, he can take only a short step; and, besides, as the knees will be bent unequally, the steps will not be of the same length. Finally, if the horse is allowed to bend his knees, it will be impossible to prevent him pawing the ground, which would necessarily make the steps unequal. We should therefore take the greatest care to have the leg perfectly straight, until the foot touches the ground. When the legs are thus extended, the steps cannot fail to be equal in length.

As soon as we get the horse to take one correct step with each leg, we should not continue this work on foot, although the progress would certainly be more rapid.

The Spanish walk is much more graceful, brilliant and regular, if the breaker teaches it when he is in the saddle. In fact, when he is on foot, he has to draw the horse forward, and he cannot then get the animal in hand, because the forward pull causes the neck to be straightened. The head is consequently placed in a wrong and ungraceful position.

Instead of pulling the horse forward, it is far better to press him up with the legs. Therefore we can teach the Spanish walk only when mounted.

Having obtained the first two steps on foot, we should mount, and try to do the work I have just explained.

My plan is as follows : I hold the curb reins and the left rein of the snaffle in my left hand, and the right rein of the snaffle and the whip in my right hand.

Having stopped the horse, I take a sufficient hold of the snaffle to keep the head and neck high, and being on the left hand, I try to get the first step with the right leg. Having the wall on my right, I am certain that the horse cannot place himself sideways when I try with my left leg, to make him raise his right leg ; but if I were to try to make him raise his left leg, my right leg would force his croup round to the left.

I carry my hands to the left, and I strongly close my left leg, which is helped later on by the spur.

The right rein of the snaffle is drawn tighter than the left rein, and both legs are kept close to the girths, so as to prevent the horse reining back ; the left leg having a much stronger pressure than the right. The effect of the reins is to put almost all the weight of the forehand on the left shoulder. The left leg of the rider should now make the horse raise his right leg, for which object, having the whip pointed downwards, I lightly touch him several times on the right shoulder, while continuing to keep up his head with the right snaffle rein.

Being ignorant of what I want him to do, the horse will always become impatient ; therefore, we should make our demands on him in a very gentle manner. Nevertheless, we should keep on at him until he raises his leg. As soon as he makes the slightest movement with his right leg, we should stop and pat him on the neck, and walk him round the school before recommencing.

In a week, the horse will extend both legs. It goes without saying that I do similar work with his left leg, but in a reversed way.

From this period, I combine the respective actions of my legs and whip, and in proportion as I obtain the desired effect, I diminish the action of the whip, and increase that of the legs, until I obtain obedience solely by the legs.

After the horse answers to the indications of the legs, and, if need be, to those of the spurs, by complete extension, I drop the whip, and it is then easy for me to press him up to the bridle, which it would be impossible for me to do on foot.

I shall now describe in detail the action of the "aids" during the entire movement : the action of the left leg and right rein makes the horse raise his right leg. At the moment he is about to place it on the ground, I press him forward with both legs, the action of which performs the double office of keeping him straight and of obliging him to put down his right leg, completely extended, and in front of his left leg. I keep an equal feeling on both reins during the forward step, up to the time he places his foot on the ground. Then my right leg and left rein, in their turn, make him raise the left leg. The connection between one step and the next one should be made in this manner, and it should be done with great care, so as to obtain perfect regularity of movement. We have then had recourse, as we should always do, to a diagonal effect.

The Spanish walk can also be practised when reining back, in which case the reins draw the animal back, the moment the extension of the leg is obtained. The difficulty in this backward movement is to prevent the hind quarters from turning to the right or left, each time we bring the leg which is in the air, back in rear of the one which is on the ground.

It often happens that the horse, by going back too quickly,

16

gets out of hand, and only about half extends his fore legs. In this case we should always recommence the work by sending him forward and requiring a complete extension.

We must not think that we are always certain to succeed even by exactly following the directions I have given. It depends on the intelligence of the rider to use all the means in his power to make the horse understand what is required of him. This is a question of tact. Besides, when a riding master breaks his first horse he is not sure of himself, and he is, therefore, obliged to feel his way. Only after breaking three or four horses, he will be able to tell if he has done well or if he has failed.

A horse ought not to be asked to do the Spanish walk unless he is very supple, and, above all things, unless he is perfectly obedient to the aids. In fact, we should be always certain of making him go forward. But in this work we require him to stand the spur without hardly going forward.

As we are obliged to have the hands high in order to raise the neck, we thus throw a great portion of the weight on the hind quarters, and consequently risk making the animal get behind his bit. It may thus happen that instead of raising one fore leg, he will, by raising two, make a half-rear, which is not a formidable defence, because it is a forward movement. Or he may rear, which is more dangerous, especially if the reins are pulled. It frequently happens in breaking, that in order to make the horse go forward, we are obliged, for a time, to give up the attempt of obtaining a movement which we are teaching. If we sometimes tolerate, even a little, a tendency on the part of the horse to get behind his bit, we will soon be powerless to make him go forward. He will quickly understand that he can get out of hand by getting behind his bit, to which expedient he will continually have recourse.

All stationary work, the object of which is to teach the

horse to bear the touch of the spurs without hardly advancing, is always dangerous. It often makes a horse restive, in which case the method is almost always blamed, although it would be safer to blame the manner of its application. Besides, it is also difficult for a riding master who is breaking his first horse or his first horses, to avoid making them get behind their bit. Very often a horse has this tendency without the breaker perceiving it. As a general rule, if a horse does not go up to his bridle, he has this fault. Hence my motto is " forward, always forward, and again forward ! "

I admit that we can never obtain a concession from a horse without a more or less lively struggle, but we must not forget that a man's authority over a horse is dependent on this struggle.* If we require a difficult thing from a horse without having prepared him sufficiently, not only will there be a struggle, but—which is a much more serious thing—the horse will win. We should, therefore, know the precise instant when each demand can be made. This is a question of tact.

If we put a horse to some work for which he has been badly prepared, we may be certain that we shall not be successful. Without a proper preparation the horse will certainly resist.

The same work can be demanded later on without any trouble. It is better to try to break a horse in a year than in six months. The more difficult a horse is, the more time should be devoted to his education. If it is necessary, we may take six months to balance him well in his three natural paces, and to make him to rein back correctly before teaching him high-school work and artificial movements.

I would attach no importance to the Spanish walk, if I were

---

* It is well to note that after each stormy lesson, if the man is the victor, the horse's docility will be well marked in the following lessons. There is no exception to this rule.

not obliged to teach it to the horse, in order, later on, to complete his high school education by pirouettes on three legs, the Spanish trot, and the canter on three legs. For this, it is of the utmost necessity that the breaker can obtain, at will, extension of the legs, and especially by the spurs, which is the only means of keeping a horse in equilibrium, of teaching him to go up to his bit, and of making him hold his legs as high and as extended as he ought to do.

There is, alas! another way for teaching a horse the Spanish walk, and I hasten to say that I never use this method of which I am obliged to speak, because it is greatly in vogue among the new school. By this term I designate the riding masters who have sprung up since the death of Baucher, and who have substituted for the school movements he executed most brilliantly, a series of strange contortions obtained by a host of accessories, the employment of which necessitates the assistance of a large number of men.

To teach the Spanish walk according to the method of the new school, it is necessary to employ an entire squad of breakers—four privates and a corporal : never less, and often more.

They begin by placing on each fore leg a hobble, to which is attached a cord, each cord being held by a man. A third person holds the bridle and a cutting whip. The corporal mounts the animal, and a fifth tormenter has the noble mission of flourishing a driving whip. We will now see the collective operations which the squad performs on the unfortunate animal.

No. 3, who has the cutting whip, taps the left leg of the horse with it. No. 1, who holds the cord of that leg, pulls the leg straight, and the corporal, who is on the back of the animal, presses his right leg against the horse's side so as to accustom him to extend his leg on being touched by the spur.

At the same moment No. 5, who wields the driving whip, touches the horse on the croup to make him go forward.

Thus, a step with the left leg is obtained. No. 2, who holds the cord of the hobble, which is on the pastern of the right leg, comes on the scene only when the squad proceeds to manipulate the right leg in the way I have just described for the left leg. This double manœuvre continues until the horse has learned the Spanish walk.

This is a case which demands the intervention of the S.P.C.A. I am at a loss for a word to express this kind of proceeding. It is certainly not breaking, and has nothing in common with horsemanship.

REVERSED PIROUETTE ON THREE LEGS.

The reversed pirouette on three legs, the fourth being held in the air, during the rotation of the croup round the shoulders, is the easiest movement to teach the horse, of course supposing that he is well balanced ; because it is an affair of uniting, in a single movement, the rotation of the croup and the extension of the legs.

Having ridden the horse into the middle of the school, we make him take a few steps in the rotation of his croup, while stopping him at every three or four steps to make him extend his leg.

As we use the same leg for both movements it ought to be kept close to the girths, the other leg being the one which stops the rotation. For example, in the rotation of the croup round the shoulders from left to right, my left leg prompts the rotation of the croup, and also the extension of the horse's right leg. When the horse has described about a quarter of the circle of rotation, I stop him by the pressure of my right leg, and I touch him with the left spur, which I keep close to the girths, while at the same time I lightly feel the right rein of the snaffle, so as to oblige the animal to extend his right leg.

By frequent repetition we can soon make a horse take a step or two in the rotation of his croup, without putting his right fore on the ground, and little by little we can make him do the complete pirouette in this manner. We ought, during the entire time, to maintain a fairly strong pressure of the opposite leg, so as to keep the horse up to his bridle and prevent him getting behind his bit. To be in a good position, the horse should have his head and neck high, and his neck slightly bent to the right. The action of the right snaffle rein is necessary to make this bend, and to help in keeping the right leg in the air.

We use the reversed means to obtain the pirouette from right to left, with extension of the left leg.

The difficulty is to keep the right leg extended; the equilibrium on the three legs being sufficiently secure to allow the horse to maintain this position, and to move his hind quarters round the left fore foot, which forms a pivot and does not shift out of its place.

In the pirouette from left to right, we should carry the hands to the left, while lightly feeling the right reins, so as to put the weight of the forehand on the left shoulder. In the pirouette from right to left, the right foot is the pivot, and consequently we should carry the hands to the right, and feel the left reins, so that the right leg, in its turn, will bear the weight of the forehand, and thus allow the left leg to be raised.

REVERSED AND ORDINARY PIROUETTES WITH THE FEET CROSSED.

The reversed pirouette with the fore feet crossed is done in the same manner as the reversed pirouette on three legs, except that the fore legs, instead of being successively extended in the air, rest on the ground, and become crossed while the horse turns.

In the ordinary pirouette with the feet crossed, the forehand turns, and the hind feet become crossed. The former is very simple, and the latter very difficult.

REINING BACK WITHOUT REINS.

This movement is not very difficult to teach ; but it is not without annoyance to the horse and danger to the rider, because the legs and spurs are the only agents employed to make the animal go back, with the consequent risk of putting him behind his bit or making him rear.

I would not advise young and inexperienced breakers to try this exercise before they have broken several horses. Until they have done so, they will not be able to exercise the necessary judgment.

We may safely try it on impetuous horses, which are always ready to go forward ; but it would be a mistake to teach a soft or sluggish animal, because the vigorous use of the legs is the only way to make him go up to his bridle. In any case, we ought not to teach it to a horse without being certain that he will not take advantage of the instruction, by reining back in opposition to the wishes of his rider ; in other words, by becoming restive. Therefore, I do not begin this exercise until the horse is perfectly obedient, and, especially, until I am sure of being able to make him go forward under all circumstances.

In teaching it, I begin in the same way as I have described for the rein back (p. 119 *et seq.*), namely, I employ both legs and hands. By degrees I diminish the action of the reins, while indicating to the horse by means of the legs, which is the great difficulty, that the hind quarters should begin the movement. It is necessary in some sort of a way that the horse should be pulled back by our thighs and seat, and that he receives a backward propulsion from his forehand.

At first, I encounter some hesitation on the part of the

horse, which is all the greater because up to this time I have always trained him to go forward at the slightest pressure of the legs.　We should keep him as quiet as possible and not insist too strongly, because the less a horse understands what is required of him, the more irritable does he become. We ought to be content with two or three steps to the rear, and immediately he has taken them, we should make him take the same number of steps forward, by relaxing the pressure of the thighs, and by touching him with the heel or spur.　We should, above all things, avoid letting him rein back quicker than we wish him to do.

I sum up by saying that at first I close the legs and feel the reins sufficiently to bring about the rein back.　Having obtained the retrograde movement, I hasten to pat the horse on the neck, and I repeat the work, while each time increasing the pressure of the legs, and diminishing the tension of the reins.　Finally, when the horse has learned, little by little, what is required of him, I leave go the reins.

ROCKING THE FOREHAND.

In rocking the forehand, the horse raises his fore legs successively, without extending them, and rocks his forehand from one leg to the other, while separating them as widely as possible from each other, at the moment when they touch the ground.

Having taught the horse to extend his legs as already described, it is easy by this means to make him balance the forehand.　With this object, his head and neck should not be raised too high, and his legs should only be half straightened, which I get him to do in the following way.　The horse being halted, I make him raise the right fore, as if to extend it, but as soon as he raises it, and before he has completely extended it, I carry my hands to the right, and, consequently, all the weight of the forehand which was on the left leg is suddenly transferred to the right leg, and the horse naturally comes down on that side, while separating the right leg from the left.

Having obtained this first step, I demand a second one from the left leg, by employing similar means. I have then one time for one leg, and another time for the other leg, and to connect them I have got only to bring them together and to put them into harmony. The separation of the legs will naturally be in proportion to the action of the hands.

The action of the legs of the rider is the same as that for the extension of the animal's legs, but it ought to be simultaneous on both sides, so as to prevent the rocking of the croup.

In a short time we will obtain the alternate rocking of the forehand to the right and to the left.

We ought not to require a great separation of the fore legs until the rocking is very regular. The wider the separation, the slower, softer and more graceful is the movement. We can easily succeed in getting a separation of forty inches, and sometimes of five feet.

The rocking of the forehand is made on one spot, and it can also be made while advancing, in which case it is more graceful, and has the advantage of not prompting a horse to get behind his bit ; but it is much more difficult, because we must add forward propulsion to the other actions I have just described.

ROCKING THE HAUNCHES.

This movement requires more tact, as regards the seat, than the preceding one. To obtain it we should feel the reins very lightly, and should make the horse take a light bearing on the snaffle while pressing him down, so as to carry his weight on his shoulders. As the haunches become lightened, their mobility will be increased.

We should take care to keep the horse stationary and very

quiet ; for we are going to require from him two times, one after the other ; because one time will not be a school movement, and will not give him any indication.

I exert a very light pressure of the right leg, which causes the horse to raise his right hind leg, as if to make a side step to the left, but at the moment this leg comes close to the left hind, and before it is placed on the ground, a pressure of my left leg pushes it back into its place, and at the same time makes the horse raise his left hind, which he places by the side of the right hind, as if he were taking a side step to the right.

If the rider does not catch with precision the moment when the horse is going to put down his right leg, this leg will touch the ground without the rider having pushed it back to the right by the action of his left leg. Under these conditions, the right leg of the horse will be placed quite close to his left leg, and they will not be sufficiently separated for him to make a small rocking movement.

The rider should be content with these two first steps until the horse does them very steadily, and then he should demand them the reverse way, namely, from left to right. He should wait until later on to do four, and should increase the number gradually. I recommend the breaker not to try to obtain a great separation of the feet before the horse rocks in a very regular manner.

The spur has to be used, in order to obtain as great a separation as possible, so to give more vigour to the movement.

When rocking the haunches, the horse has a natural tendency to carry his head low, which at first I allow him to do to a certain extent, because he will thus lighten the hind quarters. As soon as he knows the work, I make him hold his head in the position which a school horse should always do.*

* With the head low a horse is never graceful and light. All horses which are broken by means of the cutting whip adopt the faulty position of having the croup high, the reason being that by striking the croup with the cutting whip, we

By increasing the pressure of the legs, and accentuating it a little by a touch of the spurs, we can easily obtain a small *piaffer* (p. 275) of the forehand, which accompanies the rocking of the haunches.

If we press the horse forward, while making him take very short steps, we will obtain rocking of the haunches with *passage* (p. 275) of the forehand.

The movement is less graceful when done without gaining ground, than when going forward, because there is a want of propulsion, and it is less easy to keep the neck high. Finally, as it is necessary to obtain a certain elevation of all the legs, we should avoid putting more weight in front than behind. On the contrary, we should carefully try to keep him in equilibrium.*

SPANISH TROT.

Of all artificial movements, the Spanish trot is the easiest and most brilliant. With a horse which knows the Spanish walk perfectly, nothing is easier than to make him do it at the trot.

It is enough to increase the action of the "aids" to give a horse more energy. At first we ride the horse at the Spanish walk, and when we have gone a few steps, we should seize the moment when the animal's leg is raised, to touch him more sharply with the spur.

I have never had horses which took a long time to do this

cause this portion of the body to become raised, as a result of stimulating the part. On this account I condemn the use of the cutting whip in high-school work.

Horses which have been "routined," I cannot say "broken," by the cutting whip, are always ugly and badly balanced. Having the neck on a level with the withers and the croup high, the forehand is depressed, and is consequently in a position the direct opposite of that of a true school horse (Fig. 62), which has always his neck high and his hocks well bent under the body.

* I believe I was the first to make a horse do the rocking of the haunches with *passage* of the forehand in 1880, at Paris, with the thorough-bred Amour.

movement.   But, as I have often said, I content myself with a little at the beginning of a new work.

Let us suppose, for example, that at the moment when the right leg is extended, I touch the horse sharply with the left spur, he will make a small leap forward : that is the first period.   I content myself with this, and pat him on the neck. Then I begin again.

When I am sure of my first period, I do not demand a second, but I begin, quite simply, with the left leg, in the same manner as I did with the right.

When I have obtained from my horse a single time of the trot on each leg, I demand two, but only when such particular time is correct in length and height, and is done with ease.

If one leg is lazier than the other leg, which is almost always the case, I work only that leg, which is the best means of impressing the memory of the horse, and of making him understand, by means of my indications, that he uses that leg too slackly.

Having established harmony, I connect the two first periods and afterwards demand four ; but no more for a long time, not even when the horse tries to do more of his own accord.

It is better to be contented with four times well done, than to try to quickly obtain a greater number which would be doubtful.

In the Spanish trot, the horse displays great energy,* of

---

* See Fig. 51.   The thorough-bred Markir (by the thorough-bred Anglo-Arab Cyrus, out of the thorough-bred Thérésine), at the Spanish trot : right diagonal in the air ; perfectly in hand ; head a little beyond the vertical ; and jaw bent.   Fig. 52, Germinal at the Spanish trot : left diagonal in the air ; and in hand.   The cutting whip would never give extensions of the legs like those shown in these two illustrations, which were entirely an affair of the spurs. We can see in these two cases, how the hock which is in the air is brought well under the body, which is the whole secret of the elevation of the forehand.   The expenditure of energy in Fig. 51 is so great that the fetlocks almost touch the ground.

Fig. 51.—Spanish trot ; right diagonal in the air ; perfectly in hand ; head a little beyond the vertical ; and jaw bent.

Fig. 52.—Spanish trot ; left diagonal in the air ; and in hand.

which we should not take undue advantage ; because if we wish to obtain twenty or thirty steps of this movement in a short time, it is certain that the last will not be as brilliant as the first, and the horse will acquire the bad habit of not extending his legs with energy.

If, on the contrary, we know how to be contented with little, the more modest our demand, the greater will be the energy which we can obtain in its execution.

Before requiring the horse to keep up the Spanish trot for a long time, we should wait until he can do it without effort. When he is very familiar with this movement, it will not fatigue him, and we can then make him do it three or four times round the school, but we should not go beyond that.

I have already said that during breaking, we should not allow the horse to take the initiative in any movement, for if we do so, he will take advantge of our leniency, and will not obey our orders. He will frequently do what he finds easy, and what pleases him ; but not what will please us. Thus, while we are teaching him the changes of the leg at the canter, he will often do more than we demand. If we allow him to do this, we will not be able to make him do the changes regularly, because he will do them of his own accord, without our being able to regulate him.

When a horse takes the initiative in a movement which we have taught him, we should correct him, but not harshly. If we leave him to go his own way, he will quickly take advantage of our slackness, and our authority will be lost.

If I say that in this case the punishment should never be very severe, I assume that in taking the initiative in a movement which he has been taught, he gives a proof of good will. Nevertheless, I repeat, it should not be tolerated. Each time he tries to do a movement for himself, we should

replace him in the position he previously occupied, and keep
him in it until he remains in it without trying to get
out of it.

I have often seen horses which had been taught the
Spanish walk use it subsequently as a defence. To every
demand they replied by extending their legs without moving
on. This was caused by their being taught artificial *airs*
too soon. Before coming to them, the horse should be very
supple and should be absolutely obedient in all natural
movements.

Young breakers generally wish to go too fast, and it
amuses them to see their horse extend his legs. When
he does it, even of his own initiative, they pat him on the
neck, and are astonished later on at not being able to get
him to do something else which they ask him.

It is easy to understand that a horse will use the Spanish
walk as a defence, when the order of the breaking is faulty.
In fact, when we teach him this movement we force him to
bear the spur, while remaining stationary. This is the great
danger in all breaking, because, if a horse has not been
at first accustomed to go freely forward on being touched
with the spur, he extends the leg, or leans on the spur.
Before teaching a horse to bear the spur without moving
forward, we ought always be sure of being able to make him
go forward by means of the spur when we wish.

It very often happens that a horse, through softness, uses as
a defence an *air* to which he is accustomed, but will never
use an *air* which requires great energy. As I have just said,
we should of course put him back into his old position, and
should prevent him from getting out of it.*

* When a horse who knows how to do a thing very well, becomes obstinate
on some particular occasion, he should be taken in hand very resolutely and
reduced to obedience by every possible means. I advise the rider never to yield ;
for if he does so, the animal will quickly understand that if he wants to be

Besides, the horse ought to be so intently occupied with his rider, during the entire course of a lesson, that he should think of nothing else ; and the rider should mentally act in a similar manner towards the horse.

The man, so to speak, ought to take entire possession of the animal, and should make him so attentive to his orders that the horse should not think of anything except what he is asked to do. As regards myself, I take such possession of the horse I ride, that the only idea I leave in his head is: " What is he going to ask me to do ? "

Certain authors say : " It requires so much time to do this, so much to do that, at the end of so many lessons we will be able to obtain this thing or that thing," etc. This is entirely wrong. One never knows how much time will be required to succeed in making a horse do any particular work.

Some horses learn very quickly what others acquire with great difficulty. On the other hand, the former are often very unruly when an attempt is made to teach them a movement which the latter will learn at once. In breaking, we should therefore pay great attention to the peculiarities of each horse, and should not be discouraged if we do not obtain a result in the time laid down in a book.

Thus, I have had horses which learned the Spanish walk in a week, and others which required three months with the same method of instruction.

---

master, he has only to "show fight." The rider ought, nevertheless, to keep cool, and never lose his temper, or at least, not to give way to anger, beyond allowing it to stimulate his energy, and to make him forget the dangers of the struggle. |

By such faults, the breaking of a horse, instead of being finished, becomes perverted. The slightest fault which is tolerated on one day, becomes aggravated on the morrow, and is converted into a vice which cannot be cured later on, except by the most severe battles. A broken horse is not a machine which requires only to be wound up, but is a living creature who continually tries to escape from the "aids" of his rider, and who requires to be constantly kept in the discipline of work.

With certain light and well-shaped horses, I have obtained changes of the leg at the canter almost immediately ; although the majority of horses generally require six months to learn to do it properly. The same can be said of everything in riding.

SHOULDER-IN AT THE CANTER.

I have put demi-voltes at the canter into ordinary riding, because one might require, when hacking, to take a few steps at the canter on two tracks, in a more or less correct manner, in order to get out of somebody's way. I will now take up the study of the canter in high-school riding.

When the horse does demi-voltes correctly at the canter, I try by shoulder-in work at the canter, to bring his shoulders away from the wall. For this, the horse has been admirably prepared by work on two tracks at the school walk, and further by demi-voltes at the canter.

I start my horse at a canter on the near fore, and being on the right track, I keep him on it for a few strides. I then carry my hands to the right, in order to bring his shoulders away from the wall, but only about a yard. I work my right leg strongly, in order to carry the haunches from the right to the left ; whilst my left leg receives, so to speak, the haunches, which my right leg has just sent it, and throws the impulse on the hand. In fact, the left leg presses the horse forward, and thus prevents him from getting behind his bridle. It also regulates the pace by preventing the animal from sidling off to the left. If there is nothing to check the speed of the pace to the side, whether at the walk, trot, or canter, the horse will fatally regulate his pace, and will rush to the side in order to get out of hand, that is to say, he will no longer keep on two tracks. It is therefore necessary, in order for the movement to be regular, that the rider can regulate the cadence at all paces, and that he always keeps his legs close to the sides of the horse, in order to keep him in hand, and to be able to make him go forward at any moment.*

I have said that I carry the hands to the right in order to bring the shoulders away from the wall.   The pressure of the left rein on the neck should be the only means employed to bring the shoulders to the right, and it should cease the moment the shoulders leave the wall, under pain of stopping the shoulders.   We should instantly carry the hands to the left ; the left rein acting directly to its own side, and the right rein pressing, in its turn, on the neck to push the shoulders to the left.   This is an effect of the left diagonal,   The left rein, by lightly drawing the forehand to the left,† prevents the hind quarters from going in advance of the fore hand.   In "two tracks," the haunches are always inclined to go in front of

* Fig. 53.—Germinal at the canter: shoulder-in ; going from right to left. This is the second period of the canter, and the right diagonal is in support. The right hock is about to be extended, and the near fore has not yet come down.

Fig. 54.—Germinal at the canter : shoulder-in ; going from left to right. Left diagonal in support.

Fig. 55.—Germinal shoulder-in at the canter ; going from left to right in complete *rassembler*.   We will note that the horse gains less ground, and especially, that the canter of the *rassembler* is in four time, namely, near hind, off hind, near fore, off fore.   In Fig. 55, the off hind has just been put down after the near hind, and the near fore—which, in the ordinary canter, would be put down at the same time as the off hind, so as to make the third time, namely the left diagonal in support—has not yet been put down.   This canter is therefore in four time.   It should be noted that there is a moment when the off hind and near fore, which form the left diagonal, are in support at the same time ; but what makes the four time is the fact that the off hind precedes a little the support of the near fore.

† For a long time, like all riding masters since the time of Baucher, I bent the horse's neck to the side he was going ; but I found out that this was a mistake because nothing is more liable to stop propulsion.   I now restrict myself to lightly *inclining* the head of the animal to the side he is going by only very slightly bending the neck.   The rein of the side opposite to which he is moving can then have its full effect to push the fore hand, to keep the horse straight, and to secure the maximum amount of propulsion, by its combination with the other rein and with the legs.

the shoulders, especially in demi-voltes, which is a fault we should carefully check; because the moment the haunches go before the shoulders in an oblique line, the horse is behind the bit.

Immediately after I do similar work for the shoulder-in at the canter, from left to right.*

PIROUETTES AT THE CANTER.

In the pirouette at the canter, the horse's hind legs ought, so to speak, to " mark time " at that pace, while pivoting round, in order that the haunches may remain on the same line as the shoulders, which describe a circle round them. A horse should on no account rest continuously on one of his hind legs, as some authors maintain, for if he does so, he will stop cantering.

Before pirouettes are required at the canter, they should be taught at the walk, with the horse very well *rassemblé*'d. With this object, I place my horse in the centre of the school. If I wish to make a pirouette, with the shoulders turning round the croup from left to right, I carry my hands to the right, the right rein drawing the head to the right, and the left rein pressing both the neck and the shoulders to the right. Both legs are firmly closed, the left leg being carried a little back, to fix the croup and to prevent it turning, whilst the right leg presses the horse up to his bridle, so as to prevent him getting behind his bit. This work requires great delicacy and lightness of hand. If the hands are too strongly used from left to right, their action will cause derangement of the shoulders, but not a pirouette. If the hands feel the reins too strongly from front to rear, the horse will get behind his bit.

When the horse fully understands this work and does it

---

* I do not allude to the shoulder-to-the-wall; because I regard it as a bad exercise in which the horse is really held by the wall, so that he is no longer under the guidance of the rider.

Fig. 53.—Shoulder-in at the canter; going from right to left.

Fig. 54.—Shoulder-in at the canter; going from left to right; left diagonal in support.

Fig. 55.—Shoulder-in at the canter; going from left to right in complete *rassembler*.

easily at the walk, I canter him on a rather larger circle, and gradually shorten his stride ; not from front to rear, but by the shoulders, while gaining ground to the side ; and I increase the action of my legs, in order to keep up the speed. The hind legs ought to "mark time" at the canter ; but, as I have just said, the horse ought never to turn by continuously resting on one hind leg. The pirouette ought to be done as slowly as possible, The great difficulty consists in obtaining a very slow canter, without losing that pace. I employ reversed means for the pirouette from right to left.

We can also do at the canter reversed pirouettes, which consist in making the croup turn round the shoulders. This is an excellent exercise at the walk, but I never teach it to my horses at the canter, because the great difficulty in all work is to make the shoulders move. In reversed pirouettes, on the contrary, we teach the animal to keep his shoulders stationary, which is an absurdity in riding. Besides, this movement is ungraceful, because the fore legs, not being able to gain ground, remain stiff while stamping on one spot.

On the other hand, ordinary and reversed voltes are graceful and useful. We obtain them by means of the same "aids" by which we get pirouettes, only we make the horse describe a large circle instead of turning him on one spot.

When we begin a volte, it is difficult to previously determine the exact diameter of the circle which we are going to make ; but, nevertheless, this will be the only means for the rider to know if his horse is right. To find this out, it is sufficient to trace a circle at the centre of the school. If a horse follows it exactly, he does so, because his position is good, and he is well-balanced in propulsion.

When a horse does correctly at the canter all the different exercises just described, we can ask him to do any movement at the canter. Having been made supple and obedient by all

the preceding exercises, he will never refuse to obey the orders
of his rider, provided that the man is patient and tries his best
to make the animal understand.

CHANGES OF LEG AT EACH STRIDE.

I have discussed, in the hacking canter, the changes from
the outward to the inward leg upon a straight line. I shall
now speak of the changes of leg in the school canter. I teach
the horse the changes of leg from within to outside, only when
he does them from outside to within very easily, and of
course I use similar means. In the beginning, we should
carefully avoid getting the horse to do them in the corners
of the school, the outward side of the horse having, by reason
of the turning movement, more ground to cover, which fact
requires a stronger support of the rider's opposite leg * to
prevent the horse going sideways, and to press him forward
on to the hand. We should not require changes of the leg
from within outwards in the corners of the school until he
does them easily in a straight line.†

I never require the shoulder-to-the-wall ‡ at the canter
before obtaining the changes of leg in the air—that is to say,
at the canter without stopping, because when we require the
horse to change from the outward leg to the inward one, he
almost always tries to bring his haunches to the inside, as he
does in the shoulder-to-the-wall, since the same "aids" are

---

* "Opposite leg" means the leg opposite to that with which the horse changes.
If I am going to the right, and the horse is cantering with the off fore, I use my
right leg to make him change and the left leg to keep him straight. If I do not
receive the horse on my left leg, the croup will inevitably swerve towards the
wall.

† It is always very difficult to make the horse change correctly when turning.

‡ I have previously explained that I never do, properly speaking, the shoulder-
to-the-wall in the sense that I will not allow my horse to be guided by the wall.
I use this expression because it is the popular one, but as I do this work always
away from the wall in voltes, it would be more correct to call it "shoulder-out."

used. If the rider's inward leg does not instantly receive the change of leg which his outward leg sends it, the horse will naturally put his croup sideways. Under these conditions, the changes of leg are never regular or well done. And, as it always takes two or three strides to straighten a horse, it will be impossible to do these changes with short intervals between them.

On the outside the evil is less, because the wall prevents the haunches from being brought too much round.

When the changes are correctly done with both legs to the right and to the left, and especially in the corners of the school, I only then begin to regulate them, which it is impossible to do before being certain that the horse will change each time, and at the moment I want him.

At first I content myself with getting him to change in every eight or ten strides of the canter, and I demand only a single change on each leg. If he becomes excited, he should be stopped and practised again at starting.

To be on good terms with the horse, it is necessary to count the strides of the canter. For example, when going to the right, with the horse cantering with the off fore, I count 1, 2, 3, 4, 5, 6, each number marking a stride. At the sixth I make him change, and then I make him do the same work with the near fore leading. If the horse does correctly the two changes I have asked, I stop him and pat him on the neck. I then begin again by requiring him to do only a single change on each leg.

At the end of a few days, when I feel that the horse does this work freely, I demand four and then six changes, always at the sixth stride. As long as the horse does this work in a tranquil frame of mind, I gradually increase the number of changes at the sixth stride, or, as it is said, at the sixth " time," but without over-doing it.

If the horse gets excited I stop him, but I do not pat him,

for, if I did so, he might think that I was encouraging him to
get excited.   I walk him, well in hand, and then I begin again
the lesson, which I do not finish until he has done the changes
steadily.

The pitfall in the changes of leg exist entirely in the pre-
parations which the breaker generally makes to obtain them.
Of course, I do not allude to the preparation of the horse,
which is indispensable, but only to the movements of the
breaker before the exact moment when he wants the horse to
change.   It is extremely important that he remains quiet while
the horse is taking his strides, during which the animal should
not change.   Thus, during the first five strides he should not
make the slightest movement.   He ought not to change his
"aids" until the sixth time, and should then change them
together and with great precision.   If at the fourth or fifth
time he prepares to make the horse change, he will be taking
a wrong course, because the horse, being very sensitive to the
"aids" and attentive to the demands of his rider, will become
disunited.   If he touches the reins, the forehand will change,
and if he alters the position of his legs, the hind quarters will
change.   But as there will be no harmony between the "aids,"
the horse will not change his legs.

It is wrong to blame the horse for becoming disunited,
because in such cases the rider almost always provokes him
to do so, by not remaining perfectly quiet until the decisive
moment.

It also happens that the horse, thinking that he is going on
all right, does not attend to his rider's demand, and anticipates
the order, or what he thinks is the order.   Therefore I cannot
too strongly advise the rider to keep absolutely quiet during
the first five strides of the canter.

It happens with all horses, that when they have learned to
do the changes easily, they will do them of their own accord,
and without an indication from the rider.   In this case the

horse should be punished, because if we let him take the initiative, we can get no regularity in the changes.

When I say that he ought to be punished, I mean that the fault ought to be checked.   Thus, if when the horse is canter-ing on the off fore, he changes before we ask him to do so, he should simply be touched more sharply than usual with the left spur, in order to oblige him to rest on the right leg. Of course we should use the right spur in a similar way, if the horse has started with the left leg leading.   Having checked the fault in the manner I have indicated, we should avoid again requiring a change of leg in the air during the same lesson, as it might confuse the horse.   It is better to go back to the starts, while keeping him for a long time on the same leg.

If we have checked the same fault several times and have taken care to pat the animal when he changes only when we ask him, he will soon understand that he ought not to do anything without being asked.   But, I repeat, we should do the changes only when we have not been obliged to punish the animal.   It is better to devote several lessons to checking the fault, in which case the horse will understand much better, will be quieter, and his breaking will be more rapid.

I make the horse change at shorter intervals only when he fully understands what I want him to do.   Instead of be-ginning at the sixth time, I demand the change at the fourth time, by using always the same means.   For the first few times I content myself with a single change with each leg, and during the following days I gradually require a greater number of changes.

We can see that the shorter the interval between the changes, the greater will be the effort required from the horse, who is consequently apt to become irritable and con-fused, in which case he should be halted, walked for some

18

time, but not patted on the neck. After that, we should begin again starting at the canter on each leg with the horse well in hand, without asking him to change, and should not finish the lesson until he has become perfectly quiet.

Each time that I find any difficulty in the changes of leg, I go back to starting at the canter, which I find very profitable. The starts are for the horse, what scales are for pianists, and steps for dancers.

From four times I do three, then two, and finally one, in which each stride of the canter ought to be done on a different leg. I leave a sufficiently long time to elapse between each of my demands—from four to three, from three to two, and from two to one.

If we go too fast we will not succeed, for the horse cannot help making mistakes, because he has not had the chance of understanding the difference between the changes of leg demanded at different times.

By going quietly in riding, we shall be certain of succeeding quickly. Besides, the horse is the one who indicates to us the number of changes and the interval between them without spoiling his equilibrium, strength, or lightness.

Only when he is quiet, light in hand, and when he does the changes with ease, do I obtain the changes in two time, and then in each stride, during two or three turns round the school on both hands ; and I make him do the same work in two times, in voltes and changes of hand. When I am satisfied with the results obtained, I make him do the changes at each stride in these movements.

The rider who succeeds in doing the voltes and changes of hand, while making the horse change very steadily at each stride, can be satisfied with himself and with his horse, because he has overcome the great difficulty in riding.

CHANGES OF LEG WITHOUT GAINING GROUND.

To do the changes of leg at the canter without gaining ground, we should proceed in the same manner as in the changes at each stride, with only the difference that the horse should be better in hand.

It might appear that in this movement we should greatly increase the feeling on the reins, and diminish the pressure of the legs, in order to make the horse go slower. This would be a mistake; for in that case the hands would bring the hocks away from the centre of the body. We should, on the contrary, act vigorously with both legs, to keep up propulsion, without which the canter will be lost. The hand ought to take possession of this propulsion in a very light manner, and ought to drive it back to the horse's centre of gravity, which is close to the rider's legs, when the animal is well balanced.

Changes which are made without gaining any ground are hardly perceptible to the eye, on account of the very short extension of the fore and hind legs. Hence we have to be very close to the horse to see these changes.

We owe the invention of this difficult and complicated exercise to Baucher, who did it brilliantly on Turban; but not on Partisan, as many assert.

PIAFFERS AND "PASSAGES."

The natural *passage* is a very well collected, short and high trot, which is regularly cadenced from one diagonal to the other. But to fully merit the title of *passage*, the fore legs, being raised high, but gently, should pause for a moment in the air, with the knees and feet bent. The hind legs are raised and the hocks and pasterns are bent and carried

18*

under the centre.   To sum up : all four legs should be raised
high and in cadence, so that the horse is suspended in the
air from one diagonal to the other.   This natural *passage*,
which is graceful and brilliant, ought also to be slow, and as
high as possible.*

We should bear in mind that no horse will do the *passage*
of his own accord ; for it can be obtained only by teaching.
Some horses can be very easily taught the *passage*, especially
those which have slow paces and bend their knees ; that is
to say, those which have high action before and behind, and
bend their knees and hocks—in a word, slow and high
action.

A horse which goes stiffly, without bending the knees or
hocks, is not fit for this movement.   I will not go so far as to
say that he cannot be taught it, but supposing that he is made
to do it, he moves ungracefully, because he looks stiff, on
account of dragging his feet.

It is extremely difficult to explain how the natural *passage*
is obtained.   The first thing is to *rassembler* the horse,
without doing which the *passage* is not possible ; but collecting
him is not enough, for he has also to be taught to *passage*.

Having perfectly collected him, we ought to use the spur,
in order to obtain the raising of the legs, which gives the
passage.

While riding the horse at a well-balanced walk, I make him
trot, by strongly closing my legs, while keeping him well in

* Fig. 56.—Germinal at the *passage* : right diagonal in the air.

Fig. 57.—Markir at the *passage* : left diagonal in the air.   In these two
illustrations, we will note the elevation of the legs, the fore one being raised
much higher than the hind.   The spur is the only means for obtaining this
result.   The contrary takes place with horses broken by the cutting whip, which,
by being applied to the croup, fatally produces a predominant elevation of the
hind quarters.

In Fig. 57, the fetlock being extended almost to the point of touching the
ground, is preparing the energetic spring which will give height ; but in Fig. 56,
the forward movement is the more accentuated one of the two.

Fig. 56.—*Passage* ; right diagonal in the air.

Fig. 57.—*Passage*; left diagonal in the air.

hand, to prevent him extending himself. Not being able to extend his legs, he raises them, and thus gains in height what he loses in length. At the same time, with the spur helping, he makes, so to speak, little jumps from one diagonal to the other, which are the beginning of the *passage*. But the cadence is not yet correct, because he always becomes irritated at first, as he does not know what we want him to do. During the first few days we should take care not to keep at him too long, if we wish to avoid making him play-up.

The horse, being irritated by the spurs, and not understanding why they are used on him in this work, which is strange to him, sometimes gets into a state of desperation, through fear of the spurs, which are always close to his sides.*

If, at this time, we try to make the horse do what we want, we shall be wrong, and shall probably lose the battle ; because, when the quietest horse becomes maddened, he will fight like a demon.

We should keep calm, and at the slightest sign of cadence, that is to say, at the first, or later on, at the second time, we should stop using the " aids," pat the horse's neck, give him time to become quiet, and begin again.

A horseman who has great delicacy and tact, will stop the animal at the first time and pat him. But the less tact he has, the less capable is he of judging if the time is in cadence. Such a man will continue in his attempts to catch the cadence, and will succeed only in upsetting the nerves of his horse. These remarks explain the fact that a clever and tactful horseman will obtain all he wants from his mount, without making him either vicious or unsound. Being able to recognise the

* It generally happens during the breaking, that one day, or during several days, the irritated horse makes up his mind, plays his last card, and acts in the most furious manner. When the breaker, by means of tact and energy, has overcome his final resistance, the animal is submissive, but is not broken.

slightest sign of obedience, he immediately stops the work, in order to make the horse understand, by pats on the neck, that he has done well. The quickness with which he perceives the slightest signs, saves him from overtaxing and disgusting the horse, and provoking him to battle, which will wear them both out.

The unskilful rider, who is slow in catching the cadence, will continue to use the spur, in order to obtain several cadenced times, and to be sure he is right, and will thus punish the horse, who, not knowing why he is punished, will defend himself, while the rider is spurring him. The result will be, that when he wants the horse to again do the *passage*, the animal will think he is going to be punished, and will become mad at the approach of the spurs.

Hence, the important point is to recognise the slightest signs of good will, and to be content with little. If the horse does not fear the approach of the legs, and if we are not too exacting, a time will always arrive when he will take up the cadence of the *passage* with ease and pleasure. We may then ask more ; because, as the horse understands us, there will be no fear of over-exciting his nervous system.

All the work on " two tracks " can be made at the *passage*, but it is difficult to do it correctly.*

The artificial *passage* is another form, which is only an adjunct of the Spanish walk. It is an uncollected *passage*, and consequently it is opposed to all the principles of equitation. I practised it in my youth, when I had not

* Fig. 58.—Markir at the *passage* on " two tracks " from left to right, with the left diagonal in the air. The position is that of " two tracks," but the action is that of the *passage*.

Fig. 59.—Markir at the *passage* on " two tracks " from left to right, with the right diagonal in the air. Here the movement on " two tracks " is well marked. The near hind, which gains but little ground, is well raised. The off fore, after having been raised, like the off fore in Fig. 58, is carried away from the near fore, in order to gain ground to the right.

Fig. 58.—*Passage* on "two tracks" from left to right ; left diagonal in the air.

Fig. 59.—*Passage* on "two tracks" from left to right ; right diagonal in the air.

enough tact to obtain the natural *passage*.   I never teach it nowadays.*

The *piaffer* is only a natural *passage* without gaining ground.   There are two kinds of piaffers : one, which is slow, high and difficult, and which some horses will not stand ; the other, which is hurried and close to the ground, and which almost all horses can learn.

The high and slow piaffer differs from the natural *passage*, only by its being done entirely without gaining ground.   We can obtain it by shortening the *passage* step by step, until it is done on one spot.   The piaffer therefore requires more *rassembler*, and therefore more use of the legs and more delicacy of the hand, than the *passage*.†

When a horse has not been taught the *passage*, the piaffer will be a consequence of the walk.   A vigorous and impatient horse can easily be taught the hurried piaffer, which will not be regular unless he has been instructed in accordance with the rules of equitation.

It is not enough for the horse to be lively and vigorous, in order to make him do the piaffer by exciting him with the cutting whip, legs, or clicks of the tongue.   By these means we will no doubt succeed in making him impatient, but not in teaching him the manner in which he should put his feet on the ground ; and we may be certain that if he puts them

* I could make similar observations respecting certain artificial *airs* which I have long given up with horses which I break for myself ; not because they are opposed to the principles of equitation, but because I do not find them sufficiently scientific ; as for instance, the Spanish walk, reversed pirouettes on three legs, ordinary and reversed pirouettes with the legs crossed, reining back without reins, and rocking the fore and hind quarters.

† Fig. 60.—Markir at the piaffer : right diagonal in the air.

Fig. 61.—Markir at the piaffer : left diagonal in the air.

In these two illustrations, we will note the energy which is displayed and which is marked by the fact that the fetlocks come down to the ground, and by the great elevation of the fore legs, which are raised higher than the hind ones ; contrary to what takes place in the piaffer taught by the cutting whip.

down regularly, he will do so by mere chance. Almost always, the hind legs will be raised and put down at the same time, and consequently the movement will not be a pace.

We should teach the horse the piaffer by calming him down, because he will not understand what is wanted of him, unless he is in a quiet state of mind.

To obtain the piaffer, we ought to collect the horse, by closing the legs, until we touch him with the spurs. It is difficult to explain in a book the exact moment when the spur should reinforce the action of the leg; in fact, this is evidently a question of tact. It is easier to show this on the ground, because one can then see if the rider uses the spurs too much or too little. As I have already said, the office of the spur is to make the horse yield to the pressure of the leg, when that pressure is not sufficient by itself. Besides, it is necessary for the horse to feel the spurs in order to remain *rassemblé*'d.* Also, to make a horse piaffer, we must prevent him going forward, and if we do not use the spurs, he will infallibly throw himself to the right or left by forcing the respective leg. Therefore, we should use the legs sufficiently to steady the horse. Nevertheless, to hold him in check, the spurs should brush his coat.

To get the piaffer † we should use light pricks of the spurs; ‡ and, as in all other cases, we should at the beginning be contented with two times.

* The question has often been discussed, whether the spurs are an "aid" or a punishment. As I have already said, they are sometimes one, sometimes the other, according to need. During breaking, they ought always to be an "aid," and ought not to become a punishment, unless the animal openly rebels, in which case we should try to find out if the disobedience is due to pure caprice on the part of the horse or to our fault. If caprice is the cause, the spurs ought to punish him. We should remember in all cases that the English very rightly call the spurs "persuaders."

† The hurried piaffer and the slow piaffer are obtained by the same means. I practise only the slow piaffer.

‡ This is what La Guérinière admirably calls "the delicate pinch of the spurs."

Fig. 60.—Piaffer ; right diagonal in the air.

19

Fig. 61.—Piaffer ; left diagonal in the air.

I touch my horse on the right and on the left, but almost simultaneously.* My right spur brings the off hind under the animal's body, which causes the near fore to be raised ; and my left spur, acting in its turn at the exact moment when the left diagonal is in the air, produces a similar effect on the right diagonal. I thus obtain the two first times of the piaffer ; but at the beginning these two times ought to follow each other so closely as to form, so to speak, a single time,† exactly like in fencing, when the swordsman makes " one, two " very close together.‡

It often happens that the horse will plunge on feeling the first hurried touches of the spurs. If he bounds forward, not much harm will result, and we will learn that we have used the spurs too strongly. We should therefore employ them more lightly when we begin again.

If at this period of the breaking we often repeat these two first times of the piaffer, the horse will quickly understand

---

* In fact, if I exclusively attack one side without immediately receiving the horse on the opposite leg, I will succeed only in sending his haunches to the side.

† If I allow an interval between them, there will be an alternate separation of the legs to the right and to the left, as in a kind of rocking.

‡ It follows, from what I have said, that these two first times are necessarily those of a hurried piaffer. When we begin the piaffer, we cannot foretell what will happen. As a rule, the horse will try to hurry it, on account of the spurs making him impatient. Besides, the hurried piaffer being lower than the higher piaffer, will require less exertion. Having obtained the piaffer of any kind, it needs regulating, which will test the skill of the breaker. The difficulty is to prevent the hurried piaffer occurring, or, rather, to change it into the slow piaffer, by giving it height brought on by the *rassembler*. The more the *rassembler*, the greater the height. The slow and high piaffer is obtained by energetic action of the legs, lightness of hand, and, above all things, delicate tact in combining the "aids." In the hurried piaffer, the legs are kept stiff, on account of their being raised but little off the ground. In the high piaffer, the biped, which is in the air, is greatly bent, while gaining height, and the fetlocks of the biped which is on the ground almost touch it (Fig. 61), so as to be able, in their turn, to raise the body by their spring.

When we go from the *passage* to the piaffer by shortening the *passage*, we can regulate the times of the piaffer more easily on account of the cadence already obtained ; but the tact of the rider is not the less necessary.

what we want him to do. As soon as he correctly marks the
first two times, without showing any wish to escape from the
spurs, we may try to get him to do four, six or more, and we
can continue to increase the number, as long as we hold him
easily in this position ; but we should not overdo it.

We should, of course, stop the piaffer and send the horse
forward, well in hand, the moment we feel he can escape from
us, whether by bringing his haunches sideways, doing a
half-rear or reining back, which is still worse.

In the first case, we should straighten the haunches by a
sharp touch of the spur, given on the side to which he throws
himself, and by way of punishment.

If he makes a half-rear, we are forced to slacken the reins,
to avoid an accident ; but the spurs should be kept close to
the sides (Fig. 65) ; because if that were not done, he would
constantly rear. The action of the spurs ought to be increased
by small touches until the horse has become quiet in hand, in
which case he has "given in."

Running back is the most difficult and dangerous fault to
overcome. If, on being lightly touched, he violently runs
back, the reins should he left quite loose, and the spurs should
be used more vigorously. Repeated touches of the spurs
close to the girths are a means which the horse cannot resist,
if they are energetically continued. Besides, I have already
said that we should never spur a horse which is stationary,
until we have taught him to go freely forward on being
touched by the spurs. Therefore, I do not incur the liability
of combatting the defence which I have described. If, however, I had to do so, I would easily settle the matter by
repeated attacks of the spurs, which act like the roll of a
drum. But if, on account of insufficient breaking, we have to
deal with this defence, and if we cannot continue the repeated
attacks of the spurs behind the girths, we should take a
cutting whip or cane, or get an assistant armed with a driving

whip. In any case, we must make the animal go forward at all cost. Here we are in a pitched battle, and we have got to know whether the man or the horse is to be master. We should on no account yield. Any means will do, because we must win the battle, otherwise the horse will be restive. Of course, I do not advise violent spurring or other severe measures, unless the horse obstinately runs back, in which case the only alternative left to the breaker is not to be beaten.

If the horse finds out that he can escape work by running back, he will become the master of his rider ; and every time the rider uses the spurs, no matter for what movement, the horse will run back. If the man does not inflict exemplary punishment, *while* the animal is running back, he had best give up the breaking, and—which is still wiser—the horse.

We ought to remain cool, however energetically we may act. If we give way to anger, we will become more quickly exhausted than the horse. With this proviso, punish the horse coolly and severely until he learns that the more he goes back, the more pain he will suffer, and consequently he will go forward, in which case we should immediately pat him on the neck, get off, and stop the lesson.

It does not matter whether the struggle takes place at the beginning or middle of the lesson, but as soon as the horse yields we should stop it, because, if we recommence the work, we cannot be sure of obtaining a second concession in the same lesson, especially if the horse has been obstinate for a long time. Besides, we are both tired, and the animal can offer only passive resistance, which is the most terrible of all. We may kill him by blows, but he will not stir. We have gone beyond his strength, and by persisting we will succeed only in disgusting him for ever.

We should therefore profit by the smallest concession, and should, above all things, avoid prolonging the punishment when the horse goes forward.   Otherwise, he will not know when he does wrong or when he does right, because he gets beaten whether he goes forward or back.   I therefore particularly advise the breaker never to lose his temper, although retaining the utmost energy.

I once had a black thorough-bred, called Negro, which I rode in public for four or five years.   He never failed me in work, although he was peevish and screamed when touched with the spur.   When I began to break him, he ran back immediately I closed my legs.

For two months he did not stop running back under me during a lesson of twenty minutes each day.   I was in despair. All the breakers of my acquaintance said that I would never succeed in making him go forward, yet he gave in at last.   He even became an excellent lady's horse, and never relapsed into the troublesome vice, of which I had great trouble to cure him. To succeed in this, I used the spurs only by touches.   They should never be kept stuck in the animal's sides.*   The spurs which I used were very sharp, and I applied them, as I always do, as close as possible to the girths.†   I, of course, took care to pat the animal on the neck the moment he went forward. I must, however, admit that after a struggle during twenty minutes without ceasing, I was completely exhausted, and so was my horse.   To break such an animal, one must be young, have a very strong seat and good loins, because they are the first to get tired.

The reason for ceasing to keep the horse in the same place,

---

* In fact, it is the pain which is renewed at each moment that makes the horse fly from the spur.   If it is kept against his side he will rest on it, and will inevitably jib.

† There, and only there, will the touch of the spur give impulsion.   Its touch further back will cause forward movement, but without impulsion, and further, it will tickle the horse, on account of the far greater sensibility of that part.   Only a touch, as near as possible to the girths, brings the hock under the centre of the body ; hence the impulsion.   I am always tearing my girths to ribbons.

during the three defences I have mentioned, is to remain master of him. If he resists the attacks of the spurs, when he is stationary, I make him go forward at all hazards. I then close my legs, and begin again, until he yields. The point upon which I insist is, that we are always master of a horse when we can make him go forward.

These observations, of course, do not apply only to the piaffer and *passage*. My reason for having dwelt on this subject so long, is that the means I have mentioned are always the same which I use for combatting defences—always the same which the horse adopts when he is touched by the spur, while he is kept in one place.*

Men of the new school, of whom I had occasion to speak in the preceding chapter, employ, in order to teach the piaffer, means not less strange, though more brutal, than that which they use for teaching the Spanish walk. They open the door of the school, and place the horse, with his head turned to the side of the stable, close to the opening of this door, to make him impatient. One man is on his back, another holds the caveson, and a third stands behind the animal, with a driving whip in his hand.† They then put on each pastern a leather hobble, to which is attached a piece of wood in the shape of an egg.

When the horse moves a foot, or rather when he puts it down,

---

* Many breakers, when alluding to horses which have got the better of them, say, in order to excuse themselves, that nothing can be done with animals which kick, rear, or run back each time they feel the spur. The truth is that their method is faulty. Sometimes they boast that they punished their horse so severely that he could not get up for several days, a statement which only proves their brutality. In the worst battle with a horse, I have never ill-treated him to such an extent as to bring him down. I have never even fatigued him so much as to make him unable to resume his work on the following day.

† These gentlemen only work all together—always several tormentors for one victim. Besides, they are so convinced that they cannot do otherwise, that they scoff at those who say that a breaker ought to ride his horse and break him without the help of anyone, a fact which appears to them to be simply impossible.

the egg strikes the coronet, and makes him raise the foot.
The man in the saddle uses the spurs, the one who is in
rear uses the driving whip, and the operator who holds the
caveson, and is in front of the animal's head, prevents him
advancing by giving him blows on the nose with the caveson.
The horse, thus imprisoned, shows great impatience, and as the
egg strikes his coronet, and makes him raise his foot each
time he puts it down, he performs a kind of hurried piaffer,
which is neither graceful nor regular. Besides, by this
method they teach a horse to piaffer in front of the stable
door, which no doubt is very ingenious, and does not require
much skill. It has, however, the drawback that the moment
the horse's head is turned away from the stable, his impatience
vanishes, and he stops the piaffer. This is a machine-made
horse. I shall not go further in this description, for my
intention is only to give a sketch of the system of breaking
used by the new school, who use the same means for every
kind of work. I do not undertake to describe these means.

The horse which has been taught the piaffer, only by the
combination of reins and legs, will do the piaffer anywhere, at
the wish of his rider, no matter when or where.

It is no less true that the system of the new school is
practised almost everywhere. Horses are broken now without
being ridden, and by means analogous to those by which one
would break in monkeys and nanny goats. In Vienna this
system is sarcastically called " *Pudeldressirung* " (poodle
breaking).*

It is easy to understand how the piaffer, which is learned
under these conditions, is always bad. At first, progress is

---

* In the same category we should place the recommendation made by certain
authors, to hum a tune in two time to a horse which is being taught the piaffer
or *passage*.

I have never broken a horse with any music. My only orchestra is the
spurs. When my horses hear music for the first time it puts them out, but
they soon take to it.

impossible. Afterwards, as the action of the cutting whip or driving whip causes the croup to be raised, the hind legs are raised higher than the fore ones, and the neck is necessarily depressed. *But in the piaffer, as in the passage, the fore legs ought always have the loftier action,* which is the case when these movements are taught only by the help of the hands

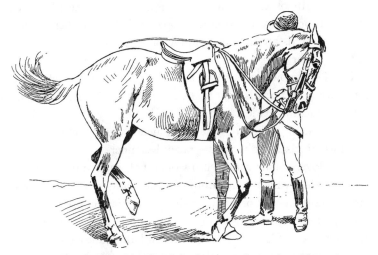

Fig. 62.—Teaching the piaffer by means of a cutting whip.

and legs; because the hocks are then brought well under the body, and the neck and forehand are consequently raised.*

We can understand that the horses of the new school are never broken in the true sense of the word. At best they are machines and automatons which the first comer can make

---

* Compare Figs. 60 and 61 with Fig. 62, which is copied from a photograph in a recent work that describes the method of teaching the piaffer by means of a cutting whip. In Fig. 62 the position of the head and neck is faulty, and the forehand is so over-loaded that the animal cannot raise the fore leg, which ought to be in the air, as in Figs. 60 and 61. In Fig. 62, on the contrary, the horse simply bends the knee, and the toe touches the ground. He does the piaffer only with his hind quarters, which are higher than the forehand. Contrary to the intention of the author, all the vices of the piaffer, *à la* cutting whip, are displayed in a striking manner by this illustration.

do this or that work, if he is only told how, and at what moment or place he should touch certain parts of the animal's body.

The riding masters of the new school take good care not to break thorough-breds, because they know by experience that wiry, energetic and strong horses will not let themselves be tortured. In order to excuse themselves, they maintain that thorough-breds are wanting in suppleness ; the fact being that thorough-breds are the most supple of all horses, but the least patient under pain.

Besides, we owe to this new school all those ladies who, not being able or not wishing to ride, find it much more easy to buy a machine-made horse and work him by touching him with a cutting whip on the legs, head, croup, and a little everywhere else, in a most ungraceful manner.

True lovers of horsemanship would not engage in this kind of equitation, which is made up of contortions, and which consists almost always of making the horse drag himself on his knees, stretch out his head on the ground like a calf which is waiting to have its throat cut, walk on balustrades, etc.

The public, knowing little of equitation, applauds in any case, but it is sad that the art of equitation should have fallen so low.

In order to know if the rider really possesses horse knowledge, it is enough to look at the horse. If the animal is light, well placed, full of impulsion, and does all his movements with so much spirit that he appears to work with pleasure, we may be certain that he is not a pupil of the new school, and is still less a machine-made horse, to which I have already alluded.

I may add that a man should ride without a whip, and that a lady should use it only to supply the want of the right leg ; that is to say, to strike on the right side and only a little behind the girths.

There is no doubt that the method adopted by the new school is the one which those who hate work would like to follow, because it is within the reach of anyone who would like to practise it after a few days' study. On the contrary, we may see a true horseman work for years without learning much. A horseman uses only his hands and legs, with such delicacy and with such slight movements that the spectator can hardly see them.

To sum up, the new school breaks a horse by means of tricks, on which account the first comer who knows these tricks can obtain certain results.

The old school is to the new school what the piano is to the barrel organ. Long study and great perseverance are required to be able to play well on the former instrument, and even then success is not always obtained; but all that is wanted to grind the barrel organ is an arm sufficiently strong to turn the handle. In the former case, one can become an artist by work and patience; but, in the latter, one has only to make a noise.

DIFFERENCES BETWEEN THE "PASSAGE" AND SPANISH TROT.

Even among those who ride well, there are many who confuse the *passage* with the Spanish trot.

In the *passage*, the knees and fetlocks are bent; in the Spanish trot, they are extended.

In the *passage*, the less ground is covered, the better is the movement, because the time of suspension is better marked, and the horse appears to raise himself perpendicularly.

In the Spanish trot, on the contrary, we should try to cover as much ground as possible in each stride. To be brilliant, the pace should be high and long, but not hurried; because, if it is too fast, the fore legs will not be able to mark the time of suspension.

There is another trot which is called the "swimmer," in which the horse ought to trot as fast as he can, while indicating with his fore legs a time of suspension in the air. But, as the speed is great, the period of suspension is much less marked than in the Spanish trot. I do not think that this is a school movement. A horse which trots well with his shoulders and knees will do it naturally. I content myself with merely mentioning it.

SERPENTINE AT THE TROT.

This movement consists in making a horse take four side steps to the left and four to the right at a well-collected trot. During the whole time the horse ought to go on two tracks, the forehand gaining a little more ground at the side to which the animal is proceeding, so as to prevent the haunches from going in front of the shoulders.

This movement appears simple, but it is very difficult to do correctly. We can quickly see that there is only a very short interval to put the horse back from one diagonal to the other gently and smoothly. All the merit and all the difficulty of this exercise consist in taking exactly four steps to each side. If the animal sometimes takes three, and sometimes five, there is no difficulty, merit, or interest.

CANTER ON THREE LEGS.

We can make a horse canter on three legs, in which case the three first times of the canter are done in a *rassemblé*'d canter (in four times), and the fourth time is done in the air. If, for example, we are cantering to the right, the off fore should be held up, without touching the ground.

Few horses can do in a brilliant manner the canter on three legs. Many can succeed in doing it ; but only a very energetic animal can hold his leg well extended in the air, without its touching the ground, during the whole period of the movement, only under which condition is this exercise interesting and brilliant.

If the reader has attentively followed my explanations, he will know that accustoming the horse to the pressure of the legs prepares him for this school movement, which is very difficult for the animal to understand and do. In fact, up to this, he has learned only to raise, extend, and place his legs on the ground, one after the other ; but now he is required to extend only one leg, and to keep it in that position.

The canter with the off fore in the air has only three beats on the ground—the first made by the near hind, the second by the off hind, and the third by the near fore. The fourth time is marked in the air by the off fore, which is fully extended and kept as high as possible.

Before putting a horse to this work, we should wait until he is perfectly broken, and until he will offer no resistance. At this time, I have at my disposal two movements which have been separately learned, namely, the ordinary canter to the right, and the extension of the off fore. From the combination of these two exercises, in which my left leg is my chief helper, I obtain the canter to the right on three legs.

It seems, in theory, that I ought to easily obtain the canter to the right on three legs, by vigorously using the left spur. But, in practice, this is not so simple ; because, having put my horse into the canter, the use of the left spur will do no good ; for it will make him bring his haunches to the right, or get away, but it will not make him extend his off fore.

We should therefore canter the horse to the right, and, having halted him, make him extend his off fore. When he has done this, we should pat him on the neck, and then begin again several times.

When the horse extends the leg without difficulty during the halt, we should make him go through the same performance, during a shorter halt.

As the momentum is not entirely checked during this half-halt, the horse who expects to raise his leg during the halt, anticipates the halt, and almost always does a time of the canter with his leg in the air, in which case we should halt him, pat him on the neck, and stop the lesson.

We can see that these two movements, which at first were separate, are beginning to be formed into one ; but that is not sufficient.

When the horse does this work easily, and without stiffness, we ought to demand the extension of the leg without a half-halt, by simply taking care to decrease the speed, and to raise the forehand. We should hasten slowly, and for a long time should be content with two or three strides during which the leg is completely extended, and above all things sustained.

If we wish to stimulate the horse to such an extent that he will hold his leg in the air, we should, ourselves, display great energy ; because, not only is the office of our left leg to make the horse keep his off fore in the air, but it also, in combination with the right leg, ought to keep him at the canter, by bringing his hind legs under him. In other words, we maintain the canter by a strong pressure of both legs, and at the same time we make the animal hold his off fore in the air, by small and repeated touches of the left spur.

We ought to use the right leg as vigorously as the left, in order to prevent the horse carrying his hind quarters to the right. If he goes sideways, we should stop him and put him straight, before recommencing the movement ; because, when he places himself obliquely, he will be deficient in propulsion, and in this position we shall be able to obtain only the extension of the leg or the canter ; but not both together. It is therefore indispensable to keep the animal very straight, and to give him a point of support on the right snaffle rein, in order to facilitate the upholding of the right leg.

The canter on three legs may be done either to the right or to the left.*

I do not know if others taught this exercise before me. In any case, I have never seen it done by anyone else, and I have never met with its description in any treatise on equitation.

"PASSAGE" TO THE REAR.

This is a very difficult exercise to do ; because ground has to be gained to the rear, while maintaining the diagonal steps in a well-cadenced manner, and preserving the same elevation of the hind legs, as in the forward movement. In every retrograde movement, the hind feet have a tendency to keep as close to the ground as possible. Unless we are absolutely sure of ourselves—as we ought to be, when we face such difficulties—we often produce, against our will, too strong an effect from front to rear, and thus transfer the weight from the forehand to the hind quarters, which consequently becomes lowered. To obviate this fault, we should make the horse

* Fig. 63. Germinal at the canter to the left on three legs ; in hand, but not *rassemblé*'d. The canter is in four time, although there is no *rassembler*, because the energetic uplifting of the forehand keeps in the air, even the leg which is not extended.

Fig. 64. Germinal at the canter to the right on three legs ; *rassemblé*'d. We can see how much the action of the spur, which is necessary for the *rassembler*, increases the extension of the leg in the air, and increases the height of the action, by bringing the hind quarters under the body.

Fig. 65 represents Germinal at the half-rear with the off fore extended, at the moment when I demanded the canter to the right on three legs in the *rassembler*. The horse had begun by a lazy extension of the leg ; but a sharper touch of the spur has made him do this half-rear, while at the same time he extends his off fore perfectly. In fact, this is a case of absolute obedience ; and the horse, immediately after the half-rear, starts into the canter to the right on three legs, in the *rassembler*. The photograph shown in Fig. 64 was taken immediately after this half-rear.

We can see, agreeably to what I have advised, that the spurs are applied to the sides during the half-rear, and the reins slackened. In fact, the reins are much less tight in Fig. 65 than in Fig. 64, in which the hands feel them ; but in Fig. 65 the hands are carried forward on the neck.

rein back by the seat, as I have described (p. 247), and not by the reins.

It is a mistake to think that we can easily go from the forward *passage* to the backward *passage*, to obtain which it is necessary to make the transition through the natural, slow and high piaffer, which is only the *passage* without gaining ground.

It is only when the horse piaffes correctly, that we can try to gain a few inches of ground to the rear at each step. With this object I increase the pressure of the legs. I try to *rassembler* the horse without pulling him back by the reins, and I sit well down into the saddle, while leaning strongly on each footfall.

On account of the *rassembler* being carried to its maximum, the equilibrium and mobility of the horse are such that the slightest displacement of the body of the rider can draw the horse in any direction, as for instance, to the rear, which is the point we are considering.

This means of obtaining the *passage* to the rear is long and difficult ; but it is the only one which gives a good result.

SEE-SAW PIAFFER.

In the see-saw piaffer, the off legs ought to be raised and put down in the same place, while the near ones make a beat forward and a beat backward, while always coming back to the same spot.

The near legs ought not only to mark the going and coming from front to rear, but the near hind quarter and near shoulder ought also to accentuate this movement without any participation on the part of the off legs, which should only piaffe regularly without gaining ground.

Baucher did this piaffer with great *éclat* on a mare called Stades. I have taught this school movement to four horses,

Fig. 63.—Cantering to the left on three legs, in hand, but not *rassemblé*'d.

Fig. 64.—Cantering to the right on three legs ; *rassemblé* d.

Fig. 65.—Half-rear (*pointe* or *lançade*) with off fore extended.

which did it more or less brilliantly, according to their degrees of energy.

It is very difficult to explain how to teach the see-saw piaffer, but I will try to do so.

It will at first be seen that this movement should not be required from any horse, unless he can do the slow and high piaffer. As such an animal, when doing this exercise, has extreme mobility, the slightest feeling on the reins will be sufficient to make him bring a leg a little back, in the same way that the smallest increase in the pressure of the spur will cause him to bring a leg a little forward.

Being at the piaffer, we ought, by means of the legs, to make the horse bring his near hind under him where he puts it down. The right diagonal being in support, the near fore— which, under the same action of the legs of the rider, has been carried forward at the moment when the near hind is placed under the animal's body—remains held up in the air, the knee bent, and the off hind also in the air (Fig. 66). Immediately the hand ought to act, in order to bring back the near fore, which is about to be placed behind the off fore, and which forms, along with the off hind, the left diagonal support; whilst the near hind, in its turn, does a time in the air, and the off fore performs its movement in the piaffer.* (Fig. 67.)

We can see that in the forward movement the near hind is placed in front of the off hind (Fig. 66), and that in the retrograde movement the near fore is placed behind the off fore (Fig. 67). This is the cause of the see-saw action from the rear to the front.

If the reader understands my explanations he will observe

---

* On comparing Fig. 67 with Fig. 66, we will see that in the movement to the rear, the snaffle reins are drawn a little tighter than those of the curb. The angle of the cheek of the curb is very little more open, and the seat presses the horse back.

that this piaffer is done, like the ordinary piaffer, by the diagonal, notwithstanding the see-saw lateral. It is very difficult to indicate, with mathematical precision the exact moment when the rider ought to use any particular rein or leg ; the action of the two reins and of two legs being made by a succession of movements which follow each other so closely that it is almost continuous. Here equestrian tact, which is the supreme quality of a rider, displays itself in all its beauty. I can only say that I increase the action of the right spur to obtain the forward movement of the near hind, and to help to keep the near fore in the air. But at the same time I strongly use my left leg to prevent the near hind from going to the left, because it gets its stimulus from my right leg.

For the backward movement I feel both reins, the near rein a little more than the off, at the moment when the near fore has to be brought back.

During the whole time the rider ought to freely use his legs and even the spurs, but the off rein hardly at all, and the near rein very little.

CANTER WITHOUT GAINING GROUND AND CANTER TO THE REAR.

The canter without gaining ground is a canter which is shortened as much as possible. It is similar in every way to the forward canter, except that the legs do not gain ground. It is very near to the backward canter, which is a regular pace of four time, exactly like the forward canter in the *rassembler*. It is the most difficult and most complicated school exercise. My advice is that it should be tried only at the extreme end of training, and with selected horses, whose loins and hocks should be exceptionally good to bear the *rassembler* at its maximum, without which it is impossible to obtain this movement.

Fig. 66.—See-saw piaffer.

Fig. 67.—See-saw piaffer.

The thoroughbred Gant, by Gantelet out of Mlle. de Romanerie, did the canter to the rear as if it were play, and after he had gone round the school at this pace he was as fresh as before.

Baucher did not know or was not able to describe the canter to the rear. The following, which is his definition of it in the fourteenth edition of his " Method of Equitation," p. 155, evidently corresponds to the way he did it :—" In the rein back at the canter the times are the same as those of the ordinary canter ; but the fore legs, instead of gaining ground when raised, are carried back, in order that the hind legs may do the same retrograde movement immediately the fore legs are placed on the ground."

How could Baucher make such a description of a canter to the rear, after having said that it was like the canter to the front ? No doubt it is like the canter to the front, and in the *rassembler* it is in four time ; but it is precisely for this reason that we cannot give the name of canter to a pace in which the hind legs do not make their retrograde movement before the fore legs are placed on the ground.

What, then, is this pace in which the two fore feet and the two hind feet respectively come to the ground at the same time. Under these conditions where is the canter ?

There is no need to be a great horseman to understand that Baucher alludes to a pace of two time, the first time being made by the hind quarters, the second by the forehand. But that is not a canter ; it is plainly little jumps to the rear. There cannot be a canter unless the fore legs and the hind legs are respectively put down one after another ; and further, when one of the hind legs is on the ground at the same time as the opposite fore leg, they form the left diagonal when the horse is cantering to the right, and the right diagonal when he is cantering to the left.

Baucher invented the expression, " canter to the rear," but

he entirely misunderstood this pace, the proof being that he never said with which leg the horse led or ought to lead.

Having broken Gant for a lady, I taught him the canter to the rear on the right leg so that the lady might be able to keep him at this pace with her spur, which is to the left. I have done more than this, for I succeeded in teaching the thorough-bred Germinal, by Flavio, out of Pascale, to canter to the rear either on one foot or on the other, according as I wished. I claim the honour to be the first to obtain this result. Whether a horse canters to the rear or to the front, the rider ought always to be able to say on which leg he is.

The canter to the rear with the near fore leading—although it is a pace of four time—ought to be made in the same way as if the horse was cantering to the front in three time— namely, first time, off hind; second time, right diagonal; third time, near fore. The great difficulty is to prevent the respective fore and hind legs being placed on the same transverse line. The off hind should be placed in rear of the near hind in order to preserve almost the same longitudinal distance between the two legs, as in the ordinary canter. I purposely say "nearly the same distance," because the strides are shorter. I need not add that the off fore should be behind the near fore, as in the forward canter.

We have seen that a stride of the canter consists of three times on the ground—namely, hind leg support, diagonal support, and fore leg support, as we see done with great precision in a good hunting canter, or what we call a hand gallop. But in the full speed gallop and in the canter without gaining ground, or the canter to the rear, which are the two extremes, the stride is in four time. In the canter to the left, for instance, the two legs which form the right diagonal, instead of touching the ground simultaneously, come down one after another, the succession of steps being as follows : off hind, near hind, off fore, near fore.

In the full speed gallop this fact is well marked, but the speed of the pace prevents it being apparent. In the stationary canter, and still more in the canter to the rear, it is much less marked, and for this reason it is almost imperceptible. In fact, at this pace the feet only graze the ground, and are drawn back for only a few inches. Instruments of precision or instantaneous photography would be required to prove this in both cases, but the fact remains. We can therefore say that in the full speed gallop and in the canter without gaining ground and to the rear, there are four successive impulsions.

Let us note, however, that in the canter without gaining ground, and in the canter to the rear, the diagonal acts in the same way as in the ordinary canter, with the single difference —which is a point I wish to bring to light—that the support of the hind leg precedes the support of the fore leg of the diagonal by an extremely short though actual interval.*

To obtain the canter without gaining ground, I begin by shortening the canter every day while maintaining the propulsion—that is to say, by pressing the horse with the legs up to his bit, the play of which should be fine in proportion to the extent of the *rassembler*. By gradually decreasing every day the length of the strides, I obtain the canter without gaining ground with impulse, but not with the horse getting behind his bit. When the animal is behind his bit in the canter, it is impossible to keep him up to his bit, and he necessarily gets away from his rider by reining back.

---

* Fig. 68.—Germinal cantering to the rear ; second time. This photograph was taken at the moment when the right diagonal was about to be used in support. The near hind is already on the ground, but the off fore has not yet come down. Hence the four times, the right diagonal making two beats instead of one.

We should note that even in this extreme *rassembler* the head remains a little beyond the vertical. We can therefore see that the reining back is done by the seat, and not by the reins, which are not drawn tightly.

We have now to convert the canter without gaining ground,
into the canter to the rear, for which purpose, when my horse
is cantering on one spot, with such ease and lightness that I
have no need for the reins, I try to bring him back an inch
or two by my seat and legs, and not by the reins. While my
legs are raising the horse, I seize the moment when he is in
the air to carry my seat back. I change the position of my
seat, and not that of the upper part of my body, by taking
nearly all my weight off the stirrups to put it on my buttocks.
The mobility of the horse is so great, at a moment when he is
in suspension,* that a movement of the rider is sufficient to
make him gain a litttle ground to the rear, which is enough to
begin the canter to the rear. By repeating and gradually
increasing these effects every day, we succeed in obtaining the
canter to the rear as I have described. If we try to get the
backward movement by the reins, the *rassembler* will be
immediately lost, because the action of the reins will send the
hocks a long way to the rear; their duty, on the contrary,
being to remain under the centre of the body. When
they are to the rear, the hind quarters being over-loaded
lose the mobility which enables them to gain ground to
the rear.

NEW SCHOOL MOVEMENTS.

I have invented a certain number of school exercises, and
will content myself by enumerating them. They are done
according to the same principles and by means of the "aids"
which have been used for the teaching of the preceding
movements :—

1. New Spanish walk, which consists in making a step

---

* This is the moment we have taken for changing the leg between the last time
of one stride and the first time of the next stride. It can be seized only with
difficulty, and then we can get everything out of a horse, because he is in the air.
A puff of wind can displace him.

Fig. 68.—Cantering to the rear ; second time.

forward and a step to the rear.   The near fore, for instance,
extends itself and takes a step forward.   Then the off fore
extends itself and also takes a pace to the front, but returns
by taking a step to the rear.   Here the left diagonal advances
and the right diagonal goes back.   I continue this movement
as long as I like.   I then change the diagonal.   The off leg,
in its turn, makes a step forward, and the near leg, after
having been extended to the front, takes a step to the rear, in
which case the left diagonal goes back.   We can change the
diagonals as we wish.

2. Serpentine at the *passage*.   This is the same movement
as the serpentine at the trot; but it is evidently much more
difficult to do.

3. Canter on three legs, to the right and to the left.

4. "Two tracks" at the canter on three legs to both sides.

5. Ordinary voltes and pirouettes at the canter on three legs,
to the right and to the left.

6. Spanish trot in two beats on each leg.   Up to the present
the Spanish trot has been done only in one time on each leg;
that is to say, one time on the right and one on the left.   In
the Spanish trot in two times, I make the horse successively do
two beats with the off fore, with the near fore extended, and
immediately afterwards two beats with the near fore, with the
off fore extended.   The rider can continue this movement as
he likes.   The horse naturally advances a little less in the
second time than in the first.

7. The Spanish trot in one and two times alternately, as
follows, the word leg being understood : right, left ; right, right ;
left, right ; left, left.   I prolong this movement as I wish during
one or two turns round the school.   I believe I am correct in
stating that this is the most complicated movement that has
been obtained in equitation.

8. The canter without gaining ground, and the canter to the
rear, on three legs.   The great difficulty of this exercise is to

obtain and preserve forward impulsion for the extended leg, while the other three are going back.*

It is, of course, understood that all these movements are done by means of the "aids" I have described. A repetition of this would be useless to anyone who has attentively read the preceding chapters.

SCHOOL HORSE FOR LADIES.

A high-school horse which is required for a lady, ought to be particularly supple, and should work from right to left with more ease than from left to right, because a lady rider does the movements from left to right as easily as a man, for she has on the left side the same "aids" as he has, namely, leg and spur. But in the movements from right to left, her whip, which is far less powerful than a leg armed with a spur, replaces the right leg of a horseman. If the horse is not very clever in movements from right to left, the action of the whip will be insufficient. This fact holds good in all kinds of work. Especially in the "two tracks," the lady's horse does not hold himself so well, and is not so completely in hand from right to left as from left to right. The changes of leg are also more difficult from right to left. In the Spanish walk, the near leg is not raised so high, and is not so well extended as the off leg. Increased severity in the application of the whip will cause

---

* Figs. 69 and 70.—Germinal at the canter to the right on three legs to the rear. Fig. 69, second time. The off hind has just come down after the near hind. For obtaining the extension of the off fore, the spur gives the impulse that preserves the seat, which makes the horse rein back. We can see that the horse's head is a little beyond the perpendicular, and that the reins are slack.

Fig 70, third time. The near fore has just been put down behind its point of departure, and the off fore, which would be in support during the fourth time, remains in the air.

The bringing together of the three legs in support shows the extent of ground which has been gained to the rear. The seat is continuously drawn back. The reins, especially the off snaffle rein, are drawn up a little, in order to keep the off fore in the air.

These illustrations enable us to appreciate the delicacy of the "aids."

Fig. 69.—Cantering to the right on three legs to the rear; second time.

Fig. 70.—Cantering to the right on three legs to the rear ; third time.

the horse to make a sudden start. Besides, when the lady uses her right arm energetically, to give a cut with the whip, the left hand will almost always move, and will consequently give a jerk to the mouth, which will make the animal assume a wrong position.

Almost all ladies bring their horse's hind quarters round to the right, because they make too much use of their powerful "aid" on the left side ; their " aid " on the right side being too weak to keep the animal straight.

To obviate these inconveniences, a lady's school horse ought to work very easily from right to left.

A lady's hack ought to be the same on both sides.

CHAPTER IX.

COMMENTARIES ON BAUCHER.

BAUCHER was certainly the greatest and most clever high-school rider we have ever had.* There is no doubt that he did not invent the high school, which is the result of the work of many generations of horsemen, but he invented and co-ordinated a new and astonishing method. Prior to his time, no horseman had obtained such marvellous results. He conquered many difficulties, and removed a great number of obstacles which a man who wishes to break-in a school horse always meets.

He invented new exercises, which he did with remarkable

* As regards myself, I claim to be a follower of Baucher. My teacher, François Caron, was his pupil. I have thoroughly studied the method of Baucher in all its parts. Without Baucher I would not know as much as I do of riding.

I would be very ungrateful to mention the name of Baucher without at the same time rendering well-merited homage to his rival, Victor Franconi, from whom I have received many excellent lessons. By his pluck, strength of seat, and by the impulse he gave to his horses, his style of equitation resembled much more that of Count d'Aure than that of Baucher.

The names of the masters to whom the horsemen of to-day are beholden would form a long list. France can boast of an admirable host of great horsemen. If Italy can name Pignatelli; England, Newcastle; and Germany, Count von Schweppe, France can put forward hundreds of illustrious names, at the head of which shine—to speak only of bygone celebrities—such horsemen as Dupaty de Clam, La Guérinière, the Chevalier d'Abzac, the Marquis of Bigne, and others. The School of Hanover, which is the most celebrated of foreign schools, is the direct offspring of the great school of Versailles. Beyond all dispute, France is the classic country of equitation.

precision. His method is specially admirable from the fact that it keeps a horse sound by proper distribution of weight, rational gymnastics, suppling, and a correct development of his powers.* Also it has the great advantage over the old methods of quickly giving results. Thus, with Baucher's method, we can break a hack in two months, and a school horse in eight or ten months. Formerly, the latter result took two or three years to obtain; and, besides, the old time horsemen never attempted the difficulties which Baucher conquered.† I go further, and say that they did not even know that such difficulties existed.

We should therefore bow with gratitude before this master of the equestrian art. Is this equivalent to saying that Baucher should be exempt from criticism? Certainly not; and for my part, I am far from agreeing with all his ideas. I even think that it is my duty to oppose those proceedings of his which I have found to be wrong. In this book I have had occasion several times to show up certain mistakes of the great horseman. I shall now criticise some of his opinions.

---

* I have adopted in my work what I call the three golden keys of Baucher's method; namely, his complete suppling exercises, with greater elevation of the head and neck; his attacks with the spurs, to enclose the horse; and his *rassembler*, which I have perfected.

Apart from this, I have worked more on the lines of the old school of Versailles than on those of Baucher, in that I always advocate fast paces, and that the horse should be allowed to extend himself.

† Up to the present time I have broken thirty-five school horses, which is more than anyone else has done. Baucher, who died when he was seventy-four, broke twenty-six. Being only fifty-six, I hope to double that number when I am as old as the great rider. I have broken hundreds of hacks.

I do not pretend to be cleverer than my illustrious predecessors. I know that before my time others have done as well, and perhaps better. I mention these facts only to show the results of my method. I am certain that every horseman who wishes to follow it will be able to obtain similar results, provided that he is properly endowed by Nature, and that he loves horses.

Few authors have described a correct method of breaking in the proper sense of the word. I have read all the books on equitation, and find that none of them are perfect.

Thus, in the first place, I say that Baucher's method, which consists in keeping the horse completely and constantly closed between the hands and legs of the rider, is dangerous for people who are indifferent riders, and also for those who work or break their first horses without being under the eye of a master.* It is, therefore, not within the compass of everyone, and perhaps it cannot be practised without trouble, except by those who have seriously studied it.

Baucher says that the mouths and sides of all horses are the same, which is an entirely erroneous idea. I maintain, on the contrary, that it is impossible to find two horses whose mouths and sides are equally sensitive. Without doubt, the difference, like that between the leaves of a tree, may not be very apparent in all cases, but it exists, and cannot be denied.

It is possible that we can succeed in making all horses light in hand and sensitive to the spurs, but I deny that we can give them all the same lightness and sensitiveness.

Baucher adds that in the case of a puller, his mouth is not at fault, and that it is sufficient to change his equilibrium. Let us test his statement by taking, for instance, racehorses in training, and leaving them to make their own distribution of weight, with their heads low, necks stretched out, and croups high. What will happen? Some will not go up to the bridle and will run badly; others will pull just enough to run well; and a third variety will pull too hard, and will run away, notwithstanding the strength of their riders' arms. What does this prove, except that they all have not the same sensitiveness of mouth, as they are all in the same position?

We should note that all horses in training are bitted in the same way, namely, with a plain snaffle. We therefore cannot blame the curb for their different ways of pulling.

The experiments I have made have thoroughly cleared up

---

* This is probably the reason why many true followers of Baucher have made their horses restive.

this point, and I have no hesitation in laying down the principle that the mouth of each horse has its own peculiar degree of sensibility, no matter what is the pace, work, or distribution of weight.

Thus, I owned and broke to high school work the thoroughbreds Redoubt by Parmesan, and Gant by Gantelet, out of Mlle. de la Romanerie, both of which had won races. I did not get them until they were five years old, and I made them remarkably good school horses.

Redoubt had a very light mouth, and could do the perfect *rassembler* almost without my having to touch the reins. Gant had a harder mouth, and required to have the reins drawn tightly, in order to do the *rassembler* to the same extent.

Riding them alternately, I went to the training ground behind Bagatelle, at a walk, trot, and canter, and observed, during these paces, the same difference of mouth which I had noticed in the *manège*, when doing the finest high school work.

Having brought them on the race-course, with the curb chain removed and the curb reins knotted on the neck, I sent them a short preliminary canter. Both of them quickly got into their racing position and speed. After that I sent them a full speed gallop of about five furlongs, and they performed in a manner which would have given no one the impression that they had not galloped for eighteen months ; but each of them showed in the full gallop the same difference of mouth which they had done in the riding school and when hacking.

During the gallop on the race-course, Redoubt pulled just enough to run well ; but Gant took a firm hold of the snaffle, pulled hard, and tried to run away. I easily stopped the former in a few strides, but I succeeded in pulling up the atter only at the end of a hundred and fifty or two hundred yards, and more by the voice than by the hands.

After the gallop, I walked them back to the stable to let them catch their wind, and as soon as I arrived, I made them do their high school work without taking off their bridles. Here, also, I found their respective mouths to be exactly the same as before.

While hacking, these horses were light in hand, without being on their haunches.* On the race-course they pulled just as much as if they had never been taught high school work; and, having returned to the school with their hind legs well under them, they were as light in hand as if they had never been galloped on a race-course.

We should note that in the experiments which I have just described, the respective weights, with these horses, were distributed in three absolutely different ways.

1. When going to the course it was distributed in the proper manner for hacking, and was the result of an ordinary feeling on the reins.

2. During the gallop, the preponderance of weight was on the forehand.

3. In the *manège*, on the resumption of high school work, the preponderance was on the hind quarters. Consequently, there were three modifications in the distribution of weight. The application of the "aids" were also entirely different, according to the nature of the work. But the essential point on which I differ from Baucher is, that a horse's mouth remains the same, no matter what is the work, use of the "aids," or distribution of weight. In the three distributions of weight I found the same difference of mouth.

I repeated this experiment with twenty thorough-breds which had been broken for high school work, and they all brought me to the same conclusion: that the nature of the mouth does not vary according to the distribution of weight.

It is sometimes evident that a horse which holds his head low makes the rider carry his head and neck; but if the rider

---

* Horizontal equilibrium is the equilibrium for hacking.

changes the distribution of weight by raising the head and neck, they will not bear so heavily on his hands.

Baucher confused the sensitiveness of the mouth with the lightness which results from a change in the position of the head and neck.

Let us now consider the sides of a horse.

Who will believe that the sides of a common, heavy, lymphatic horse are as sensitive as those of a strong, wiry and free-going animal?* It is possible to make the former do almost the same exercises as the latter; but at what cost? We would have to dig the spurs into him to make him move; but with the free-goer, the mere approach of the heels would be enough.

A ticklish, impatient horse will never bear the spurs with the same docility as a good-tempered, placid animal. In no case can we succeed in completely changing the work of nature. Further, a horse which is naturally ticklish, becomes still more so from the continual contact of the spurs. It may even happen that a horse which is not naturally ticklish, becomes ticklish from the use of the spurs during breaking.

Also, a horse which has bad loins, weak hocks, or any other defect, will not be cured by Baucher's method. Often his imperfections will only be increased by the sufferings which he will endure, on account of being made to take up certain positions, as in ordinary reining in, without the pressure of the legs,† or in the complete *rassembler*. Baucher, therefore, was far from being right when he asserted that his method cured all ills.

As a general rule, the weaker and more unsound a horse is, the less should be expected from him, under pain of making him incapable of any kind of work. With such an animal,

---

* We might as well believe that all men are equally ticklish.

† Besides, I have already said that we should not use the simple *ramener* except with a high-spirited horse which goes freely up to his bridle.

there is no question of fine equitation, for he cannot bear the *rassembler*. We should simply require him to go forward, and we should feel happy if we make him a passable hack.

Baucher appears to me to be absolutely wrong in stating that we should destroy the "instinctive forces" of the horse, and act only on the "transmitted forces." This theory is so strange and so contrary to the nature of things, that I cannot help thinking that the expression used by Baucher incorrectly translated his thoughts.

The "instinctive forces" are apparently the natural forces, or muscular power. If it is destroyed, what remains? What are the "transmitted forces" of which Baucher talks? Whence do they come? We can transmit an electric current or a moral effect, but to transmit a force we must, first of all, produce it, and we know that the rider should not display force, because he ought always to remain supple; and even if he displayed force, it would be insignificant as compared to that of the horse.

What means can the rider employ? He has only his legs and hands.*

Without doubt the legs awake the vigour of the horse when they are well closed, but they do not add any force to it. They simply stimulate him to put forth the energy he possesses.

The hands ought not to display force. If, in an exceptional case, they make an effort, its object will only be to thwart that of the horse. They do not transmit force to him, but more or less check his force.

Supposing that two jockeys are finishing almost together, and that their horses are equally exhausted. If one of them is very strong, he can, by displaying great energy of hands, legs, and whip, appear to communicate the force of propulsion to

* The legs are "aids" of impulsion; the hands, "aids" of retention and direction.

his horse, and thus obtain two or three powerful strides, which will enable him to win. Such a force has the appearance of being transmitted, but in reality the jockey simply stimulates by his vigorous action, all the remaining energy of the horse, and makes him go at his maximum speed for two or three seconds.

Let us take another case of horses being exhausted when returning from a long hunt, and when going down a steep incline, at the bottom of which there is a ditch, at which some of them, not being well supported by their rider's legs, stumble or fall. One of the riders, on the contrary, spurs his animal sharply and thus prevents him making a mistake, by doing which he appears to transmit force to him at that moment. In reality, he only stimulates the energy of his horse, whose natural force saves them both.

Let us take a high school horse, when he is at the end of his work and has lost his "go," as sometimes happens. If I wish him to do some energetic movements, I am obliged to have recourse to the spurs, and I use a certain amount of vigour to make him answer to their attacks ; but instead of trans-mitting force to him, I merely awaken his energy, which he puts into action.

To sum up : the rider does not transmit force to his horse, whose natural forces he directs, moderates, or excites at his pleasure.

I am inclined to think that Baucher simply wished to say that whenever a horse tries to take the initiative in using his own natural forces, the rider should stop or direct them, especially if the animal wants to "play up," as, for instance, by plunging, rearing, or spinning round. But when a horse puts forth all his energy to do a good walk, a grand trot, or a well-marked canter, I don't think that we ought to try to destroy it. Baucher neither destroyed nor transmitted forces ; he directed them. He obtained control of the horse's powers by suppling

22*

exercises, and by rational training, and consequently he ruled his horse by preventing him using these forces in his own way.

Finally, a horse can always escape from strength by strength, in which case the rider will soon be exhausted. Therefore the rider ought always try to prevent the horse knowing his own strength, so that he may hinder him from using it against himself. He can do this by feeling and divining in advance the intentions of the animal. A rider who has tact foresees the defences of his mount, feels them coming, and wards them off before the animal can make them.

Baucher, after having passed his life in breaking horses such as Partisan, Buridan, Capitaine, Stades, and others, complains that his horses were not always light in hand during changes of direction. The reason which he gave was that, with his way of working, he obtained only *equilibrium of the second kind*, which I call "*imperfect equilibrium*" or "*incomplete rassembler*." According to him, "*equilibrium of the first kind*," which I call "*perfect equilibrium*" or "*complete rassembler*," is obtained by using the hands without the legs, or the legs without the hands. But in this, Baucher seriously deceived himself, because the fact of his finding "equilibrium of the first kind" towards the end of his career was due to the elevation of the head and neck, which he finally adopted at a time when he was no longer able to ride. He was not able to obtain the complete *rassembler* by placing the head and neck of his horses in the way he used to do. The head was too low, and the neck was bent in the middle. Therefore it frequently happened that his horses were badly balanced.

It is simply absurd to say that the "complete *rassembler*" can be obtained by the hands without the legs, or by the legs without the hands.

We read on page 82 of the fourteenth and last edition of Baucher's book that "my method places the horse so much under the control of his rider that, by the combination of the effects of the legs and hands, our slightest movements suffice to direct the energy of this powerful animal, according to our will." Nothing could be truer. But why does he maintain on page 178 of the same edition, that the only true kind of riding should be done by "legs without hands, and hands without legs"? How did he not see that these two assertions are contradictory? The office of the legs of the rider is to make the horse energetic in his hind quarters, and that of the hands, to make him "amiable in his mouth." Without the simultaneous co-operation of these two "aids," we may do wonderful tricks, but not good horsemanship.

The fact that Baucher broke his horses with the two "aids," and afterwards used only one of them, proves that he deceived himself by thinking that he had obtained perfect equilibrium with "legs without hands and hands without legs." But as the legs are necessary for impulsion and the hands for direction, he hastened to go back to the two "aids."

Under these conditions, why did he abandon an "aid" which he was obliged to use every moment? Is the proof required? When working on "two tracks" without the legs, there will be nothing to indicate to the horse that his haunches should move, especially if we want him to do the "two tracks" at the canter or *passage*. If we demand the Spanish trot without legs, the horse will raise his fore legs a little without gaining ground, but nothing will give him the impulsion necessary for the trot. Change the "aids," and demand the same work without using the hands. The action of the legs to obtain the elevation and extension of the fore legs will have the result of sending the horse abruptly forward, because there is nothing to restrain him and to raise the fore hand. It will be the same in all other movements.

I admit, however, that when the education of the school horse has been carried to its highest degree of perfection, he

will do, so to speak, all the movements without the help of the
" aids, " it being sufficient to indicate to him what he has got
to do, by the slightest approach of the leg, with the reins slack
on his neck.   In fact, this is a question of *nuances* (minute differences) : but all art is made up of *nuances.*

Be that as it may ; but since Baucher acknowledges that he
could get only the "equilibrium of the second kind" (incomplete
rassembler), I am justified in thinking that my school horses
are superior to his ; because, for the last ten years, I have obtained "equilibrium of the first kind " (complete *rassembler*).   I
hasten to add that, thanks to Baucher, I succeeded in finding
this *rassembler*, which is possible only when the head and neck
are kept very high.   Also, when I say that my school horses
are superior to those of the illustrious master, I do not pretend
that they were more precise in their movements than his, which
were perfectly correct.   I wish simply to say that I obtained
the same school movements in as good form as my learned pre-
decessor, but with greater elevation of head, neck, and limbs ;
that is to say, with more complete equilibrium, which consequently required less effort, and above all things with more
impulsion.

In his books on equitation, Baucher said little about riding
in the open.   This was an evident omission.

The fact is that Baucher never rode outside.   Without
being his pupil, I followed and studied him during his journeys
to Austria, Italy, Switzerland, etc., from 1847 to 1850, But
during these three years I never saw him go out on horseback.
It has been very incorrectly stated that his seat in the saddle
was weak, and for this reason he was afraid to ride hacking or
hunting.   I admit that he was not such a fine rough rider, and
had not such a strong seat as the Count d'Aure, but that does
not prove he was afraid to ride outside.   The fact that he
broke many horses proves that he had a strong seat ; because
there are always more or less violent struggles during break-

ing. We must therefore seek elsewhere for the reason which prevented Baucher from riding in the open.

Baucher being a reformer and consequently a seeker, had no pleasure in leaving a horse to himself, as is done when hacking. He devoted all his life to his work in order to show us the way, which was the only thing that interested him, Riding without working was only a weariness to him. Therefore he never studied the character or manner of riding a hack or hunter; or the enormous difference between a "closed-in" school horse and an ordinary saddle horse, which is left a good deal to himself.

As he did not ride outside, he never rode his horses at fast paces, which was wrong; because a horse passes very easily from an extended position to the *rassembler*. Full speed, provided that it is not too prolonged, has the advantage of allowing the animal to extend himself, and consequently to obtain rest, by changing his equilibrium, while at the same time it develops and strengthens his lungs.

The chief fault of Baucher was that of keeping his horse constantly "enclosed." I think we ought to observe the principle of letting the horse extend himself after each concession, during breaking. Finally, I maintain that as a general rule during breaking, we should accustom our mount to extend himself from time to time at the walk, trot and canter. Every form of equilibrium and position ends by fatiguing the horse. If we change one of them, the horse will return to it with pleasure.

As a last observation I may remark that on page 103 of the fourteenth edition of his book, Baucher repeats a conversation which he had at Berlin with some German officers who were supposed to know something about horses. They said : " We like to have our horses *in front* of the hand." Baucher replied: " I like mine to be *behind* the hand, and in front of the legs."

Personally, I share neither the opinion of the German officers nor that of Baucher. The horse ought to be in front of the legs and lightly *on* the hand. It is always a question of *nuances ;* at least, when army horses have not been considered, because with them there is something quite different from a *nuance*, and in this case I differ entirely from Baucher. I even dare to say that the single fact of his stating that horses should be behind the hand, ought to be sufficient to exclude his method from the army. Such an opinion put into practice would only make the horse hesitating ; because the hand directs him. The horse always hesitates when he does not feel the hand, But if he is *behind* the hand he does not feel the reins. The army horse ought always to go freely up to his bridle (*on the hand*).

These are the principal points of Baucher's method with which I disagree. Nevertheless, I have a sincere admiration for him.

Baucher was a creator, and every one who rides ought to respect him as a master. He had the great merit of not describing anything which he could not do. Many who have come after him have written at great length on riding, and often with the object of describing magnificent movements which they have never done. Baucher proved the superiority of his theory by putting it into practice.

CHAPTER X.

TESTS OF HORSEMANSHIP.

To be an accomplished rider, or at least to be a fair performer in the saddle, a man should be able to pass the following tests :—

1. To ride a difficult horse.
2. To ride in a steeplechase.
3. To ride a trotting match.
4. To ride a flat race.
5. To be able to break and ride a school horse.

Riding a difficult horse, when it is only a question of remaining on his back, is simply an affair of strength of seat and pluck. It is sufficient to be a good rider and a bit of a dare-devil. But we require a knowledge of reasoned-out equitation to anticipate and thwart his defences.

I place steeplechase riding in the second rank, although it requires great strength of seat and pluck. A cross-country jockey has to be a good rider, rather than a good horseman ; but steeplechase riding requires less delicacy of handling and tact than the following tests.

I think match trotting comes in the third rank as regards judgment and knowledge. It is evident that if the rider of a trotter cannot accurately tell when his horse is at the top of his speed, he will continue to push him, and will make him break into the gallop. But judgment of pace is much more easy in trotting than in flat-race riding, to succeed in which a jockey should know what is the highest speed of his horse, should always keep near it, and should demand it only at the critical moment.

I put flat-race riding in the fourth rank, considering that it is truly an art which only such men as F. Archer, Watts, Cannon, Webb and others can acquire. A flat-race jockey has to be an exceedingly good judge of pace, and if he does not know what speed his animal can maintain without becoming exhausted, he will never make a name for himself. When we think that the highest speed of a racehorse is about five furlongs in a minute, we will understand how difficult it is to judge pace within a second or two.

If it is simply a matter of one following the other, the first comer can do it. The difficulty is to set and maintain the pace which suits the horse best, and if the jockey cannot place him as he likes, without fighting with him, he will do no good.

If the jockey takes too strong a bearing on the reins, the horse will exhaust himself by the efforts he makes against the hands, in which case his mouth suffers much less than his loins and hocks, the result being that the animal will not be able to finish in good style. If, on the contrary, the jockey does not keep a proper hold of his horse's head, the animal will go too fast, and will be unable to struggle at the critical moment. The jockey should therefore have sufficient sense not to fall into either of these extremes.

Breaking a school horse comes under the last term. To succeed at it, a man should possess knowledge, delicacy of touch and tact to a supreme degree, and should have an exact acquaintance with the capabilities of a horse, so that he may break him without making him unsound.

In the breaking of a school horse, we require not only a perfect knowledge of the effects of the hands and legs, but we

should also, by our seat, be able to feel the slightest movements of the hind quarters, for we learn by our seat what
passes under us.   Consequently, we can check the slightest
fault, and immediately reward the faintest sign of good will.
This is the entire secret of breaking.

Further, the riding master who breaks a school horse, acts
alone, and depends only on himself.   Every fault committed
and every good movement done are his work.   This is true,
only in the school.

The racehorse, to mention his case only, passes through
many hands, such as those of trainers, riding lads, and jockeys,
and if the animal commits a fault with any of them, the man
can put it down to his next-door neighbour.   Only the school
horse is the exclusive work of the person who broke him.
Count d'Aure replied one day to a criticism of Baucher
that, "I am not a horse breaker."   Then, what did he break?
Did the word breaker jar on his ears?   For my part, I know
no other.   Of course we should not regard in the same light
the horseman who breaks a horse in good style, as the groom
who takes the rough edge off him, and I venture to say that
no one can be a real horseman, if he cannot break-in a horse.
Breaking is the horseman's touchstone.   The broken horse is
the proof of the *breaker*.

CHAPTER XI.

WITH BELGIAN OFFICERS.

I WAS giving performances at Brussels, when Count d'Oultremont asked me to give an exhibition with my horses at the Royal Circle of which he was president.

He expressed the desire that this performance would be accompanied by explanatory remarks, "Your 'aids' are so delicate," he said to me, "that we do not always see the precise means you arrive at a result which we witness. We wish to know how you obtain so much with such a small effort. Give us explanations."

The exhibition took place one afternoon in the month of December, 1890. All the superior officers who were members of the Circle were present. I worked my horses, but not as in a public show. Sometimes placing my mount in a good position to obtain the desired result under correct conditions; sometimes placing him in a bad position, in order to show its fallacy by making a mistake; I accompanied each part of the work by explanations, which were practically confirmed on the spot.

After the performance, the officers of the second regiment of Guides asked me, through Commandant Fivé, to be good enough to make out a course of instruction for their use. I accepted with great pleasure, and the riding school of the 2nd Guides was placed at my disposal every day from ten o'clock to half-past twelve. The course consisted of thirty lessons.*

The following was the programme which I laid down, and which was carried out consecutively :—

2ND REGIMENT OF GUIDES
of H. M. the King of the Belgians.

PROGRAMME OF HORSE-BREAKING,
done under the direction of
MR. JAMES FILLIS.

1ST LESSON.

Lunging the horse for some days, to the right and to the left, to make him obedient.

1. Putting him in hand. Flexion of the jaw, standing still, and then in movement. (The right hand holding both reins of the bridle at two inches from the bit, and high, in order to raise the neck. The left snaffle rein in the left hand, which is carried forward in opposition to the right hand.)

Pat the horse on the neck and begin again as soon as he yields.

2. Make the horse yield to the right leg and to the left leg.

2ND LESSON.

1. Flexions of the jaw, the man being on foot; same flexions when mounted.

2. Short trot : (*a*) On the left diagonal biped.
   „ „ (*b*) On the right diagonal biped.

Rising in the stirrups at the trot.

3. Shoulder-in : To the right hand, and to the left hand.

4. Reversed volte.

* It was the same with the 1st Regiment of Guides, who placed their *manège* at my disposal every day from nine till half-past ten.

3RD LESSON.

1. Repetition of the 2nd lesson.
2. Change of the diagonal hand, to two-thirds of the change of hand, ; making the horse yield to the leg on two tracks (to both hands).
3. Shoulder-in : Repeat this movement to both hands.

4TH LESSON.

1. Repetition of the 3rd lesson.
2. Short trot, and change of hand on the diagonal.
3. Canter to the right and to the left.
4. Getting the horse into hand.

5TH LESSON.

1. Repetition of the 4th lesson.
2. Canter on the diagonal.
3. Circling.
4. Change of hand by passing into the trot.
5. Collecting the horse.

6TH LESSON.

1. Lateral flexion of the head on the neck (the reins held as in the flexion of the jaw).
2. Canter on the diagonal.
3. Circling and changing the hand.
4. Shoulder-in.
5. Canter on a straight line and change of hand.
6. Collecting the horse.

7TH & 8TH LESSONS.

1. Collected trot.
2. Direct and lateral flexions on foot.

3. Repeat the flexions while moving.
4. Short trot. Collecting the horse.
5. Canter on the inward and outward leg.
6. Shoulder-in.
7. Shoulder to the wall.
8. *Rassembler* while moving.

9TH LESSON.

1. Repetition of the 7th lesson.
2. Cadence of the trot, and continued *rassembler*.
3. Increase the collection.

10TH LESSON.

1. The same order of work.
2. *Rassemblé*'d trot, and movements on two tracks.
3. Half a turn on the haunches.

11TH LESSON.

1. Repetition of the preceding lesson.
2. Canter on the inward and outward leg in a straight line

12TH, 13TH, & 14TH LESSONS.

1. Repetition of the 11th lesson.

15TH LESSON.

1. Repetition of the preceding work.
2. Increase of the *rassembler* and of collection.
3. Shoulder-in on the circle.
4. Shoulder-out on the circle.
5. Starting into the canter from the halt.

16TH LESSON.

1. Short trot. Collecting the horse.
2. Flexion with the curb, on foot.

3. School walk : Shoulder-in.

    ,,   ,,   Shoulder-out.   Change of hand on two tracks.

4. The same movements on the circle.

5. Canter on the inward and outward leg.

6. Changes of hand by passing to the trot.

7. A higher degree of collection.

17TH LESSON.

1. Same succession of work.

2. Increased collection.

3. Half turn on the haunches.

18TH LESSON.

Repetition of the preceding lesson.

19TH LESSON.

1. Collecting the horse at the trot

2. Flexions with the curb on foot.

3. Shoulder-in and shoulder-out at the school trot.

4. Half turn on the shoulders.

5. Canter on the inward and outward leg.

6. Change of hand at the canter, by arriving at the opposite track, at the walk, and starting at the canter by the position of the head (to each hand).

7. On a straight line : canter to the right : a few strides— at the walk—canter to the left—repeat several times the same movement.

8. On the circle : Shoulder in—shoulder-out.

9. At the canter : Shoulder-in. (Never shoulder-out at the canter, so as not to accustom the horse to go sideways.)

10. At the walk : getting the horse completely in hand.

1. Trot with the horse in hand.
2. Flexion with the curb on foot.
3. School walk : shoulder-in.
   „ „ shoulder-out. Change of hand on two tracks.
4. Same movements on the circle.
5. Canter on the inward and outward leg. Change of hand by passing to the trot.
6. Getting the horse completely in hand.

1. Flexions with the curb (by going with the head high).
2. *Rassembler*—school trot—shoulder-in—shoulder-out.
3. Halting—Reining back—Forward. (Repeat the same movement several times).
4. School walk : demi-volte and shoulder-in by finishing the demi-volte (to both hands).
5. Canter on a straight line with both fore legs alternately leading.
Change of hand at the canter by passing into the walk and changing the leg.
6. Demi-volte at the canter ; change of leg at the track.
7. Shoulder-in, a canter, to both hands.
8. Circling at the canter on the inward and outward leg.
9. Collecting the horse completely at the walk.

1. Repetition of the preceding lesson.
2. Canter down the centre.
Reversed volte, straightening the horse on the same leg, change of leg.

3. Ordinary volte with shoulder in, same movement to the other hand.
4. Walk.
5. Canter to the right, canter to the left, three strides on each leg.
6. Collecting the horse.
7. Preparation for the *passage*.

23RD LESSON.

1. Repetition of the preceding lesson.
2. Getting the horse more completely in hand than before, to finish.
3. Preparation for the *passage*.

24TH LESSON.

1. Repetition of the 22nd lesson.
2. Each day more complete *rassembler* than before, so as to obtain the *passage*.

25TH LESSON.

1. Repetition of the 22nd lesson.
2. Getting the horse more completely in hand than before, to finish.

26TH, 27TH, 28TH, 29TH, AND 30TH LESSONS.

1. Repetition of the 22nd lesson. Getting the horse in hand more and more completely.
2. A few strides of the *passage*, pat the horse on the neck, begin again.

F. DE HASE, Commandant Adjutant-Major.
Brussels, 5th January, 1891.

The results were excellent, as the following letter shows, and I most cordially thank the gentlemen who signed it :—

" DEAR MR. FILLIS,—

"At the moment when you are going to bring out a new edition of your 'Breaking and Riding,' we are anxious to express our admiration of the excellent principles you have taught us.

" You have shown us, in breaking, how to combine reasoned-out energy with victorious patience.

" No more excitement! No intemperate punishment, which is prejudicial to success.

" Also, thanks to your method and your instruction, we have succeeded in thirty lessons to break horses of entirely different tempers without injuring them, and we fully recognise that the principles we previously employed did not give us such rapid and satisfactory results.

" We are anxious, dear Mr. Fillis, to add our tribute to the numerous testimonies of admiration which you have received everywhere, and we beg you to accept the expression of our distinguished regards.

" F. DE HASE, Commandant Adjutant-Major.

" LAMBERT, Captain Commandant.

" FIVÉ, Commandant.

" CEC. HERG, Lieutenant.

" DE FORMANOI, Captain.

" P. BIOURGE, 1st Lieutenant.

" LE GRAND, Lieutenant.

" G. JEIDELO, Lieutenant.

" M. LECLERQ, Captain.

" F. DOCQ, Lieutenant.

" COMTE JEAN DE MEROD, 1st Lieutenant.

" M. D'HESPEL, 1st Lieutenant.

" R. PYCKE, 1st Lieutenant.

" VANLOQUERE, 1st Lieutenant.

" BIA, Captain."

I ought to mention that in Belgium no one ever thought of blaming me for riding in a circus, which is considered in that country to be the only place for equestrian work, and that it is as natural for a horseman to ride in a circus, as for a lyric artist to show himself at the opera, or for an Academician to dress himself in green, in order to croak out an address under the cupola of the Institute. I ought also to mention that at Brussels I did not meet any military distrust of civilians. The people only required a riding master to thoroughly know what he taught. Cavalry officers are obliged to learn not only riding, but also an infinite number of other things which make it very difficult for them to afford time to study equestrian science to its utmost limits. Hence the necessity for specialising, as well for the instruction of the military rider as for others. I believe I faithfully convey the opinions, on these matters, of the Belgian cavalry officers whom I had the honour of meeting.

INDEX.

———◆———